A STAR IS FOUND

A
STAR
IS
FOUND

OUR ADVENTURES
CASTING SOME OF HOLLYWOOD'S
BIGGEST MOVIES

☆

JANET HIRSHENSON

AND

JANE JENKINS

with Rachel Kranz

Harcourt, Inc.

Orlando   Austin   New York   San Diego   Toronto   London

Copyright © 2006 by The Casting Company, Inc.

All rights reserved. No part of this publication may be reproduced or
transmitted in any form or by any means, electronic or mechanical,
including photocopy, recording, or any information storage and retrieval
system, without permission in writing from the publisher.

Requests for permission to make copies of any part of the work should
be submitted online at www.harcourt.com/contact or mailed to
the following address: Permissions Department, Harcourt, Inc.,
6277 Sea Harbor Drive, Orlando, Florida 32887-6777.

www.HarcourtBooks.com

Library of Congress Cataloging-in-Publication Data
Hirshenson, Janet.
A star is found: our adventures casting some of Hollywood's biggest movies/
Janet Hirshenson and Jane Jenkins, with Rachel Kranz.—1st ed.
p.   cm.
1. Motion pictures—Casting.   I. Jenkins, Jane.   II. Kranz, Rachel.   III. Title.
PN1995.9.C34H57   2006
791.4302'8—dc22   2006009242
ISBN-13: 978-0-15-101234-3   ISBN-10: 0-15-101234-2

Text set in AGaramond
Designed by Cathy Riggs

Printed in the United States of America

First edition
A C E G I K J H F D B

*We'd like to dedicate this book to actors everywhere.
Thank you for your talent and for the courage to share
heart and soul, bringing words on a page to life.
Without you we wouldn't be here.*

CONTENTS

A STAR IS FOUND

INTRODUCTION

Casting is a part of filmmaking that most people never think about—but once you become aware of it, you might be startled at how central these decisions are to your experience of a film. Just recall Hollywood's casting legends—*Casablanca,* for example. The studio's first choice for the role of Rick was George Raft, then a major leading man. Only when Raft wasn't available did the studio grudgingly accept minor contract player Humphrey Bogart, known mainly for playing gangsters in a slew of second-rate crime films. Matching Bogie with Rick turned the actor into an icon for world-weary, cynical heroes with hearts of gold— and it endowed the film with near-mythic status. Who knows what would have happened if George Raft had been the one to murmur "Here's lookin' at you, kid"—but it's hard to imagine that a new type of film hero would have been the result. Bogart seemed so right that, once he was cast, the part seemed made for him—even though he hadn't actually been anyone's first choice.

Or think of *The Wizard of Oz* with first choice Shirley Temple as Dorothy. When MGM couldn't get "America's sweetheart," they reluctantly awarded the role to Judy Garland, then known mainly for her teen musicals with Mickey Rooney. Of course, even without Judy, *Oz* would have been endowed with magic, a gripping story, and a stunning score, but Garland brought to the film her extraordinary combination of vulnerability, longing, sweetness, and hope—qualities that made a potentially good movie into a great one.

Or consider *The Godfather,* early candidates for which were Ernest Borgnine and Ryan O'Neal. Just take a moment to picture those two in the roles that Marlon Brando and Al Pacino ultimately played. At this point, the roles seem to have been written with Brando and Pacino in mind—but that's only because they did, finally, get cast in them; it was hardly a foregone conclusion. Likewise, Charles Grodin has long been notorious as the guy who turned down the part eventually played by Dustin Hoffman in *The Graduate.* Perhaps the movie would have been equally good with Grodin in the part—but at the very least, it would have been a different movie if Grodin, not Hoffman, had been the one to stammer, "Mrs. Robinson, are you trying to seduce me?"

The essence of a good casting decision is that you simply take it for granted. Only when you imagine a cast being different do you realize how great an impact a casting choice can have. To take a relatively recent example, think of the movie *Good Will Hunting,* which introduced Matt Damon and Ben Affleck to a broad audience. We didn't cast this movie, so we're commenting on it purely as viewers. In that film, Matt plays the innocent math genius; Ben is his tough and knowing friend—casting choices that seem to work very well. Now imagine the two actors swapping roles—think of

Ben as the math whiz and Matt as the working-class guy who's left behind. We're not saying the movie wouldn't have worked that way, but it becomes a different picture. Imagining these roads not taken helps illuminate the kind of magic that can be generated when an actor's persona, talent, and style mesh perfectly with his or her role.

The two of us have been casting directors through the last three decades of Hollywood history. We got our start in what we thought of even then as the University of Zoetrope, working with Francis Ford Coppola in his extraordinary effort to create another type of Hollywood studio. Francis is a true artist who dreamed not only of making his own groundbreaking movies but also of creating an environment in which other film artists could collaborate on a new kind of American cinema. Unfortunately, his utopian venture only lasted a few years, but for those of us who were privileged to be a part of it, it was a life-changing experience.

When Zoetrope Studios went under, we went out on our own. We founded The Casting Company and began relationships with some of Hollywood's most exciting young directors: Ron Howard, Rob Reiner, Chris Columbus, and later on John Hughes and Wolfgang Petersen—men of artistry and integrity whom we're still lucky enough to be working with today. Throughout the 1980s and 1990s, we also cast movies for such directors as Tim Burton, Brian De Palma, David Lynch, Steven Spielberg, Jerry Zucker, and many others. Then and at Zoetrope, we discovered such stars as Alec Baldwin, Steve Carell, Tom Cruise, John Cusack, Matt Damon, Benicio Del Toro, Leonardo DiCaprio, Anthony Edwards, Emilio Estevez, Brendan Fraser, Andy Garcia, Scarlett Johansson, Diane Lane, Rob Lowe, Michael Keaton, Kyle McLachlan, Virginia Madsen, Dylan McDermott, Joaquin

Phoenix, River Phoenix, Tim Robbins, Julia Roberts, Meg Ryan, Winona Ryder, Nicollette Sheridan, Elisabeth Shue, Kiefer Sutherland, Patrick Swayze, Lili Taylor, Billy Bob Thornton, Bradley Whitford, Forrest Whitaker, and Robin Wright (later to become Robin Wright Penn). More recent directors we've worked with include Peter Berg (*Friday Night Lights*) and Nancy Meyers (*Something's Gotta Give, The Holiday*), while among our twenty-first-century acting discoveries are Paul Bettany, Daniel Craig, Linda Hardy, Josh Lucas, Mike Vogel, and the *Harry Potter* kids: Daniel Radcliffe, Emma Watson, and Rupert Grint.

We gave some of those actors their first parts. There were others whose talent we recognized, and if we weren't able to give them significant roles, we were at least able to help them pay the rent until something better came along. And then there were those who had maybe worked a bit—but we gave them the part that put them on the map.

You would think that with a list like that, we'd both be unshakably confident whenever a new script crosses our desk. Alas, no. Like the veteran actress who never fully gets over her stage fright, neither of us has ever quite learned to greet a new movie with equanimity. The moment we take on a new project, the anxiety sets in. The typical Hollywood script contains roles for fifty to a hundred actors, not counting the extras—those faces in the background who have no speaking parts. (Luckily for us, "extras" casting—an entity unto itself—usually takes care of those roles.) The sheer volume of parts can be daunting, let alone the commitment we both feel to finding candidates who are truly right for each role, actors who will fulfill the director's vision and help the movie reach its best potential. We take our cue from Konstantin Stanislavski: "There are no small parts, only small actors."

Casting is a complicated, delicate, and almost alchemical business. To be a good casting director, you need instinct, patience, and the ability to remember hundreds of diverse faces, voices, and performances. You also need the kind of empathy that enables you to know, almost before he or she does, what your director wants in a particular part, as well as the sympathy that allows you to put a nervous actor at ease or to help a potentially stellar actress find the great audition that you sense she can give. Perhaps most important, you need the kind of wild faith that enables you to keep believing in miracles—to know that the part that's gone unfilled for months will eventually be cast, to find the performer who's eluded you for so long, to see the talent in the awkward but brilliant kid whom no one else will consider. When that kind of faith is rewarded, it's a thrill like nothing else we've ever known. Those are the moments we live for, the times that make all the anxiety worthwhile—and the closest thing we'll ever know to magic.

1 ☆ THE CALL

JANE

It began, as it usually does, with a phone call—this time, from Louisa Velis, Ron Howard's longtime associate producer at Imagine Entertainment.

"Russell Crowe's deal for *A Beautiful Mind* is done, so we're ready to go ahead. The budget is going to be tight, but of course there are great parts, and I'm sure you'll come up with great actors, as always. Can you start putting a list together and meet with Ron on Friday? The wife and the roommate are especially important to him."

JANET

Whether it's a big film, a small one, or something in between, our job always begins with the Call. Sometimes the Call comes from a director we know well—Chris Columbus, Ron Howard, Wolfgang Petersen, Rob Reiner. With such long-standing relationships, the Call is almost a formality, a confirmation that it's once again time for us to get to work.

When the Call comes from a director we've never worked with, his first step is usually to schedule a meeting. (The director is so rarely a "she" that in this book, we're just going to say "he," with apologies to Hollywood's female filmmakers. Although there are now lots of powerful women in Hollywood—producers, top agents, even the heads of several major studios—it's still unusual for women to direct films. We've never been able to figure out why—surely if a woman has life-or-death power over someone else's movie, she ought to be able to make her own—but with a handful of exceptions such as Nancy Meyers, most directors are men.)

At this point in our career, we don't exactly go on job interviews. But this initial meeting with the director—and, perhaps, his producer—pretty much serves that function, as we all figure out whether or not we want to work together. The director already knows that Jane and I have a long string of successful movies to our credit—but so do lots of our colleagues. So should he choose us, or one of Hollywood's many other casting directors?

Sometimes this decision is based on the type of film that is being planned. Perhaps the director is looking for someone to solve a particular problem—finding 300-pound jugglers for his circus movie, or getting access to the Latvian community for all those folk-dance scenes he's planning. Most likely, though, he's looking for the "vibe," trying to feel out what our relationship will be like for the long, arduous months that casting a movie usually takes. I once heard of a producer who described filmmaking as a long road trip—he didn't want to work with anyone with whom he wouldn't enjoy traveling for eight, ten, twelve hours a day, week after week after week. This initial meeting is the director's chance to find out what sharing that journey might be like.

Such meetings usually start with the director describing his vision, with maybe a few additional words about the movie's overall budget. Then Jane and I toss out some ideas, almost as though we already had the job. All of us are trying to act as though we actually *are* working together, to see what a real relationship might be like.

At these types of meetings, we try to walk a fine line. We don't want to give away too many good ideas—that's what we do for a living—but we do want to let the director know that we *have* good ideas, suggestions that go beyond the obvious. After all, you don't need to be a casting director to think of Harrison Ford or Julia Roberts—stars that many movies can't even afford. On the other hand, we don't want to give away our best alternate ideas until we know we've got the job.

Even though this isn't really a job interview, Jane and I still get nervous about these meetings. Sometimes it's simply because we need a job. A couple of years ago, Jane had just finished casting *A Beautiful Mind* and I'd just come off *Harry Potter*—two of the year's most high-profile movies. But a possible actors' strike was looming and production had ground to a virtual standstill. Clearly, the phrase "job security" isn't in the showbiz dictionary.

Sometimes we're eager to work with a particular director, and we want to be chosen. Or maybe we just can't wait to get our hands on a delicious script. Like actors, though, we try to do our best and then leave everything at the door, hoping that our past work speaks for us.

Of course, we don't always come out of these meetings with a job. I remember two meetings that were especially disappointing—not to say mystifying. One was with Peter Howitt, director of *Sliding Doors,* which we'd both loved. Peter seemed equally fond of us, since he was nice enough to announce that we had cast five of his all-time favorite films, which he then proceeded to list. When we didn't get the job, we had to laugh. Maybe whomever he finally hired had cast *six* of his favorite films?

The other was for a movie called *Mr. Wonderful,* which was to be Anthony Minghella's first American movie. You'll recall that Minghella later became known for directing *The English Patient,* but at this point, his only U.S. release was a terrific but relatively obscure British film called *Truly, Madly, Deeply.*

His British producer called our office. "Is it possible," she asked in her impeccable accent, "that the truly *legendary* casting directors, Jane Jenkins and Janet Hirshenson, are available for a meeting?"

As it happened, Jane had seen *Truly, Madly, Deeply* at Sundance, before its U.S. theatrical release, which made her one of the few Americans at the time who actually knew the director's work. She loved it, I loved the sound of it, and the whole meeting dissolved into a love fest. Surely *this* time we were in. We were "the legendary Jane and Janet," after all.

Then weeks went by with nary a word, until finally the terribly polite British producer sent us an awfully nice note saying that they'd absolutely *loved* meeting with us—and had decided to go in a different direction.

Jane gave me a sardonic look across the office. "Going with someone *less* legendary, no doubt?" You can never fall too deeply in love in these meetings. Like actors, you never know why you don't get a job.

☆

Meanwhile, we, too, are trying to figure out whether this is a trip we want to take. Can we deliver what the director needs? Does he envision the movie in a way we can understand? If our idea of cute and perky is Reese Witherspoon and his is Paris Hilton, we're clearly not speaking the same language. That's okay—as long as we can learn his. If his vision remains mysterious to us, even after a long discussion, we're probably the wrong match.

We might also turn down a job if we think the director's expectations of casting don't match the reality we know. You always want to reach high, but if the director thinks he can get Brad Pitt for a one-page cameo as the waiter, or if a first-time director expects us to guarantee the latest hot commodity for his low-budget film, we may wish him luck with somebody else. Certainly if someone wants us to go through personal channels to convince a well-known actor to consider a script—contacting a performer by any means other than through an agent or manager—we'll say no to that job.

We're also reluctant to take scripts that are full of extreme violence or that seem particularly degrading to women. Sex is fine, violence is fine, even sexual violence is fine—up to a point. But if we can't stomach the thought of working on a script for months at a time, if we can't imagine talking about it enthusiastically with the director and the actors, then we've got to pass.

Sometimes we simply can't face the demands that a particular script will involve. If I had it to do over again, I'd say "yes" to *Witness,* which I think is a wonderful movie. But the script came to me right after I finished *The Outsiders* and *Rumble Fish,* which had kept me on location in Oklahoma for several months, and the thought of spending a big chunk of time in Lancaster, Pennsylvania, was just too much. What a mistake that was!

Likewise, we've never gotten over our "no" on *Risky Business.* But Jane had just finished doing Ron Howard's *Night Shift* and auditioning yet another round of hookers didn't appeal to her. When we saw *Risky Business,* we knew we'd made the wrong choice. It was a terrific movie—without our name on it.

JANE

A lot of our discussion with directors centers on artistic considerations—who are the actors that fulfill his vision? But the context in which these discussions are held includes several other factors, all of which interact with one another. Sometimes we mention them explicitly. Other times, they're simply implied. All play at least some role in determining the final decisions.

First, last, and always, there's money. When we start working on a movie, we usually have some general idea of how big the budget is and how much we've got to spend. We need to make our casting decisions accordingly so that we don't run out of money before the movie is cast. Still, Hollywood budgets tend to be flexible. A picture that's budgeted at $6 million might go up to $14 million if the studio thinks they can get a more expensive star to come on board. Sure, the new guy costs more money, but he'll also bring more people into the theater. Magically, the money for his salary—and a lot of other things—suddenly appears.

An actor's price is also flexible. Stars who demand huge salaries for studio films may be willing to do an indie for less, especially if they like the director, the script, the topic, or the part. And while some of the non-stars will be working for "scale"—union minimum—others will negotiate higher salaries. Here, too, you've got to expect the unexpected. A lesser-known actress whom you could once hire for scale may have just done a small role in a movie that's getting a lot of buzz: suddenly her price goes up. Or an actor whom we feared might cost too much is eager to work with our director and tells his agent to give us a break.

Money affects our work in a variety of ways. The budget we get from the studio allocates a certain amount of money for each role, and if we end up getting someone more cheaply for one part, maybe we can use it to hire someone more expensive for another. Or maybe the studio will simply grab the money we've saved and hand it over to Art, Wardrobe, or Special Effects, who want that extra cash as much as we do.

Another consideration is the studio itself. While theoretically the director has the final say over all the movie's roles, studios and other financial interests often want veto power. They're less likely to second-guess an A-list director like Rob Reiner or Chris Columbus, especially for the non-starring parts. But if a new guy is making a film, or if a veteran has been having a string of flops, the studio may want more of a voice even on less-significant roles.

Studios may also have made two- or three-picture deals with certain actors, whom they naturally want to use as soon as possible to complete their obligations. And studio execs have their preferences, like anyone else. That's often where a studio casting department comes in, to let us know whom the studio wants—or doesn't want.

That indefinable factor known as "hotness" also plays a role—both "sexy hotness" and "popular hotness." All things being equal, you usually want a certain number of good-looking actors in your movie—sexually attractive people whom audiences will enjoy looking at, fantasizing about, identifying with. You also want players who are professionally desirable: Who just got an Oscar or a nomination? Who had even a small part in last week's top-grossing hit? Whose indie film just made a big splash at Sundance? All sorts of events can make a significant difference in an actor's desirability.

Recently we auditioned the handsome young Australian actor Alex O'Loughlin, first to become the next James Bond and then for a part in Nancy Meyers's *The Holiday.* Even though he didn't get either of the parts, this relatively un-known guy's stock took a big leap skyward. Being courted for two significant projects gave his desirability a nice little bump. He's a wonderful actor, and he deserves anything he gets, but the increased "hotness" factor from two unsuccessful auditions increased his chances of being cast in bigger parts and more significant movies.

An actor's history can also be a factor in casting decisions. Some parts call for an actor whom no one has ever seen before, so that our past associations don't interfere with our ability to be carried away by the film. Thus, then-unknown actor Edward Norton made a huge splash in *Primal Fear,* where he played an altar boy accused of murdering a priest. The whole movie turned on our uncertainty about whether the boy was lying when he claimed the priest had molested him. *Was* this kid telling the truth, or was he running a scam? Because we'd never seen this actor before, we had no idea whether we should trust or despise him. The film was far more unsettling as a result.

By contrast, whenever Madonna or Courtney Love shows up on-screen, we're incapable of separating their racy personal histories from their on-screen presence. This familiarity can work for a movie—the minute we see either woman, we know we're looking at a femme fatale. But their off-screen personas do make them hard to buy as spinsters or sexually repressed women. If they ever are cast that way, part of the fun will be to see if they can pull it off, the way we were all watching to see if Jack Nicholson could turn himself into the nebbishy everyman in *About Schmidt.* (Trust Jack—he could!)

Sometimes a movie will deliberately invoke your expectations of a familiar actor—only to turn them against you. The marvelous George Clooney has built a durable reputation as a charming, powerful hero, which cued audiences to expect similar heroic achievements from his CIA operative in *Syriana.* The film kept setting us up, teasing us with the idea that Clooney's guy would ultimately save the day. When he couldn't, the effect was more powerful than if a lesser man had failed. When even George Clooney can't solve a problem, you know you're in serious trouble.

☆

Beyond all these other considerations, there's an implicit hierarchy that governs who's eligible for which roles, indicating who's big enough to play the hero or who's too big to play the mother or best friend. From the cop on the corner to the leading man, every role is evaluated according to this hierarchy, so that you've got actors of the appropriate "size" in every part.

Of course this hierarchy varies according to the context. An actor who's a huge catch for a TV series may play only a small part in a big movie; an actor who takes a supporting role in a Steven Spielberg film may be courted for an indie lead. And, as we've seen, an actor's stock is continually fluctuating. That gorgeous woman who only yesterday played leading ladies is today relegated to the role of understanding mother or wacky aunt; the kid who was the second-rate hit man in last year's movie is suddenly the romantic hero in this week's hit.

Still, there are some basic guidelines. So here—with all caveats duly noted—is a rough outline of the Hollywood Hierarchy:

At the bottom of the ladder are the Wannabes. Those are the people just out of acting school or fresh off the bus from Kansas or New Jersey. They're still trying to get a SAG card—a union card from the Screen Actors Guild—not to mention an agent, some good head shots, and enough work experience to put together a résumé.

Moving up a rung, we find the Unknowns, the actors no one has heard of (yet!). They do have their SAG cards and maybe even an agent, and they finally have a credit or two or three. But even Janet and I don't know their names, and we can be pretty sure that our directors don't, either.

Next is the category generally referred to as Working Actors. These are the performers familiar to industry insiders and film buffs. We actually do know their names—in fact, we call them all the time—but you've probably never heard of them, though you may well recognize their faces. These are the best friends, the doctors, the gangsters, the cops—the bedrock of day-to-day moviemaking.

JANET

Like most casting directors, Jane and I have our favorites among the Working Actors—people whom we think have interesting faces, big talents, and a gift for making the most of the small but juicy parts. Edie McClurg, for example, is the plump, purse-lipped lady with the strong Midwestern accent whom I first cast as Grace the Secretary in *Ferris Bueller's Day Off*. Although she's unlikely ever to star in a film, she's a terrific comedienne who worked for a decade with the famous comedy troupe known as the Groundlings, and she used to perform her own trademark characters on David Letterman's daytime show. If you've watched TV or gone to the movies during the past three decades, you've almost certainly seen her, probably several times.

I picked her out immediately for *Ferris Bueller* because I knew that director John Hughes liked to populate his film with offbeat, distinctive characters. John never considered a small part a throwaway—no good director does—and he was always looking for someone who could contribute an unusual flavor or quirky line delivery. In fact, I think one of the reasons he came to us was because he felt that our company did an unusually good job with the smaller parts, granting them the same meticulous attention that we'd give the major roles.

I'd realized right away that with John, I'd need plenty of backups for every role—he likes to see a lot of people—but in Edie's case, I knew it wasn't necessary. Sure enough, as soon as she walked into the audition room, he began to smile. "Oh, yeah," I thought. "This was meant to be." Edie made even the tiniest role sing, and from then on, whenever we were casting a movie, John would say, "Okay, here's the Edie part!" or "Wait a minute, how are we going to use Edie?"

Another classic Working Actor is Troy Evans, whom you might know as the surly Frank Martin, emergency room desk clerk on the long-running TV show *ER*. Or maybe you saw him as Sergeant Bob Pepper, the tough soldier engaged in a poignant, passionate love affair on the award-winning series *China Beach.* Like Edie, Troy is an excellent actor who gets supporting parts in films and somewhat bigger roles on television, a medium that tends to be far more hospitable to actors who aren't young, thin, and gorgeous.

But in movies, too, you need someone like Troy. All too many actors *look* like actors, but Troy looks and feels like a regular guy. Cast him as a mechanic, police officer, or football coach, and you immediately add a dose of reality to your film, a sense of texture and color. I first cast him as a trucker in another John Hughes film, *Planes, Trains and Automobiles.* With his sardonic features and bulky body, Troy is known for bringing bite, heart, and depth to even the most minor roles.

To some extent, Troy and Edie are prisoners of their physical type. They're both strong presences but very specific. I'd actually love to see someone cast Troy as the insecure nerd or the sensitive painter and allow him to play against type. Not that he's done so badly with the typecasting. When we put him in *Planes, Trains and Automobiles,* the small part of the trucker turned into a windfall for him. The movie required snow, and there wasn't any that year. Usually you try to avoid bad weather when you're shooting; in this case, the production was actually chasing it! Troy's moment on camera kept being delayed—and he just kept getting paid. At the end of the film he thanked us: that little part had earned him the down payment on a house.

Likewise, Edie can ring more changes on the nosy, bossy, prudish-but-prurient middle-aged lady than any other actress I can think of—but there's something so coy and playful about her that you could never cast her as a sexy broad or a mean old bird. I'll never forget her wonderfully annoying car-rental clerk in *Planes, Trains and Automobiles.* Looking every bit the proper Midwestern matron, she smiles ever so sweetly as Steve Martin explains frantically why he needs the car she's just told him that he can't have. "Oh!" she exclaims brightly in that cute little voice. "Well, you're fucked, then, aren't you?" No one has ever been able to make the word "fucked" sound so prim and cheerful. Her extraordinary comic sense is a true gift to a John Hughes film—but she's just too funny for the tragic, terrifying world of, say, a Wolfgang Petersen thriller.

Connie Britton is a slightly better-known Working Actor whom I cast as the coach's wife in *Friday Night Lights.* TV viewers know her from her work on the long-running series *Spin City* and her occasional appearances on *The West Wing,* but most people who recognize her face probably couldn't tell you who she was. I think she's a terrific actress with a lot of range—she's proven her comic abilities on *Spin City,* while her quiet support of her husband added depth and warmth to *Friday Night Lights,* giving us a glimpse of Coach Gaines's private side. We were all happy to use her in that role, but we didn't expect viewers to leap up in recognition.

JANE

Like Connie, Working Actors who have a bit more range may have a shot at moving up to become Names. These performers might lack the youth, looks, or charisma to be considered Stars, but they make a solid, essential contribution to any film they're in.

William H. Macy, for example, is an actor who has attained his own kind of stardom. His presence can green-light an independent film or a TV movie. He writes and produces.

He's got extraordinary range—we cast him as the cynical fast-talking investigator Charlie Crisco in Rob Reiner's *Ghosts of Mississippi,* and he was equally brilliant when we cast him in *Air Force One,* his first action movie. He's also a well-known stage actor who co-founded New York City's Atlantic Theater Company with his longtime colleague, the playwright and filmmaker David Mamet. Lots of moviegoers know his name, and people who know acting think the world of him.

Likewise, Allison Janney, whom we cast in one of her first film roles in *Miracle on 34th Street,* is well known and well respected. Famous in the TV world for her work on the hit series *The West Wing,* she works a lot in movies, and, like Bill Macy, she does her share of theater, where she can expect to play the lead. As a woman in her forties who's attractive, strong, and funny, she's part of the glue that holds a film together. On the big screen, though, she's usually a supporting player—Meryl Streep's girlfriend in *The Hours,* Chris Cooper's wife in *American Beauty,* Jennifer Aniston's sister in *The Object of My Affection.* Allison is a good example of how a talented, attractive—but not drop-dead gorgeous—woman can do brilliantly on TV and yet not quite reach movie stardom. Her career makes clear that TV and the name recognition that goes with it can open up significant opportunities, especially for women. Edie Falco—star of *The Sopranos* and a featured player in the film *Freedomland*—is another example of how an "attractive but not gorgeous" woman has built a solid career based on quality TV.

Yet TV stardom can be a bit of a double-edged sword when it comes to casting a film. While independent filmmakers are usually delighted to get TV Names, A-list producers may not want an entire cast of actors who can be seen every week for free. There's still a bit of snobbery about television in the film world, even though so many movie stars came out of television—Tom Hanks, George Clooney, Bruce Willis, Queen Latifah, Jennifer Aniston, Will Smith, Denzel Washington—and despite the ways that HBO and Showtime have boosted TV's prestige. Even so, crossing over from TV stardom to a film career can sometimes be difficult, especially in A-list movies.

At the very top of the Name category are the people like Philip Seymour Hoffman, Paul Giamatti, Frances McDormand, Laura Linney—actors who are Stars in some contexts and top Names in others. In the bigger movies, these performers play the tasty supporting roles, but they may well get the leads in small, independent, or otherwise offbeat films: *Capote* for Hoffman; *American Splendor* and *Sideways* for Giamatti; *Fargo* and *Laurel Canyon* for McDormand; *You Can Count on Me, Kinsey,* and *The Squid and the Whale* for Linney.

None of these fabulous actors are likely to become Superstars, and as of this writing, they probably can't get a big movie green-lit on the strength of their presence alone (though they are certainly able to green-light smaller films). Still, they're all solid, versatile performers whose roles go well beyond the best friend or plain sister.

Since the Hollywood hierarchy favors men—conventional wisdom has it that movies with strong men in the lead do better than films anchored by women—we can make one more distinction: between the woman who takes second place *only* to a man and the woman who'll take supporting roles under a female lead. Laura Linney is an example of the first: at this point in her career, she's always the most important woman on the screen. If her part is smaller than someone else's, that someone else is a leading man, as with Liam Neeson in *Kinsey* or Jeff Daniels in *The Squid and the Whale.*

Frances McDormand, on the other hand—though sometimes the female lead—was willing to support Diane Keaton
in *Something's Gotta Give* and Charlize Theron in *North
Country.* She might not have taken either part in the wake of
her acclaim for *Fargo,* and she may still star in independent
films, but she's also open to taking parts on a level that
Linney probably wouldn't consider.

At the top of the hierarchy, we have the Stars—people
like Halle Berry, Cate Blanchett, Robert De Niro, Cameron
Diaz, Will Ferrell, Jake Gyllenhaal, Samuel L. Jackson, Kevin
Kline, Heath Ledger, Al Pacino, Meryl Streep, Owen Wilson, Kate Winslet, Reese Witherspoon. These are the actors
who become the selling point for the movie, one of the main
reasons people will come to see it. Stars usually take only starring roles—the movie's biggest part or biggest male/female
part; the hero or heroine; the focus of the film. If they do
play second fiddle, it's probably to someone in the next category: the A-list.

A-list actors are the Stars who can get a picture made:
their mere presence in the cast is enough to guarantee funding. Almost by definition, there are usually fewer than a
dozen names on it, and almost all of them are men. As conventional wisdom has it, women will go see a "guy movie"
but guys won't go see a "women's film"—unless it stars Julia
Roberts. So as of this writing, Julia Roberts is pretty much
the only A-list actress in town, although Reese Witherspoon's
Oscar for *Walk the Line* and her overall popularity with both
men and women may have put her into Julia's category, and
Cameron Diaz is a close runner-up. Guys on the A-list include George Clooney, Russell Crowe, Johnny Depp, Eddie
Murphy, Vince Vaughn, Mark Wahlberg, Denzel Washington, Robin Williams, and Bruce Willis.

But we've still got one more rung to go: the true Superstars. You might say they're the guys on the A-plus list, guys who can not only get a picture made but who can practically guarantee that it will turn a profit. As of this writing, that would be Tom Cruise, Matt Damon, Harrison Ford, Mel Gibson, Tom Hanks, Brad Pitt, and Will Smith. Pretty much any movie those guys want to do will get made.

At least that's what we thought when we were first drafting that paragraph. By the time we were revising the book, we had second thoughts. Maybe we should move Harrison down to the A-list—he's gotten a bit older. And doesn't George Clooney deserve an A-plus?

Then, *Capote* was released and the Oscars were given out, and we changed our minds again. By the time this book hits the stands, I'm sure the lists will have changed once more; by the time we're in paperback, they'll almost certainly have changed yet again. But what never seems to change is the hierarchy itself. Some parts need to be filled with Stars, others with Names, still others belong to Working Actors. Keeping track of who goes where is a big part of our job.

JANET

The story of how we got into this business is both unusual and typical. We are two of the approximately seven hundred casting directors and associates working in the United States, most of whom operate on a freelance basis. The notion of a freelance casting director was a relatively late development in motion picture history because for the first several decades of filmmaking—under the studio system— every studio had its own casting department. In those days, even the stars were under contract, so a director didn't have to go out looking for new talent every time he wanted to make a picture. And for the lesser roles in a movie, he simply asked the casting department to send over some choices. Casting was considered more of an administrative function than an artistic endeavor, and a separate function from the talent scouts, those legendary guys who scoured the country for the next Lana Turner or Clark Gable.

In the 1960s, however, the studios began breaking up. The production companies that took their place didn't have the resources to keep track of all the actors in town, let alone to audition all the people who kept coming, or to go out and search for new performers to fulfill a particular casting need.

The New York–based television industry was likewise hungry for talent. As in Hollywood, casting began as an administrative function: a (usually female) assistant or associate producer was sent to find some actors to audition for each available role. But the need for actors was so great—especially after shows began shooting weekly—that a distinct profession of casting directors soon emerged. This new profession—still predominantly female—now had two functions: to supply directors and producers with lots of actors for every type of role, and to keep restocking their supply with new talent.

When we got into the business in the late 1970s, the profession looked more or less the way it does today: a few casting people still on staff at the bigger studios, and hundreds of freelancers working from project to project. While the on-staff casting people might do some of the work, usually an outside casting director is asked to supply lots of good choices for every part. The director, producer, and studio execs make their final selections from that pool. Casting was the only major department in the industry that was never covered by unionization. We have a professional association, the Casting

Society of America (CSA), one of whose early goals was to try to affiliate with a union. In 2006, after twenty-five years, we finally managed to affiliate with local Teamsters in L.A. and New York—the Teamsters already covered the drivers, animal handlers, location managers, and some other workers on movies, and now casting directors, too, can enjoy the benefits of union representation in our negotiations with the studios.

Most casting is done in either New York or Hollywood, but regional casting companies have also sprung up in places like Boston, Austin, and Florida to provide actors for local productions as well as for studio films shooting on location. These regional casting companies are a terrific source of talent, and we often work with them when we need to hire local actors.

Most full-time casting directors work in Hollywood though—and almost all of them work freelance. In fact, most of our colleagues don't even have permanent offices. They get hired onto a movie and set up operations at its temporary production headquarters. Occasionally they're given space at the studio that's financing the film. Or if they're working on a TV show they'll be given space in that production company's offices. When the movie wraps, they take their photos and their notes and go home until they're hired onto a new picture. Usually they work solo, with perhaps a few associates and assistants hired for the length of the project. Some casting directors are on staff with major studios; they may cast a movie or two, but they're more likely to serve as supervisors and collaborators for the freelance casting directors brought on board for each project.

We operate a bit differently. Jane and I have pretty much always worked as partners, and after a brief stint at Zoetrope, we've always maintained our own office and staff. While we,

too, work freelance—hiring onto one picture at a time—
we've developed long-standing relationships with some major
directors who tend to hire us again and again.

Likewise, our career path has been a bit different from
most of our colleagues'. The usual career route for a casting
director is to start as a casting assistant on someone else's
movie, then go from one picture to another, working for several different casting directors. Eventually you move up to
slightly more responsibility as an associate, again working
under a variety of people. Finally, when you think you're
ready, you start casting your own films. Depending on your
connections, you might begin with low-budget films and
work up, or you might know enough people to be put onto
major films early in your career.

That's how most people have done it. But not us.

JANE

I never intended to be a casting director. I started out
wanting to be an actress. Growing up in Queens as a star-
struck teenager, I had a crush on Marlon Brando, and I fan-
tasized that if I became an actress, I might get to work with
him.

When I was a kid, someone told me, "You know, you
never look at people when you talk to them." So I worked
really hard to meet people's eyes, though it was fairly painful
for me. People also told me that I tended to be aloof—but I
wasn't, only shy. Acting seemed to offer a way to meet people's
eyes, to be friendly and gregarious, to achieve all sorts of
things that I could never do "as myself" but that I could accomplish in the persona I adopted. Years later, when I was living in L.A. as a single mother and I absolutely *had* to be able
to drive, I was in despair at having failed my driving test—

twice. One more failure and I'd have to wait several months before being allowed to try again. I finally passed the damn test by *playing* a person who could drive, a person who felt entitled to have a license. So for me—and, I think, for many actors—acting was a way to deal with shyness.

It was also a fascinating craft. I studied at the High School of the Performing Arts (of *Fame* fame), and later with the highly respected acting teachers William Hickey and Charles Nelson Reilly, both marvelous actors in their own right. I loved studying, and I found acting itself great fun. But when I started looking for professional work, I found out that acting in front of somebody in order to get a job is really terrifying—especially when you need the money. I'd stand in front of the casting director, my knees literally knocking together, the saliva evaporating from my mouth so quickly that I could hardly talk.

Meanwhile, I had gotten married very young to a man I met in acting class. Pretty soon we had a baby, and somebody needed to be the breadwinner. I'd already given up my dreams of stardom; now I was ready to abandon the whole damn profession. Still, what else was I equipped to do? Apparently I was good for nothing better than glorified secretarial work with fancy titles like "assistant to the director" and salaries barely above minimum wage.

A few years later, I got divorced. Those starvation salaries were even more problematic now that I was the primary support of a growing boy. But there I was, working as assistant to writer/director Frank Pierson on a film called *King of the Gypsies,* wondering what came next.

The work itself was actually interesting. Frank had me doing research in the Roma community—I even got to attend an extraordinary Gypsy wedding—and I began to get a real feeling for who these people were, how they spoke, moved, danced. Great, I thought. I've become a Gypsy maven. Now *there's* a salable skill.

One day I happened to be watching the casting sessions, and I had what I would now consider a very naïve thought, though at the time it struck me with the force of a revelation: *These people weren't right.* Gypsies weren't just dark-haired people, some exotic version of Italian or Jewish or Eastern European. They had their own unique spirit, their own distinct sensibility—and many of the good-looking, talented, mainstream actors coming in to read for us didn't have that quality.

Realizing that I could tell the difference between who was right for the movie and who wasn't led me to an exhilarating thought: *I* could cast a movie. Maybe not right away, but someday. After all, I had trained as an actress, even if I hadn't succeeded as one. I understood how different actors brought out different qualities in each other, why one talented performer might be right for a certain part while another— equally talented, equally attractive—was simply wrong for it. I could even tell, after years of watching my fellow actors in classes and plays and movies, which performers might have abilities that weren't being tapped, who might need only a bit of encouragement or a chance at the right part in order to suddenly shine.

Oh, my God, I thought. *I don't have to spend my life working for a secretary's pay, schlepping around from one job to another. I could actually have a career, a paying, respectable place in this industry. I could be a casting director. And I could be a good one.*

Once I'd figured out that casting might be my true calling, I couldn't wait to get started. The work on *Gypsies* would soon be coming to an end—along with the paychecks—so you can imagine how desperate I must have been to take my next step: I called up an ex-boyfriend. My relationship with Ralph Waite, better known as "Pa" on *The Waltons,* had always been stormy, but theoretically, at least, we'd parted as friends. So I put on my most confident tone and asked Ralph to help me get an assistant's job in the casting department at Lorimar, the production company for *The Waltons.*

"You know," Ralph said, "Lorimar just gave me a million dollars to direct my own little movie—*On the Nickel,* about a bunch of winos on the Bowery. Why don't you cast that?"

"Are you nuts?" I asked him, surprised into bluntness. "I'm not ready to do my *own* picture. For one thing, I don't know anything about contracts or SAG rules or—" (SAG is the Screen Actors Guild, whose complicated union rules governing actors' salaries, hours, and working conditions still plague us.)

"Oh, we don't have enough to pay more than scale anyway," Ralph said. "Just get the SAG rule book and read it. You'll be fine."

Then there was one of those pauses that I'd learned to know and distrust so well. "So," Ralph added with apparent casualness, "do you think you could do it for free?"

"Um, I have a kid, Ralph, remember?" I said as calmly as I could. "And the kid has to eat."

We settled on a hundred bucks a week, off the books. It wasn't much, but it would cover rent, car payments, and my grocery bills—and it was enough to get me into the business.

JANET

Typically, Jane charged into the world of casting full speed ahead. Also typically, I fell into it backward. Although

I was interested in show business, I never thought I could actually be part of it. True, I had grown up in a community in Los Angeles. But Pacoima was the blue-collar L.A. that has virtually nothing to do with movies. The only bit of showbiz in my background came not from living near Hollywood but from living with my English grandmother, who in 1949 had followed my English war-bride mother to America.

Nanna was an enthusiastic devotee of the silver screen and of the newly emerging rock and roll. She bought me my first Elvis and Beatles records and reminded me that we actually had "show people" in our family: an ancestor who was an original "Christy Minstrel" in the 1850s as well as other turn-of-the-century forbears who'd worked in the theater until they discovered their virginal young daughter snogging with a stagehand. I would watch *American Bandstand* with Nanna and pore over her movie magazines. Maybe it was training: I developed a good memory for actors' names and can still recall a lot of obscure 1960s casting trivia.

I went on to enjoy Hollywood's hippie scene and to marry my husband, Michael Hirshenson, with whom I spent five glorious years in Hawaii. But when we finally came back to the real world, I discovered that I needed a license to return to my former job as a medical assistant. Better to sign with a Los Angeles temp agency. I couldn't type very well, but for minimum wage, I was pretty sure I could answer the phones.

The prospect didn't exactly fill me with enthusiasm, so Michael had to prod me. "Go down to the office this morning," he said one day. "If you wait till afternoon, all the good jobs will be gone." It was easier to listen than to argue. But here comes the showbiz part: I was sitting alone in the temp office, filling out my application form, when a call came through. The receptionist looked around and saw only me.

"We just got a call from Columbia Pictures," she said. "They need someone to answer the phones. You interested?"

"Sure." It seemed a fitting tribute to Nanna.

At quitting time, the office manager asked if I'd like to come back. Now I was in showbiz!

The second day I was sent to Jennifer Shull's office. Jennifer was the casting director at famed producer Ray Stark's company, Rastar Films, a subsidiary of Columbia. I soon discovered that Jennifer was the most wonderful boss in the world—a true gentlewoman, thoughtful and generous. She saw something in me that made her think I could be a casting director, so she hired me as her assistant.

Every so often, Jennifer would describe a part she was casting and hand me the *Players Directory,* a compilation of actors' photographs. "Who do you think might be interesting?" she'd say. Soon she was giving me more and more responsibility—having me read with actors who came in, or letting me sit in on auditions and talking about who'd done well.

My first assignment for Jennifer didn't even involve people: I had to find a pregnant horse about to foal so a film crew could record the little one's birth.

The movie was *Casey's Shadow,* a racehorse epic starring Walter Matthau. Casey's Shadow was the horse around whom the movie revolved, and the script called for a scene portraying the birth of the champion. That's Hollywood for you: we were scheduled to shoot the birth scene in December, a time when foals, according to racetrack regulations, are not supposed to be born. (Any foal born earlier than the traditional spring season has a considerable advantage in size and weight over its future competitors.) So it was no easy matter finding a horse owner willing to admit that he or she had a pregnant mare with a due date in December.

Somehow I managed, and one day I got a call that the mare I'd found had delivered the night before. Although we had horse painters standing by, we turned out not to need them: the little foal came out perfectly, with the exact markings to match the full-grown racehorse we had already cast as Casey's Shadow. My first casting job was a success.

JANE

We both ended up working with Jennifer, and went on to join her as the casting department of Zoetrope Studios, a story that we'll continue in Chapter 2. But our time at Zoetrope helps explain why our career paths are so unusual: after the studio failed, our reputation as "Francis's girls" enabled us to get hired onto major films right from the beginning. We also had the extreme good fortune to make early films with several guys who became major directors—Chris Columbus, Ron Howard, Wolfgang Petersen, and Rob Reiner—men who've worked with us through virtually all of their U.S. careers. John Hughes started working with us about halfway through his career and just kept bringing us back. As a result, our credits include a uniquely long list of major films.

We're also among the few casting directors who maintain a permanent office and staff. Although sometimes keeping our office has seemed like a real extravagance, it gives us a home base that we both cherish. Sometimes we've wondered where the next rent check was coming from, but so far we've managed to maintain a sense of permanence that's unusual in our profession.

We're also among the few casting directors who work as a team. When we sign on to a movie, we work on it together. Though one of us will have primary responsibility for the film, the other is always there for backup.

Most casting directors don't specialize in any one type of film, and in that way, we're no exception. However, a few broad categories apply. Studio versus independent is one: we tend to get called mainly for large studio films, while a whole other group of casting directors focuses on the indie features that make up an ever more prominent part of Hollywood's output. Film versus television is another: although we've cast some TV pilots and made-for-TV movies, we tend to work more on the film side of things, and we basically avoid casting the episodes themselves, which require dozens of actors to be assembled each week. Early in my career, I did do some episodic casting, and the strain of finding all those actors on such short notice—not to mention keeping with the constant new demands generated by ongoing script revision—was enough to convince me that this area of the business was not my thing.

Commercials, reality shows, and live productions are considered separate domains from fictional film and TV, so people tend to specialize. Within the realm of film and TV, you also might find yourself specializing, but only as a function of how a résumé grows: producers tend to call you based on what you've already done. If you cast a successful horror picture, you'll probably get called to cast another; if you're known for doing big-budget flicks, you're likely to keep on doing them. We're lucky to have a fairly broad range of work to our credit, though early in our career, we sometimes had to prove ourselves. I'll never forget the director who looked at our then-short list of credits and said, "Oh. You don't do comedies."

"Well," I replied, "if the script is really funny, I'm sure we can find a bunch of actors to deliver the lines in an amusing way."

Needless to say, we didn't get that job—but after we'd made *Night Shift, The Sure Thing,* and *Ferris Bueller's Day Off,* we didn't worry about our ability to find comedic actors.

Likewise, after we made *The Outsiders* with Francis—the movie that introduced such stellar teenage talents as Tom Cruise, Matt Dillon, Emilio Estevez, Diane Lane, Rob Lowe, Ralph Macchio, and Patrick Swayze—we got the reputation of being the ones who "knew all the kids." As a result, we had the opportunity to do a lot of teen movies, though I'm not sure we really had an edge on that market. We just happened to have done a successful movie about young people.

There is a network of people who'll put together an entire cast for low-budget films. If you get a reputation in this field, you'll have a whole circle of indie directors knocking at your door. You might like this independent world, or you may only be using it as a stepping-stone to more expensive projects. We never had to make that choice: from the beginning, we did a lot of bigger movies and we've been lucky enough to continue doing them.

Smaller films are definitely more of a challenge. When we make a film like *The Da Vinci Code* or *Poseidon,* every agent in town is calling us; on an indie, we're the ones begging for a response to our offers. At least agents who know they'll be coming to us for Ron or Wolfgang's next project will give us the courtesy of a quick "no," rather than making us wait months for an answer.

JANE

One of our favorite Calls has always been the Bond Call. Almost as soon as we left Zoetrope, we formed a close relationship with famed producer Albert "Cubby" Broccoli and the rest of the James Bond production team. As a result, we've worked on pretty much every Bond movie since *Octo-pussy,* usually filling in the bits that British casting director Debbie McWilliams can't do from London, though we were the primary casting directors on the U.S.-based *License to Kill.* We've also been involved in three Bond searches, part of the process that gave us Timothy Dalton, Pierce Brosnan, and Daniel Craig.

Our first Bond Call was back in 1982, when they needed a heroine for *Octopussy.* Debbie was doing the rest of the film in London, but the filmmakers wanted a broader search for the exotic leading lady and her diabolical friends.

I must admit, that particular Call had me almost beside myself with excitement. Besides the reassurance that Janet and I actually *were* going to be able to get a business going, there was the fun of working on the famous Bond series. After all, I'd grown up on James Bond. And now *I* was going to find the next Bond girl? Frankly, I was thrilled.

And a bit daunted. "Now, for the heroine's sidekick—" Michael Wilson, Broccoli's stepson and a producer/writer on the project, was telling me the story of the movie. Then he interrupted himself. "Shouldn't you be taking notes? How else are you going to keep all the characters straight?"

"I thought I'd wait until I got the script." If there was anything in the business that I thought I understood, it was the importance of the script. Respect, no, *reverence* for the almighty script had been dinned into me first as an actress, then at Zoetrope, and I'd read every word of every screenplay I'd ever worked on—often several times. How else would I know who the characters should be?

But now the producer was laughing at my naïveté. "This is a Bond movie," he told me. "Top secret! You're not getting a script." I don't think even the actors got scripts much before the days on which they shot their scenes. To cast a Bond movie, you got a list of characters and a brief set of descriptions—usually oral—and then you were on your own.

Sometimes you couldn't even count on that. The one thing I thought was certain about the new Bond heroine was that she was an "exotic East Indian dark-skinned beauty." For plot reasons, the woman had to be East Indian; for Bond reasons, she needed wickedness, wit, and steamy sexuality. In those days Hollywood was a lot whiter and more European than it is now, and I just couldn't find a dark-skinned actress who fit the bill. I looked at actual ethnic Indians, such as Persis Khambatta and Susie Coelho, and I also auditioned some women who could pass for Indian, such as the sultry brunette Barbara Parkins, who played the bad girl in *Peyton Place*. But no one had the right combination of looks, style, and je ne sais quoi that screamed "Bond girl."

Then one day Broccoli came into the office with a different idea. "You know, *The Man with the Golden Gun* was on TV last night," he said casually. "Maud Adams was awfully good in that—let's use her."

It was all I could do to keep from shouting out in disbelief: "Maud Adams? But she's *Swedish*! *I* look more Indian than she does!"

Luckily, I kept my mouth shut, made some calls, and managed to get Adams on board—the only woman in the history of the series who ever appeared in two Bond movies. They dyed her hair, the writers threw in some lines about her having been raised by an Indian family, and as far as the producers were concerned, problem solved.

I learned a valuable lesson from the Maud Adams saga: no casting problem can ever be solved in only one way. True, most of the time you move heaven and earth to cast the character who's already written. But sometimes—especially if there's a terrific and gorgeous actor you're just dying to use— you simply change the script.

☆

Of course, the heart of all Bond movies is Bond himself. When we joined the team, Roger Moore was the man with the license to kill. Soon, though, he would have to hand over his martini shaker to a younger replacement, and the search for that guy was shrouded in more secrecy than a mission "for your eyes only": even Roger himself was not to know about the effort, in case the producers wanted him to do a few more movies before they actually made the switch. So they brought me over to London to play myself, Jane Jenkins, American Casting Director. Barbara Broccoli—Cubby's daughter and a budding Bond producer—played my assistant. Our cover story? We were casting a new American TV pilot, whose hero just happened to bear a striking resemblance to that British secret agent, James Bond.

This story provided the perfect opportunity to audition a lot of potential Bonds without anyone ever catching on. Debbie McWilliams was much too well known as a member of the Bond team to take part in the scam, so her role was limited to feeding us a list of names. Someone in London set up the meetings, and I swooped in, very much the grande dame, with Barbara—who was really my boss—giving her all as my efficient young assistant. "Can I get you another cup of tea, Miss Jenkins?" she'd ask as I auditioned actor after actor. Everyone read through the scenes that had been specially written to test for Bond-ish qualities—basically, we had to see how the guy handled a girl, a gun, and a martini, and, of course, we wanted to know how he'd look in a tux.

Although no one ever saw through our subterfuge, it yielded nothing. The Broccolis were also looking at other British actors, and they eventually settled on Timothy Dalton, one of the most charming and funny men I've ever met. Like pretty much everyone since Sean Connery, Tim was reluctant to take on the Bond persona, fearing that he'd become trapped in the part. He might have been spared that temptation, because the Broccolis' first choice was Pierce Brosnan, then known mainly as the extremely handsome and witty star of a TV show called *Remington Steele*. Alas for Pierce, when the network found out about the Broccolis' interest, they renewed his show, which they'd actually been on the verge of canceling. So the Broccolis moved on to Tim, who never really hit his stride in the part. After only two movies, the mantle passed to Pierce, since his show was, predictably, canceled as soon as the Bond-generated interest had died down.

Pierce went on to make several films for the Broccolis before they decided that Her Majesty's Secret Service once again required a new man. By 2005, the franchise had moved to SONY, and Cubby's heirs—Barbara Broccoli and her half-brother Michael Wilson—were now completely in charge.

At this point, everyone felt the need to regenerate the franchise for today's younger, hipper audience. When the Bond series first began, no one had ever seen anything like its combination of espionage, wit, sexiness, and high-tech gadgetry. Now that type of thriller was far more common, putting enormous pressure on the producers to choose a Bond who was charismatic enough to compete with today's new crop of film, TV, and video-game action heroes.

This new search was opened up to pretty much everyone in the English-speaking world—the British Isles, the United

States, Canada, Australia, and New Zealand. The only condition was that Bond be perceived as an Anglo-Saxon Brit, with a bona fide British accent. But an American, Aussie, or New Zealander with good linguistic skills had a genuine shot. (Although we, too, read the rumors of a female Bond—perhaps Angelina Jolie—we never looked at any women.)

Debbie started seeing people, and so did we. Having already run through pretty much all of the Ian Fleming novels on which the character was based, the producers were planning to start over with stories from Bond's early career. So we were hoping to find a young Bond, ideally someone in his mid-twenties, though we'd settle for mid-thirties if we had to.

The age issue turned out to be stickier than we'd expected. We were all very excited about Alex O'Loughlin, for example, partly because he was so young. Alex is a terrifically sexy, masterful, and take-charge guy—just the type who can make you remember that James Bond is a seriously dangerous man. And he might make a fabulous Bond in a few years, but when we saw him, he just didn't seem old enough for that 007 sense of command.

Another young actor, also incredibly talented, was Henry Cavill, who was even younger than Alex—probably no more than twenty-two or twenty-three. You'd never hire Henry to play a college kid, though; he already seems to be a mature man, and I know he's going to have a long and exciting career. But he, too, lacked the sense of mastery that James Bond requires.

At one point, we approached Julian McMahon, of *Nip/Tuck* fame. Julian decided not to pursue the possibility, since he'd just done *Fantastic Four,* which had options for its own set of sequels. We were also interested in Karl Urban— you've probably seen him in *The Bourne Supremacy* and the

Lord of the Rings movies—but he never seemed to be available for the screen test. An interesting young man named
Sam Worthington—whom a reviewer called "one of Australia's most likeable young leading men"—made it to the
screen-test level, but the thirty-year-old actor had a boyish
quality that didn't seem quite right for 007.

Meanwhile, the names of some better-known people
were bandied about—Colin Farrell, Orlando Bloom, Heath
Ledger. Ewan McGregor actually got a screen test. In the
end, these people all seemed too big, too expensive, and too
well known. This is one of those cases where you don't want
a performer's history interfering with your perception—
when you look at the sexy, powerful secret agent, your view
shouldn't be clouded by memories of the actor as a lovelorn
husband or drug-ravaged youth. You just want Bond—pure
Bond.

Eventually, Barbara and Michael became quite interested
in Daniel Craig, even though at age thirty-six he was pretty
much at the upper end of the desired range. They knew
Daniel from his work on the London stage, and he'd also
done a few well-regarded films. U.S. audiences had seen
Daniel as the weak brother in *The Road to Perdition,* Sylvia
Plath's husband in *Sylvia,* Lara's friend in *Lara Croft: Tomb
Raider,* and an Israeli agent in *Munich.* Despite this impres-
sive body of work, he'd remained barely recognizable to most
Americans—yet he had an undeniably Bond-like combina-
tion of danger, wit, and sex appeal.

Like the other serious candidates, Daniel had a full-out
screen test—lights, makeup, tuxedo—to make absolutely
sure of his look. It's rare these days to put actors on film before they're cast; most studios don't want the expense of
lights, a set, and a film crew when they can videotape some-

body for a fraction of the cost. For Bond, however, it was crucial to be certain that the actor would indeed look and "feel" the part. Daniel's test was fabulous, and the franchise decided that he was their guy.

For a while, Daniel was reluctant. A dedicated actor, he didn't want to feel that no one would ever let him do more serious films, and he had to be reminded that Pierce, while still playing Bond, had also made such movies as *The Tailor of Panama* and *The Thomas Crown Affair*. He wouldn't be confined to Bond alone, Barbara promised him—by this time she was wooing him quite heavily—and becoming an international superstar might well open some new doors.

Eventually Daniel agreed and the announcement was made. Janet and I breathed a sigh of relief—and settled in to wait for the next Call.

2 ☆ GETTING STARTED

JANE

Casting a movie usually begins with the reading of the script. But the Bond movies never let you see the screenplay, and even for other projects, we might start casting before a script is ready.

With *The Da Vinci Code,* for example, we relied on the book to start the casting process. Like millions of other people, I had read the best seller, so when producer Brian Grazer acquired the rights and Ron Howard signed on, I was all ready to jump on board. In fact, *everyone* seemed to have read *Da Vinci,* because as soon as word got out, I started getting calls from agents and managers who were sure their client was perfect for one of the leads. Even friends who had nothing to gain—including some casting directors!—called to make suggestions. Proposing dream casts for *The Da Vinci Code* seemed to have become everyone's favorite parlor game.

A Beautiful Mind wasn't quite such a high-profile project, but the process was similar. As soon as I heard that Ron was thinking about making this movie, I picked up my own copy of Sylvia Nasar's book. True, the movie might not ever have gotten made—most movies don't, even when a producer has acquired the rights or commissioned a screenplay. Usually, by the time we come on board, the movie has financing and *will* get made—though sometimes we've gotten hired and then learned that financing was pulled. In this case, Ron's early interest in *A Beautiful Mind* might have translated into an actual production or it might not have; the story of a mentally ill mathematician hardly seemed like the stuff of blockbusters. But there was no harm in being prepared.

Normally we wouldn't even start "thinking" until we actually had the job. But we'd worked with Brian and Ron for twenty years, making our relationship somewhat different. So for the next several months, I let the characters from *A Beautiful Mind* percolate through my consciousness, pulling photos or making notes whenever I thought of someone who might be right. Things can move awfully quickly once a picture is green-lit, and if Ron or Brian called to ask me for ideas, I wanted to be ready.

Meanwhile, Ron was also thinking about casting, but his concerns had a single focus: Who would play John Nash? Even with such a well-known and successful director as Ron, a project is rarely green-lit until one or more actors of substance sign on. Then we cast around those leads, though once again, there are exceptions. Sometimes the director's track record, the funding sources, the picture's topic, or some other factor will enable a movie to get funded with no big stars attached, though such situations are increasingly rare in today's financially conservative Hollywood.

For *A Beautiful Mind,* we definitely needed a Star at Russell Crowe's level to play John Nash, and once he was cast, the green light came fairly quickly. Now, this question of green-lighting is a bit tricky. It's not accurate to say that Russell "got" the movie green-lit: a director of Ron Howard's caliber isn't dependent on any particular Star to assure his movie of funding.

On the other hand, nobody—including Ron—wanted to go ahead with *A Beautiful Mind* until they knew who Nash would be. For both artistic and commercial reasons, the movie needed a box-office draw and a brilliant actor in the lead. So once Russell said "yes," we got the Call—and our work began.

JANET

Agents, too, are eager to see scripts, at least for high-profile movies. Top agents in particular want to start thinking about which of their clients might be right for the bigger parts and may even want a Star or two to read the script.

Often we're happy to oblige, but sometimes we need to keep a tighter rein. All of Hollywood may be talking about a project whose screenplay is not yet ready to be seen by outside eyes. And in these Internet-happy days, scripts seem to end up in cyberspace at a moment's notice, which producers—hoping to sell tickets—are just as happy to avoid. Particularly when the script is based on a well-known story, the production team usually wants to preserve some mystery about exactly how the screen adaptation relates to the source material. Thus, *The Da Vinci Code, Poseidon,* and *A Beautiful Mind* all had carefully guarded scripts that only a few agents and actors were allowed to see. *Godfather III* was so top secret that we even used a code name for the title.

Of course, agents don't have time to read every studio film and TV script that crosses their desk, not to mention all the independent film and theater productions. Instead they rely upon the "breakdown"—prepared from the script by a company called Breakdown Services, Ltd. Each breakdown includes a brief plot summary along with thumbnail descriptions of every character—just enough information for agents to decide which of their clients to submit: age, gender, ethnicity, and type ("an innocent girl," "a con artist," "a grizzled old man"). The breakdown also identifies the leads, tells how many scenes and lines the smaller roles have, and gives the page number on which each character first appears.

Before a breakdown goes out, it comes back to us so we can tweak the character descriptions, making sure they fit our own vision of the part. If we're trying to keep a story confidential, we might change a summary or character sketch that gives away too much information. And if a character description doesn't give an age range, we add one, if only to save our own sanity—no need for agents to send us actors aged twenty to seventy when *we* know the part should be played by someone in her forties. Finally, we might specify an ethnicity or add "any ethnicity" to the parts for which that's appropriate.

Once we've approved the breakdown, it goes out to everyone who subscribes to the service, which is pretty much every agent and manager in Los Angeles and New York, as well as lots of people across the country and in Canada and London. Every working morning, these folks receive up to a dozen breakdowns for movies, TV shows, and sometimes even theatrical productions, which they must then sift through and compare against their client roster. But at least they don't have to read (or have their interns read) a dozen scripts.

That hasn't always been true. More than thirty years ago, Breakdown Services founder Gary Marsh was a mere college student with a summer job in his mother's talent agency. As agents did back then, Ms. Marsh had Gary running around to all the studios reading scripts, looking for parts that her clients might be right for. Gary invented his own system of notation to help his mom keep the roles straight—a system she found so helpful that he began to realize he was on to something. The enterprising young man started a company that turned ninety-page scripts into four- or five-page break-downs, saving everyone the trouble of finding their own col-lege kid to do all that reading. At this point, it's hard to imagine Hollywood without the breakdown.

JANE

Of course, sometimes the breakdown changes. A few years ago I was casting the Martin Lawrence comedy *Rebound*. The movie was a kind of *Bad News Bears* of basket-ball: a group of lovable misfits finds a reluctant coach and becomes a championship team. "Big Mac" was to be the school bully recruited by the coach in a desperate effort to improve his team. As the original breakdown explained:

BIG MAC
Built like a brick s_ _ thouse, this middle school juvenile delinquent finds his life changed when he's plucked out of detention to receive a special opportunity at the school . . .
16 lines, 8 scenes (50) [That last note means that the character first enters on the script's page 50.]

For some reason, we just weren't finding the kid we needed, and the producers were starting to lose patience. In a conversation with director Steve Carr, the idea was raised that maybe a girl could play the part. Both Steve and the studio loved that idea, since a girl also offered possibilities for a team romance. And so the breakdown was rewritten:

BIG MAC
FEMALE, 15 years old, all ethnicities. A hulking wall of a girl, she is the school bully. Everyone is intimidated by her. However under the tough exterior there is a sweet lovable girl waiting to emerge . . .

We still didn't have a candidate—but at least we had a whole other gender to search from. Then one day our casting assistant, Devra McMullen, said, "You know, my daughter Tara might be right for Big Mac. She's a big girl, and she plays basketball."

Tara turned out to be an extraordinary natural actress with a mixture of anger, despair, and sweetness that made Big Mac one of the most important characters in the movie. From sixteen lines, her part expanded significantly, and her transformation from a tomboyish bully to a team player who was sweetly in love became a key part of the movie's emotional appeal.

So usually, yes, our job is to serve the script. But sometimes an actor will come along whose quality is so striking that the script ends up being rewritten to serve her.

JANET
Even though *we're* allowed to change the breakdowns, we hope that the agents will follow them, sending clients that actually fit the descriptions we've approved. When the breakdown calls for a "brilliant nuclear physicist at the top of her field," it makes us cranky to be sent sultry young starlets; when we're asked for a "world-weary drifter," we're not happy

about seeing angelic-faced surfer dudes who look as though they should still be in high school. We prefer agents who don't waste our time—or their clients'—by sending us people who obviously aren't right, although sometimes getting past our own typecasting can lead to a creative breakthrough.

We probably spend from one- to two-thirds of each working day talking to agencies of all sizes and descriptions. Like everyone else in Hollywood, agents operate on a hierarchy. The top five agencies are Creative Artists Agency (CAA), Endeavor Agency, International Creative Management (ICM), United Talent Agency (UTA), and William Morris Agency. These companies represent the industry's top talent—actors, writers, directors, producers—but they also work with promising newcomers according to the ever-present Hollywood Hierarchy: top agents tend to speak directly with A-list directors and producers (many of whom are also their clients); mid-level agents call us to pitch their Names and Working Actors; and brand-new agents trying to get started attempt to interest us in their Unknowns.

Lots of our best submissions have come from the smaller Hollywood agencies, though it's become increasingly difficult for them to stay in business: since their clients tend to get the smaller parts, the agents also get the smaller paychecks—and these days, the trend is to squeeze the players at the bottom in order to have more money for the top. Unless a small agency represents someone in a TV series, with a regular weekly paycheck, it can be hard to stay afloat.

Some agents are clearly so desperate to get their actors hired that they submit everyone and her sister for every part, whether she's right for it or not. One agency used to have its half-dozen agents each make separate submissions—some 150 people per agent—in response to every breakdown.

Getting a thousand photos from the same agency was simply overwhelming, so I called their office.

"Do you think you could have just one person make submissions for each breakdown?" I asked. "Maybe put a little more thought into which of your clients is right for a particular part? You're submitting the same actress for the wife, the cop, the hooker, the teacher—she can't possibly be right for *all* those roles! And you're sending us so many people, we can't look at any of them—to be honest with you, we don't actually open your envelopes anymore." I even invited them to send someone over to have a chat with us and learn more about the way we work.

I don't know why they didn't take us up on our offer. Maybe it's not too surprising that they eventually went out of business.

On the other hand, we know another small agency whose submissions are so intelligent that they're a pure pleasure to receive. Clearly they read the breakdowns carefully and put a lot of thought into which clients are right for each part. When we meet their submissions, we see that they're good, strong actors, so the agency obviously puts a lot of care into whom it represents, as well. Their small size—which probably means that their clients get extra attention—doesn't seem to make them any less reliable.

Agents we know well often ask us to meet someone on a "general"—an informal session with an actor whom we've never met, more of a conversation than an audition. Of course, if we have a part that someone might be right for, we'll read them. But if nothing is available and the agent wants us to meet the actor for future reference, why not? This is a town of favors, so it's not only agents who ask us to see people: directors, studio people, and even a few well-known actors have put in a word for some promising newcomer.

Recently, an agent we like asked us to meet with Mark Strong, an English actor who's trying to establish himself over here. We'd seen Mark on a BBC-TV series as a 1960s "swinging London" gay Mafia man, and we also knew him as the creep who beats up George Clooney in *Syriana*. Though we didn't have him typed exclusively for the bad-guy roles, we didn't realize how funny he could be. When we met him, though, he was lovely—gracious and charming—and we chatted happily for at least half an hour. As it happened, he lived on the same London square as lots of the English guys we'd been seeing for the Bond search, so we had a nice talk about how they all took their kids to the same park. By the time our conversation was over, we had a much broader range of parts in mind for him, and we'll look forward to calling him for one of the many different roles he might play. Certainly we'd have considered him on a straight submission—but now we're in a better position to suggest him for parts as well.

Sometimes we'll also hear from an actor's manager. An agent is allowed to solicit work for an actor and can only accept 10 percent of whatever the actor earns. A manager is not supposed to solicit work but only to advise the actor on how to build his or her career, in exchange for up to 20 percent of the actor's salary. Under California law, agents are very tightly regulated, while managers are left pretty much to their own devices. Agents have to register, but your best friend could set herself up as your manager and no one would be the wiser. In fact, there was once an actress who put on an English accent and pretended to be her own manager—which might have boosted her career except for the fact that she wasn't a very good actress. She kept calling and calling after we'd already seen "her client," and no matter how many hints I dropped, she wouldn't leave us alone. Finally Jane, willing to play the bad cop, said, "Look, we've seen your actress and she's not that talented and not that beautiful, so please, stop calling!" We'd never have knowingly said such a thing to the actress herself—so maybe that was poetic justice?

If you're a beginning actor, we advise you to check out your agent and your manager very carefully. *Never* go with anyone who wants money up front—they're supposed to make all of their salary out of the work they find for you (or, in a manager's case, the work they advise you to take). And if they insist that you use their photographer or makeover artist or anyone else who requires cash in advance, make sure you talk to other clients who've used those people, so you can be sure it's legit. We don't deal with sleazy agents, and you shouldn't either.

Certainly, though, we couldn't live without our favorite agents. We've got about twenty of them on speed dial right now, and they're the first folks we call when we desperately need an actor or want some fresh ideas to suggest to a director. We also depend on these agents to do some of our talent scouting for us. We can be sure that they'll be at Sundance and the other film festivals, and they'll come back with a long list of new clients that they'll then ask us to see.

JANE

Once a breakdown is completed, we might use it, too, rather than thumbing through the script for every part. As I worked my way through the *Beautiful Mind* breakdown, I came upon a small but significant role:

BECKY
This blonde co-ed is the woman whom Nash tried to pick up at a bar. The socially inept Nash offends her with a clumsy remark, and she retaliates by swatting him across the face . . .

To make the scene work, Becky has to be sexy and self-possessed—clearly out of Nash's league—but poor, awkward Nash approaches her anyway. His "clumsy remark" is world-class:

> *Look, I don't know exactly what things I am required to say in order for you to have intercourse with me. But could we assume I've said them? I mean essentially we're talking about fluid exchange, right? So, could we go right to the sex???*

At first, the young woman seems intrigued. We think for a moment that Nash's bold gambit might actually pay off. Then, almost without warning, she slaps his face.

The Sexy Coed is the kind of role both of us love to cast—the small part that can make or break a scene without anybody ever really noticing why. A lot of our job involves talking about money or scheduling, but this aspect of our work is pure craft, and we both take great pleasure in it. Our first step is to look at the glossy eight-by-ten photos that every actor uses as a calling card, known as head shots.

To cast a part like the Sexy Coed, I might have some ideas of my own, in which case I'll pull those actresses' head shots from my files. If Janet has any suggestions, she'll pull them for me as well.

Our files are organized by sex and age range (males,

25–35, females 45+, and so on), as well as by ethnicity and some special skills. If we've done a movie about magicians, for example, we'll have a magician file. We've done enough searches for little people that we have a little-people file. And we have files of people who speak foreign languages. These days, the Internet makes it less necessary to keep many of these files, and we've begun to rely on Internet Movie Database (IMDb) and other sources.

Once we're past the specifics, the search gets less organized and more intuitive: whichever one of us is primarily doing the movie pulls out huge armfuls of head shots and begins flipping through them at approximately the speed of a blackjack dealer in Vegas. We only stop when someone leaps out at us—when an actor catches our eye and makes us pause. We're looking for that indefinable something—different, perhaps, in each case, but always unmistakable—which makes us say, "Well. Maybe . . ."

Once we've made our piles, we'll bring in maybe fifty people for each part, even the small ones, and then put the top candidates on tape to show the director. Almost everybody starts by being considered for parts at the level of the Sexy Coed, though we have cast some newcomers in starring or featured roles—Brendan Fraser in a film called *School Ties;* Kyle MacLachlan in David Lynch's *Dune.* But most actors start here, including Matt Damon, whom we cast as the rich boyfriend's kid brother in *Mystic Pizza,* and Leonardo DiCaprio, whom we chose to get beat up by a tough girl in an episode of the TV version of *The Outsiders.* Famous actors whom we turned down at this level include Kevin Spacey and George Clooney, who both missed out on the snooty boyfriend in *Curly Sue.* We also passed on Clooney for one of the control-room guys in *Apollo 13.* Instead, the *Curly Sue* role went to John Getz while the *Apollo 13* part went to Todd Louiso, both Working Actors who have a long string of credits, familiar faces—and names you probably can't quite place.

JANET

So when we look at a head shot, what are we looking for? What makes a great face?

Most of the time, we want actors who look like people, not like Actors. If we're casting a stunningly beautiful woman or a gorgeous guy, a little actor-ishness may not be so bad. But if we're looking for a gas station attendant, a therapist, or a business executive, we need someone with some kind of reality about them, even if they're also exceptionally attractive.

Then we want someone who looks alive and intelligent—someone who seems to have something going on behind the perfect features and beautiful eyes. You'd be surprised how many otherwise attractive people don't come alive on-screen—it's as though they withdraw deeper into themselves, leaving the camera with nothing but a blank face. Actors who "the camera loves" are just the opposite—their very being seems to emerge through their pores, surrounding them with that indescribable aura known as "screen presence."

Basically we want someone who catches our attention. That's why Jane and I shuffle through the photos so quickly. Of course, some of that is simply to save our sanity—there are just so *many* of them!—but some of that is a test. You're shuffling along, one photo after another—and then suddenly, one of them makes you stop. You might not even know why, and it probably doesn't matter. If the picture caught your attention, there is at least the possibility that the real-life person will do so, too.

Once I've pulled a head shot, I look at the résumé on the back. First, I'll check out the actor's credentials. This isn't necessarily a make-or-break issue—if someone has a great face and the part isn't too big, I might not care where he trained or who she worked with before. But unless I'm desperate, I'm very unlikely to suggest a genuinely inexperienced person for a large part, or even a small one. Making movies is a very technical business. You've got to be able to repeat a fragment of a scene again and again and again, and always at the same level of intensity. Unlike the theater, where you have the chance to work up to an emotional moment, movies demand an instant ability to hit the right note—and then to repeat it through Take 2, Take 5, Take 27—whatever it takes to get it "in the can." All other things being equal, we prefer actors who have done commercials, television, independent films, bit parts—anything that assures us of their ability to meet the basic professional demands of being on-camera.

Besides the emotional demands, there are the physical ones. You've got to be able to hit your marks—to sit, stand, or walk in exactly the place the director has marked out for you, so you can be lit and shot as he intends. If Cop #3 keeps flubbing his one line or needs four tries to hit his marks, the director is going to wonder why I've sent him an actor who's wasted so much expensive shooting time.

Still, we can filter out the incompetent actors in the audition process. At this point, a great face trumps a poor résumé. If I really like someone's look—if my gut instinct is saying *yes,* or *see her*—I'll give even an inexperienced actor a try.

Finally, if I'm going through head shots from our own files, I'll check the back of the photo for one more thing: evidence of whether we've auditioned this person before. If we have, there'll be a note, such as "Great reading" or "Smart, charming, interesting—keep in mind."

The notes are almost always positive. If we've seen someone we don't like, we'll probably just toss their head shot. Why load up our files with mediocre actors when we already know more good ones than we can hire? Of course, if your agent submits you again and you look right, we won't hold your past against you. To be honest, we probably won't even remember that we've seen you before. (Sorry, actors, but we see *hundreds* of people. We can't possibly remember every one—although if we do remember you, yes, indeed, that is a very good sign.)

Occasionally there are some actors who are so bad—or who have behaved so rudely or unprofessionally, with us or on a set—that we keep their head shots precisely to remember *not* to give them a second chance. On the back of those photos goes the dreaded notation "NTBSA," which stands for "never to be seen again."

Now, actors, don't worry. We don't use this notation lightly. You won't get it if you're just "not very good"—maybe you were having a bad day, or maybe you'll take some more acting lessons and get better. You have to be really, truly awful to get the NTBSA, and even then, you may be able to get out of it. For example, then–Working Actor Tate Donovan once lost control during an angry scene and literally punched a hole in our plasterboard wall—but we forgave him when he returned, with flowers and apologies, to replaster it himself. On the other hand, the actor who was rude to the receptionist, brought in a real knife for a scene, and then used it in a threatening way with no concern for anyone's safety got the NTBSA. Of course, he wasn't a very good actor. If he had been, maybe we would have forgiven him, too.

JANE

One of the hardest qualities to convey through a head shot is sexuality, especially for actresses. In our society women are encouraged to be sexually attractive, but they aren't necessarily given a lot of leeway to expose their own sexual feelings. So it's often hard to cast a part that requires an actress to reveal her sexuality—it's such a personal, intimate part of her that she may not be willing to share it with a camera and several million filmgoers.

I remember years ago when I was casting the remake of *Breathless,* with Richard Gere in the role originally played by the French actor Jean-Paul Belmondo. For the part previously played by the American Jean Seberg, we were looking for a Frenchwoman, someone who could express a sexuality that would make the couple's passionate affair come alive.

A young woman named Elisabeth Leustig was our associate at the time, and she happened to be French. So she brought in a bunch of French fashion magazines—French *Elle,* French *Vogue,* and so on. There was one gorgeous model whom we kept seeing—collegiate and fresh-faced but with the sexual quality that we wanted. "Wow," I said. "If this girl can walk and talk as good as she looks, she's in. Do you think we've got to fly to Paris to see her?"

Indeed, we did have to go to Paris, where we met a whole slew of French actresses. And, indeed, Valérie Kaprisky—the girl in the magazines—was exactly the person we thought she was. She was only twenty at the time, and hardly a naïve girl, but just the sort of unspoiled, unfettered person we needed, and totally open to her own sexuality. It turned out that most French girls shared her openness, which both intrigued me and made me sad. Why couldn't American girls enjoy an equally relaxed relationship to their sexual feelings?

It might make all of us happier—and it would definitely make *our* jobs easier!

☆

Certainly sexuality was a big element in casting *A Beautiful Mind*'s Sexy Coed. For this brief appearance, we weren't looking for a big star or even someone with a huge résumé. But we did need someone who could make that pause work, someone who could hold that suspended moment between Nash's invitation to exchange bodily fluids and the climactic slap on the face.

First, our Coed had to seem sophisticated enough for the audience to think that she might actually go for Nash's direct approach. Then, she had to pull off the indignant look—a 1940s good girl who's conventional enough to be offended. You had to believe both that she might like Nash's crudeness and that she didn't.

If you start to think about all the famous actresses who *couldn't* play that part, you'll start to get a sense of just what it is that we do. A Meg Ryan type couldn't manage it—she'd seem too sweet. A Catherine Zeta-Jones look-alike wouldn't work, either—she'd give Nash a withering look before he made it halfway across the floor and he'd turn back, abashed and ashamed. Renée Zellweger, on the other hand, would be too approachable. It wouldn't seem nearly as brave for Nash to go after her in the first place. If the actress appeared too shy or uncomfortable with her own beauty—think Calista Flockhart or Maura Tierney—the slap would come off as virginal or scared, and the joke would be lost. Someone like Michelle Pfeiffer would make the Coed too vulnerable; the focus would shift to how much the slap cost her, distracting you from Nash and his pain. An Angelina Jolie type, though, would be too tough; you'd cringe every step of the way, knowing long before he crossed the floor that Nash would get shot down. And if the actress seemed too smart—with, say, the kind of intelligence that Jennifer Connelly would bring to the much bigger role of Alicia, Nash's wife—the Coed's rejection would take on too much weight. Nash's romance with Alicia works because we viewers believe that only someone of unusual intelligence can appreciate Nash's genius—and we believe this partly because we've seen the kind of girl who turns Nash down. So for this scene we needed a woman who was smart, sexy, sophisticated—but not too much so. Oh, and she also had to look like she belonged in the 1940s and be the right age for a college student.

Most likely, not one person in a thousand who watched *A Beautiful Mind* would notice the amount of labor and judgment that went into casting that scene. Only if we (or Ron Howard) made the wrong choice would you notice the casting, because instead of focusing on Nash and his miserable social life, you'd spend the whole scene thinking about how pretty the actress was, or how big her breasts were, or how contemporary she looked. Or the slap would seem mean or strange or well deserved, or you'd like Nash less, or your belief in the movie would be disrupted even if you didn't quite know why. For our job to be done right, it has to be invisible.

Ultimately, for a part that required less than three minutes of screen time, I'd go through hundreds of head shots and spend the better part of two days meeting and reading actresses in close to thirty auditions. From this group, I'd bring Ron several candidates, out of which he would choose three finalists—a blond, a brunette, and a redhead—to read with Russell.

JANET

Jane didn't start seriously pulling head shots for *A Beautiful Mind* until she had a script, but sometimes the head shots come first. When I was casting *The Perfect Storm* for Wolfgang Petersen, I knew there'd be a lot of men on the fishing boat, so as soon as I got the Call, I headed for our files. By that point, we'd worked with Wolfgang for so long that I had a pretty good idea of what he'd be looking for, so I started pulling interesting people whose look or style I thought might appeal to him. When I finally read the script, I saw that these top candidates were indeed right on.

Among the head shots I pulled were John C. Reilly, William Fichtner, and John Hawkes, so I had their agents send us their "demo reels"—excerpts of their best work. Wolfgang likes to look at tape, so Jane, Wolfgang, and I watched these tapes during our first sit-down, and we continued to look at them for several weeks. (Every director has his own process—this is Wolfgang's.) The three of us were also working on casting the leads—the parts eventually played by George Clooney and Mark Wahlberg—and we couldn't decide on these supporting roles until the leads were set. (For more on that process, see Chapter 4.) But I told the actors' agents to alert me if they got other offers. In fact, all three of my first-instinct choices were eventually cast. (By the way, *The Perfect Storm* was also a chance for us to reunite with one of our favorite assistants, Jackie King, who'd met Wolfgang the first time we worked with him, on *Shattered.* Jackie was happy to leave the world of casting and work for Wolfgang while studying to become a psychologist—so you never know where the casting business will take you!)

For the local bit parts in *The Perfect Storm,* we hired Boston casting director Carolyn Pickman, so I didn't get to go to Gloucester. (Carolyn also worked with us on *Mystic Pizza*, and she's the person who brought both Ben Affleck and Matt Damon in to read for Steamer, the snooty younger brother role that Matt eventually got.)

When I first started casting, I often found myself on location, including for *The Outsiders* and *Rumble Fish*, both of which I cast for Francis Ford Coppola in Oklahoma. In those days, if you wanted a movie done anywhere outside of Hollywood, you were likely to have to go there yourself. Over the past twenty years, though, as location shooting has become more popular, a network of local casting directors has sprung up on which Jane and I both rely. Regional casting directors are generally based in midsize cities and cover a pretty decent amount of territory, often over several states. A whole local community of professional actors can make their livings from movies of the week, commercials, and other location shooting in their region, and the local casting person will know this cadre well. She (it's almost always a "she") will also know where to hire child actors, which locals have special skills, and pretty much anything else you need to know. Most of the biggest film roles are still cast on one of the coasts, but gone are the days when location shooting meant either working with amateurs or flying in an entire cast.

JANE

My first experience with location shooting was also my first casting job. By rights, I should have had to work my way up, but there I was, flying solo my first time out, casting my ex-boyfriend's low-budget film out of a scuzzy hotel on L.A.'s version of the Bowery. My fourteen-hour days seemed barely long enough for all I had to do, but there was so much going on I didn't have time to remember how inexperienced I was—and I loved every minute. Along with the low pay, Ralph had given me a tremendous opportunity, the chance to scramble up a steep learning curve that would stand me in excellent stead for the future.

I went on to work with the skillful and generous Joe Scully, casting a TV movie of the week called *The Million-aire*. I also met two wonderful women whom I thought would be extraordinary mentors, Terry Liebling and Jennifer Shull, both of whom were nurturing, smart, and extremely good at what they did. But neither one of them had a job for me, so I signed on to cast a TV show over at Universal.

If it had been my first casting job, I would have been over-joyed. But it was my third, and I was miserable. There I was working in a windowless basement office on a mediocre show for barely enough to live on. The script came out on Thursday and the episode had to be cast by the following Wednesday. It was all so fast and furious that you couldn't really find the actors who were *right*—just the ones whom you could get.

To cast a pilot, you get four to six weeks, time enough for the kind of care that goes into casting a film. TV episodes are turned out every week: you get five days to cast a half-hour show and seven or eight days for an hour show. With up to twenty new parts to cast each week, speed puts a lot of pressure on quality. And when writers make their inevitable last-minute changes, you might find yourself with just a couple of hours to cast the doctor, friend, or neighbor role they just wrote.

In those days, too, many good actors were reluctant to do TV. Today, the Will Smiths and Jennifer Anistons and George Clooneys have increased the medium's prestige, but back then the best of the acting pool was holding out for film work. (Commercials, too, used to be hard to cast until Sir

Laurence Olivier's famous Polaroid commercial suddenly made them acceptable. When Janet and I cast one of our very few commercials, we hired British actor Jonathan Pryce to be the on-camera spokesperson for Infiniti—and the ad actually helped to raise his U.S. profile.)

So there I was, working with actors who saw TV as a bitter compromise, and I was miserable. Then Jennifer Shull called out of the clear blue sky and spoke the words that would change my life. "I know this is really short notice," she said, "but do you think you could start working for me next Monday?"

I probably would have said "yes" if she'd asked me to pay *her*. But she went on to add, "I'm really sorry—I can only get you $800 a week. Will that do?"

That was more money than I'd ever heard of in my life, and I thought my brain was going to explode. But in my best actory, stay-calm voice, I said, "Oh, well, $800 a week, that could be okay."

So I took the job with Jennifer, where I also had the pleasure of meeting Janet. A few months later, Francis Ford Coppola asked Jennifer to head the casting department at his new Hollywood studio, Zoetrope. On the condition that she be allowed to bring Janet and me, she said "yes." And off we went, to the place we'd come to call the University of Zoetrope.

JANET

Zoetrope was, frankly, amazing. Francis was one of the most exciting and well-respected American directors of the 1970s, and his plan to reestablish the studio system under the supervision of an artist, rather than the businessmen who had run the old studios, seemed poised to create an American film renaissance. We all thought that if anybody could make commercially viable artistic cinema, it would be Francis, and we had the heady sense of being present at the birth of a whole new artistic movement.

Sadly, it didn't work out that way. But during its brief run—from 1980 to 1984—Zoetrope was an almost magical environment, with people like Marlon Brando and Gene Kelly routinely wandering through the corridors; Michael Powell (director of *The Red Shoes*) available to us as Director Emeritus and all-purpose adviser; and Francis manically devising new plans and discovering new talent every day of the week. (Though poor Jane never did meet Marlon—the one time he showed up for one of Zoetrope's famous Friday night beer-and-pizza parties, she'd gone home early with a cold.)

To be sure, as financial problems worsened, some Fridays we'd all get called into the little screening room, where emergency meetings were held, to be told that the company didn't have enough money to cover our paychecks that week. "Maybe on Tuesday," someone would suggest, and the rest of us would say, "Okay, no problem." Who needed money? Being part of this groundbreaking movement was reward enough.

Jane and I were in seventh heaven. Not only were we working under Jennifer, our beloved mentor, but we were also the colleagues of former casting director Fred Roos—famous for having cast such films as *The Godfather, American Graffiti,* and *Five Easy Pieces.* Now Fred had signed on as a producer for the fledgling studio.

One of the most remarkable aspects of Zoetrope was the wide range of projects that Francis explored there. Although this very openness probably led to the studio's downfall, it was thrilling while it lasted. Once, I remember, Francis decided to do an old-fashioned children's musical and I spent months auditioning child singers and dancers. I'll never forget the five-year-old nymphet who sang "I Will Survive." She showed up at the audition with her mother *and* her grandmother—clearly two ex–child actors themselves. As the game little girl bumped and grinded like a miniature Gypsy Rose Lee, I noticed the bags under her eyes and the desperate look on her face. Thank God, I thought, *that* hadn't been my introduction to show business.

I continued to worry, though, that my personality might be working against me. I wasn't anxious or timid, but I was definitely somewhat quiet, and in the flamboyant world of Zoetrope, I sometimes felt like a fish out of water.

Then came *The Outsiders,* based on the best-selling adolescent novel by S. E. Hinton. A librarian and some students from a Fresno junior high sent Francis a copy of this, their favorite book, along with a petition begging the director to make it into a movie. Francis was a big believer in education, so he glanced at the novel and agreed. Originally some up-and-coming Zoetroper was slated to direct—a documentary filmmaker who was doing his first feature—and I didn't feel particularly nervous about being asked to cast it. After all, I told myself, it wasn't as though I were doing it for Francis.

Then Coppola read the book on an airplane and fell in love with it. He decided to direct the movie himself—and suddenly I *was* doing it for Francis.

Francis made it clear that he not only wanted Unknowns, he wanted *great* Unknowns—a bunch of fabulous, heartthrob kids with movie-star good looks and an authentic kind of toughness that could evoke the alienation and longing so beautifully captured in the novel. My challenge was not only to find individuals who could play the roles but to put together a community, a vital but conflicted group of boys.

As it happened, these great Unknowns turned out to be great indeed—and remarkably nice people as well. Plus they were all, frankly, gorgeous. Rob Lowe is still a very handsome guy, but in those days, he was just stunningly beautiful. I needed someone to play Sodapop, who's described as "movie-star handsome"—even more beautiful than the rest of the boys. But Sodapop can't be cocky or taken with himself; the character is actually very sweet, the peacemaker of the group. As soon as I saw Rob, I knew he was that guy. He's still pretty much that way. All these years later, whenever we run into him, he's always happy to see us, bubbling over with enthusiasm for whatever he's working on at the moment.

Tom Cruise was also always warm and friendly. Years later, when we were casting *A Few Good Men,* he was set for the leading role before we ever came on board, but Jane saw him when he read with actresses for the female lead. Tom asked not only about me but about my husband, Michael. How many movie stars would even have remembered our names, let alone asked after us?

The first time I saw Tom, arriving for a casting session with the other guys, it was as though he had a kind of force field around him, setting him apart. He was only nineteen, but he already seemed to have an incredible drive and an inexhaustible enthusiasm. You could tell he was game to do anything that the picture needed, and that he had a powerful long-term vision of the kind of work he wanted to do.

The Outsiders had so many parts to fill that it took us a while to figure out who'd play what. One day I found myself in a huge casting session in New York City, set up to show us different performers in different combinations. Fred Roos was running the show, but so was I, organizing little groups of guys, giving them their parts, sending them off to one corner of the room to rehearse together while some other little group read for Francis. As the session continued, I felt I was weaving a seamless web of energy—reassuring this actor, explaining a scene to that one, reminding Francis of what came next, making silent eye contact with Fred as we nodded and smiled at each other across the room. Although I'd often felt intimidated by the oversize personalities at Zoetrope, Fred and I were both on the quiet side—and suddenly, that didn't seem to matter. In fact, the "talent" probably found our laid-back approach kind of restful.

When it was all over, I joined Fred and New York casting director Jane Iredale at one end of the room, sinking into my folding chair with an exhausted sigh. Jane was staring at me, and I wondered what was wrong. "That was amazing, the way you ran that session," she said.

"Really?" I said. "I didn't feel like I was doing anything, really." But to myself, I had to admit that I knew exactly what I had done.

JANE

Janet's New York casting session for *The Outsiders* was just a prelude to her time on location in Oklahoma, back in the days when we often cast on location. These days, we're more likely to use local casting directors, sparing us from such adventures as casting an entire Soviet army in New Mexico, as I had to do for *Red Dawn*. We needed several young men who spoke Russian well enough to make us believe they were indeed the Soviet soldiers whose occupation of the United States sets the plot in motion, but where in the world would we find Russian speakers in Las Vegas, New Mexico, a little country town seventy miles east of Santa Fe?

Even though it would be expensive to fly people in, I started lining up Slavophones from L.A., just in case.

Then I made an amazing discovery: the University of New Mexico in nearby Albuquerque has an entire Russian Studies department. Well, if you were a college kid studying Russian, wouldn't you love to play a Soviet soldier in a John Milius movie? The students were more than happy to turn out in great numbers, sparing us the trouble and expense of flying people in. And if the Albuquerque locals hadn't been enough, guess what? Santa Fe was also home to a Russian émigré community.

By the time we came to cast *The Da Vinci Code,* we were able to rely more upon local casting directors, though I was very involved as well. One of our earliest casting challenges was Sophie, the French woman who helps hero Tom Hanks crack the code. At first, Ron and Brian weren't sure how to define our Sophie search. A number of prominent actresses had expressed an interest in the part, including Jennifer Connelly and Cate Blanchett, both of whom spoke French and had worked with Ron.

But when I heard those names, I was surprised. "Don't we want an actual Frenchwoman?" I asked. "It's such a great opportunity to put together a really international cast, with people actually from all those countries in the book. That seems so much more interesting than Actors Doing Accents."

Both Ron and Brian were intrigued by the notion of an authentically international cast, and eventually they decided to go with it. But now I had to find a French actress, and I wasn't all that familiar with the Gallic movie scene. I went through the usual channels—U.S. agents who represent European actresses, French agencies, the Internet. I also reached out to anyone else I could think of: my friend, the French lawyer; an L.A.-based French potter I happened to know; a reporter whose name I'd gotten from a manager friend. Somehow I got a sense of who I should be looking at, and I started renting their movies. When I had a list of French actresses in the appropriate age range, I began showing their films to Ron.

One day, Ron and Brian were planning their next trip to Paris to scout locations and start the incredibly complicated negotiations for shooting in the Louvre. "You know," Ron said suddenly, "we really should meet some of these French actresses we've been thinking about."

"Uh—*when* are you leaving again?"

"Friday," Ron said casually, and I leaped for the phone. Somehow I managed to put together meetings with about a dozen French actresses. There was no time for anyone to prepare an audition, especially since most of the people I talked to claimed not to be all that familiar with the book— or with Ron, either, for that matter. Hell, most of the primary agents I contacted didn't even speak English (or claimed they didn't), and since I didn't speak French, I had to conduct my business with their assistants, who did speak English.

We managed to book a hotel room where one of Ron's production assistants could conduct the meetings, running down to the lobby to escort each actress up to the room. "How will I know who these women are?" she asked.

"Just go to the hotel desk," I suggested. "The clerk can probably point out anybody who's been asking for Ron Howard and Brian Grazer."

I'm not saying it *wouldn't* have worked that way. But I began to realize that we really needed a French person in the room, someone who knew the actresses and could help manage the situation a bit more gracefully.

By this point, the lovely French actress Linda Hardy had made her way to Los Angeles, where I'd cast her to play a young Arab woman in a film directed by Mitch Davis now called *A House Divided.* Linda was also up for Sophie, but I was planning to have Ron meet her in L.A. She'd sent me a terrific audition tape when she was still in Paris, so I contacted the casting director who'd shot it for her. As it turned out, he wasn't available, but he did find me Paula Chevallet, another casting director who agreed to serve as my Parisian stand-in. Of course she knew all the actresses we'd invited, and she even suggested a few people of her own. She was a lovely presence in that hotel room—ready to translate, explain, introduce—and the entire day was a great success.

From those initial meetings, we picked out a handful of women we really liked and flew them to L.A. to read with Tom Hanks. In some cases, you might audition actresses before bringing them in to read with a star of that magnitude, but here it wasn't necessary: each of these women had a body of work that spoke for her.

Meanwhile, Ron was continuing to assemble his international cast. He kept going back to Europe to scout locations, and I kept setting up meetings. Once, he was in Paris and we arranged for him to have breakfast with the distinguished French actor Jean Reno. And when Ron was in London, he breakfasted with Sir Ian McKellan, who had a few questions about the script. That worked out well, too.

Since most of the film would be shot in London, the majority of the smaller parts would be cast there. If I'd only had to hire a few stars, I might have gone to London myself, but for what we needed, it made more sense to use a local person who knew the London agents and all the local day players. (A day player is hired by the day, generally for a smaller part, so they tend to be the less expensive—and less well-known—actors.) We were delighted to hire the courtly John Hubbard as our British casting director.

Meanwhile, we still hadn't cast Sophie, though Linda Hardy was shaping into a strong contender. Ron had long ago considered and then rejected Audrey Tautou, the charming gamine who made an international sensation in the French film *Amélie* and who then surprised audiences as the desperate immigrant in *Dirty Pretty Things.* Audrey next went on to play the courageous war widow of *A Very Long Engagement.* But when we started casting *Da Vinci,* Ron had only seen *Amélie,* and he'd retained an initial impression of Audrey as young and delicate. She was lovely, he agreed, but hardly the woman to play the strong, determined Sophie.

Then I happened to catch Audrey on an episode of Charlie Rose, where she was promoting *A Very Long Engagement.* I was so struck by the strength of her presence that I made Ron a tape.

Ron, too, was impressed with Audrey's persona. She is, after all, a very focused and dedicated young woman—not the childlike creature she seemed to be in *Amélie* but a strong-willed woman in her mid-twenties.

"Maybe I've made a mistake," Ron said after viewing the tape. "Maybe we should get her over here."

Mlle Tautou was not only promoting her most recent movie—she was in Japan—but was also in the process of preparing for her next one, a French film to which she was deeply committed. Somehow, though, she found the time to

fly to L.A. to read with Tom. By this point, she was the only
one of our actresses who hadn't read the book—in fact, she'd
only had the material for the length of her plane ride from
Japan to Paris to Hollywood. Altogether, she'd spent twenty-
four hours en route, so, frankly, I was surprised that she
could stand up straight by the time she got there. And indeed, her first two attempts were subdued and tentative as
she gradually found her way into the scene.

Then, on the third take, something started to happen.
She really caught something about the character, and the
whole room responded. Tom—who had read with every Sophie candidate and given each one of them his all—immediately kicked into a higher gear. For the first two takes, he,
too, had gone slowly, giving Audrey time to find her way. He
could see, as could we all, that this was the first actress who
had shown up without an entire vision of the character that
she was ready to present; instead, she had allowed her performance to unfold, and Tom had given her the space to do
that. But when she found an approach that worked, he
matched her energy—and the two of them began to create a
powerful chemistry.

Watching them, I was impressed all over again with what
Star-quality presence does to a room. We'd seen lots of good
actresses read for Sophie—but Audrey was more than a good
actress; she was a Star. She had three big movies under her
belt and she wasn't the least bit intimidated by the presence
of the *Da Vinci* team. After all, she was already doing another
film (one of her conditions for *Da Vinci* was that we schedule her participation around that other commitment), and
she felt no need to show us how good she was. Instead, she
simply worked on the character the way an actress does,

trying different things, allowing the character to inhabit her, letting things take their own instinctive course. She didn't need to impress us—and as a result, she could take bigger risks. I'm very fond of Linda Hardy and I expect big things from her, but for this project, we needed someone who was *already* a Star—and that Star was Audrey.

3 ☆ AUDITIONING
THE UNKNOWNS

JANET

Casting a movie requires a Zen-like balance between two polar-opposite principles: *Know exactly what you want,* and *Prepare to be surprised.*

These factors come into play the moment we begin looking at head shots, and they become even more important when we start auditioning, especially because lots of actors don't actually look like their photos. Retouchers can make people look younger, sexier, and prettier—which may get you through the door, but which ends up wasting a great deal of everyone's time. You won't win any brownie points with us, either, after we've wasted fifteen minutes seeing you for something you're not right for. Actors, please, send us head shots that actually look like you, so we can call you for something you've got a chance at.

Sometimes head shots are deceptive in more subtle ways. Women who can look extraordinarily sexy in a still photograph often turn out to be either girlish or uncomfortable when asked to display the same affect in a scene. Male charm is also tricky: lots of guys who look warm and genuine in their photos read as wooden, phony, or just not so interesting when they show up. (If you've ever struggled with Internet dating, you know exactly what I'm talking about!)

When an actor comes in, your first step is to measure his or her quality against the ideal character you've already envisioned based on your reading of the script and your discussions with the director. A clear image of the character is especially important when the part is small. The actor may have less than thirty seconds to establish a character, so you ask yourself immediately if he or she has the quality you're looking for: Innocent? Wise? Virginal—but available? Virginal—and repressed? Should the character seem comforting? Dangerous? Charming and a little wacky? Tragic and haunting? Do you believe this woman as a truck-stop waitress? Do you buy this guy as Lord of the Manor? And, never to be forgotten, does the performer read as the right age?

JANE

To gauge the candidates for the Sexy Coed in *A Beautiful Mind,* I started by calling them in for a reading. As our assistant videotaped each performance, I stood off camera and recited Russell's shocking line ("So, could we go straight to the sex?"), while on camera the actress conveyed her offended reaction and pantomimed her slap.

Thank God for video, I thought more than once during this process. In the old days, actors were often reluctant to go on tape because they were worried about being badly lit. Maybe, too, they thought they'd have a better shot at meeting a director if they refused to be taped, or perhaps they feared that a bad audition tape would be around to haunt them forevermore.

Now, thank heavens, actors are used to working on video, and we routinely tape everyone who comes in. From our master copy of all auditions, we edit a second-generation tape of our top choices, which we'll send to the director. Sometimes directors will cast the smaller roles right from the tape.

Video also allows us to review our own decisions. We might see a hundred or more actors over a three-day period, and by the time you get to #98, you tend to wonder whether #43 was really was wonderful as you thought.

Studios, too, might want to see this early tape. Usually they're only interested in the larger parts and maybe the very top candidates for some smaller roles, but there are always exceptions. When I was doing *Rebound* for Fox, studio people wanted to see our first-round tape on several dozen candidates for such tiny roles as Referee Freddy, Preacher Don's Sidekick, and Vulture Mascot. How closely a studio wants to supervise such minor parts varies depending on the studio, the budget, the director's experience, and a host of other idiosyncratic factors.

Tape is also useful for revealing how an actor works with the camera. Some performers' energy seems to fill the room in person but somehow flattens out on-screen. Don't ask us why—it's one of the great mysteries of how the camera interacts with the human face—but it's definitely something we want to find out *before* we cast them. The opposite is also true: a performer who seems ordinary, even dull, in person can come suddenly to life on-screen.

Video is particularly useful when you're looking for a tiebreaker—trying to choose between two strong candidates who may nevertheless reveal noticeable differences on tape. An experienced performer really knows how to work the

camera—how to use the flick of an eye or the flare of a nos-
tril to convey worlds of emotion. Meryl Streep is famous for
being able to milk enormous meaning out of a tiny lift of the
chin or an extra-long blink.

Of course, live auditions also have their advantages—you
can direct actors on the spot, and you see exactly what you're
getting. The contrast between live and tape is especially key
when we're reviewing videotape from an actor's previous
films, or when the tape is produced by the actors themselves:
the right use of lights, filters, and makeup can do wonders
in hiding an actor's flaws. Most of our directors rely on a
combination of tape and live auditions, though Wolfgang
Petersen vastly prefers to cast actors from tape, and Nancy
Meyers insists on multiple live auditions for everyone who
makes it past Round One.

For *Beautiful Mind*'s Sexy Coed, we used a combination
of taped and live auditions. I chose a dozen first-round audition videos to show Ron Howard, and together, we chose our
top three candidates to read with Russell Crowe. Star auditions at that level are rare—you don't usually take up the
star's time with the smaller parts. But because this scene was
so specific, Ron wanted to include Russell in the choice.

JANET
A typical audition scene for a small part might have only
one to three lines:

> CLERK: Will that be all, ma'am?
> HEROINE (*looking around anxiously*): I—I'm not sure.
> CLERK: Well, make up your mind, lady—there's people
>   waiting.

Despite—or maybe because of—the part's size, we'll need quite a bit of information to cast that Clerk. Should the scene build tension or add comic relief? Is it meant to demonstrate how dull the Heroine's life is, or should it expose a timidity that the Heroine must learn to conquer? Is the Heroine supposed to reveal her charm, demonstrate her bad temper, or succumb to her absolute despair about what to do next? The answers to those questions determine how the Clerk should read those lines—and tell us what to look for in an audition.

As you can see, the qualities a role demands aren't always obvious. *In the Line of Fire* opens with a scene in which hero Clint Eastwood sits in a bar and chats with a fifty-year-old woman. The script specified the actress's sex and age, but no more. We needed to know whether Wolfgang Petersen saw that woman as an uptight businesswoman, a bored housewife, a sexy broad, or a tough dame. (With a director I hadn't previously worked with, I'd probably just ask. After having done so many films with Wolfgang, I guessed he wanted a dame—and I was right.)

Likewise, if all we know about a role is "Clerk," then we have to find out if we're going young or old, sassy or exhausted, Brooklyn or Korean, heartthrob (with a little comic moment as the Heroine checks him out) or slightly menacing (to build an already growing sense of danger). A decisive director may have already told us exactly what to look for. Or we might be working with someone of the "I'll know it when I see it" persuasion, in which case, we may suggest our own vision of the Clerk. Or maybe the director wants us to bring in a range of options. Nancy Meyers is notorious for needing lots of choices for parts like this—I hate to tell you how many people came in to read for the one-line part of the Customs Officer in *The Holiday*.

Of course, some scenes are written in such a way that even a tiny role calls for specific qualities. For example:

TEENAGE HERO: Um, Ashley, would you, um, be willing to go to the prom with me?

ASHLEY *looks at her fellow cheerleaders and bursts out laughing. The girls walk away together, giggling.*

ASHLEY (*as she walks away*): So Brad called last night, and he is just sooooo dreamy . . .

Obviously, whomever we cast as Ashley has to read as pretty, sexy, self-confident, and a little bit mean. She also has to appear to be a teenager, even if in real life she's twenty-seven. Since she's rejecting the Hero, she probably could be taller than he is; heroines, of course, must be shorter or should at least match the hero's height. Ideally, the evil Ashley will be a strong physical contrast to the Nice Girl who eventually accepts Our Hero—so Ashley and the Nice Girl should have contrasting looks. For starters, they probably shouldn't both be blondes, brunettes, or redheads. Since the Nice Girl is likely the bigger part, maybe even the heroine, Ashley's hair color will be cast around hers (or we might ask her to dye her hair). Likewise, if the Nice Girl is an athletic type, Ashley should be delicate; if the Nice Girl is a wispy little thing, Ashley might seem more sturdy, and so on. For a part that's clearly all about looks, we're unlikely to choose an Ashley who reads as a "diamond in the rough" or who's unusually tall, short, heavy, or rail-thin. And if the Hero is white, Ashley probably will be, too—or will at least read as white—otherwise, we risk sending a message we don't intend. As you can see, there's not a lot of leeway here.

Having said this, we could still bring in enough Ashley candidates to populate a small Midwestern city, so we can't stop with the basics. Even for a small part, we're going to hold out for an actress with a great sense of timing, a lot of personal magnetism, and the ability to convey with a glance that she's a queen and he's a worm.

So we start every audition reminding ourselves to *Know what we want*—but then we must definitely *Prepare to be surprised.* We've imagined a sexy scene played in a slow, sultry voice, but an actress finds a way of rushing through the lines as though she can hardly wait to jump into bed. We've visualized a brusque Clerk, annoyed and preoccupied, whose neglect will make the beleaguered Heroine feel even more alone in the world. Instead, the actor plays against the obvious meaning of the lines ("Well, make up your mind, lady!"), turning an apparent dismissal into a weird kind of overly solicitous concern—something so creepy and unexpected that he's just ratcheted up the scene's menace another few notches.

Sometimes, too, Jane and I surprise each other. When she was casting *Night Shift* for Ron Howard, for example, she was having trouble finding someone to play Bill Blazejowski, the slacker who convinces his straight-arrow co-worker (played by Henry Winkler), that they should start a prostitution ring in their morgue.

Bill was not an easy character to cast. Frankly, he was a pain in the butt, and his ethics were borderline, to say the least—not to mention his lack of respect for the dead. To make that part work, you needed someone who could be annoying, reckless, and relentlessly committed to bad behavior, while still finding a way to make you like him.

Jane had looked at a number of up-and-coming actors: Jim Carrey, Tom Hanks, the young comic Howie Mandel. But none of them were quite what Ron had in mind.

"You know," I said one day, "there was this guy I saw a couple months ago . . ." At one point, we'd been working on a Zoetrope musical called *Sex and Violence* about a movie-obsessed man who gets off a studio tour bus and just sets up his own office on a movie lot, and a young actor named Michael Keaton had read for the part.

Michael seemed like the most annoying bad puppy in the world—but a puppy so endearing that you could never quite bear to hit him with the rolled-up newspaper. I'd never forgotten his unique brand of intensity and charm, though his career hadn't yet taken off. By this point, Michael had done some TV—he'd even played a stagehand on *Mister Rogers' Neighborhood*—but he'd never done a feature. Jane did indeed cast him in *Night Shift*—and launched his career.

JANE

Sometimes we neither get what we want *nor* are we pleasantly surprised. The early audition process can be enormously discouraging, particularly when we're reading actors who are Unknown even to us. We're periodically shocked at the lack of craft we encounter at this level—actors who can turn on the charm and personality but who don't seem to know how to create a character. On *Rebound*, for example, we saw fifty—count 'em, fifty—teenage girls read for the part of the "quirky, bookish" high-school reporter, and not one of them could pronounce the word "Pulitzer." ("Do you know what that is?" I asked one young auditioner. "Sure," she said in her perfect So-Cal drawl. "My mom told me it's kind of like an Academy Award for writing.") Likewise, when casting the Sexy Coed, I saw all too many actresses who could *indicate* sexy—flirting with the camera, batting their eyes—but who didn't have the moment-by-moment skill to make the scene work.

In acting terms, we're always looking for someone who can play actions and make choices—a performer who doesn't just speak the lines but uses them specifically to accomplish an objective. The right actress will make you sense an entire history behind her face, a person with a distinct if mysterious past that somehow shapes her response to this encounter, a woman whose personality shines through every word, every pause, every lifted eyebrow or parting of the lips. If the actress is good enough, she'll make you feel as though she herself has left the room and another person has come strolling in. In fact, a skilled actress's belief in her alternate reality is so powerful that it can force the person who's reading the scene with her to believe it, too. If the actress sees you as a dorky, awkward adolescent guy, you'll start to feel, act, and talk like one, almost against your will.

A good actor also needs to be able to shape her performance. For example, in the Sexy Coed scene, we'd look for someone with a strong sense of comic timing who knows just how long to stretch out that pregnant pause before it stops being funny and simply seems silly. And if we asked her to play the scene a bit differently—with more comedy, or more disdain, or simply with greater intensity—we'd want her to incorporate that instruction into her performance, revealing her all-important capacity to take direction.

These are the bottom-line abilities that we expect to find in any actor—even a complete Unknown.

JANET

Zoetrope was a virtual gold mine for Unknown talent. Many of the actors we first met there went on to remarkable careers, even as Jane and I sharpened our talent-spotting abilities under Jennifer's—and producer Fred Roos's—guidance. Then, sadly, the studio fell and we were forced out on our own.

Zoetrope's demise looks inevitable now, but at the time, we couldn't quite believe it. How could lack of financing and the new teen-oriented blockbusters win out over Francis's extraordinary artistry? How could a special-effects movie triumph over serious adult films about love, loss, and the human spirit?

Still, the signs were unmistakable. Instead of getting our paychecks a little late, we suddenly found ourselves working for half pay, and then for no pay. The studio was falling apart, literally—the roof was leaking, the toilets didn't flush. Eventually all the buildings and their contents would be auctioned off to pay the enormous debts that had accumulated. Financing for Zoetrope had always been shaky—Francis's ambitions were as massive as his talent—and the final nail in the coffin was the well-publicized failure of Francis's 1982 musical love story, *One from the Heart*.

We came to call those last days at Zoetrope the Fall of Saigon—a tribute to Francis's more successful movie, *Apocalypse Now*. Yet despite the downward spiral, good movies were still being made right up until the end. I was lucky enough to miss some of the worst times by being in Tulsa in 1982, casting first *The Outsiders*, then *Rumble Fish*.

Being part of those two movies—which I still consider Hollywood landmarks—was a special treat. For *The Outsiders,* we discovered several new actors who became a virtual Who's Who of 1980s Hollywood: besides Tom Cruise and Rob Lowe, we also cast Matt Dillon, Emilio Estevez, Leif Garrett, C. Thomas Howell, Diane Lane, Ralph Macchio, and Patrick Swayze.

Matt was the perfect actor for S. E. Hinton movies—he seemed to be the exact embodiment of what she wrote, other than being from New York! He was a very bouncy, friendly guy who by age eighteen had already become a movie star— he'd been working since he was about fourteen. He was always being written up in teen magazines as the cute, hot, dangerous teenager of the time, but he wore his fame lightly. I never saw him be anything less than charming, though I think it freaked him out a bit when he'd go somewhere and instantly be surrounded by hundreds of screaming fans. Part of what made him so appealing was the way he combined the bravado of the undeniably hot guy with an underlying vulnerability, which, as far as I could tell, was not an act at all but exactly how he felt.

Diane Lane came to us at age seventeen, but she'd also been working for years, having done a stint at New York's famed La Mama Theatre when she was seven and a wonderful Laurence Olivier movie, *A Little Romance,* when she was fourteen. Zoetrope producer Fred Roos had his eye on her from the beginning, but we all respected the body of work she'd amassed by such a young age. *The Outsiders* and *Rumble Fish* were real boys' movies, with Diane as virtually the only girl, so I don't think she had quite as much fun as the guys, who horsed around and let off steam together when they weren't on camera. But Diane was always a very serious actress who even as a teenager brought a quiet dignity to her work. She'd had a difficult life by then—apparently her parents had engaged in an ugly custody battle—but whenever I saw her she was calm, friendly, and ready to work.

The Outsiders created a new kind of filmmaking, especially about teenagers—a more naturalistic look at how young people talk, act, and experience the world. This movie was one of the few Hollywood offerings to deal realistically with kids from the wrong side of the tracks, and to portray honestly children whose parents had abused, neglected, or otherwise failed them. Films about miserable, badly treated kids are almost a cliché now—but in 1982, when *The Outsiders* was made, Hollywood's idea of a teen movie was *Beach Blanket Bingo,* a movie Francis gently lampoons by having his anguished characters watch it at a drive-in. The contrast between traditional Hollywood teen fare and *The Outsiders* couldn't have been stronger.

Rumble Fish is also a story of alienated teens from the wrong side of the tracks, young people whom the adult world has grievously failed. The movie's plot is episodic and its shooting style is hallucinatory, trying to capture the day-to-day disorientation of a confused teenage boy. It featured strong performances from Mickey Rourke and Laurence Fishburne—who were just starting to make their mark—as well as giving new prominence to Nicolas Cage, who was called Nicolas Coppola when we cast him. (We cast him first in his uncle's movie, but then *Valley Girl* made him famous before *Rumble Fish* came out.) *Rumble Fish* also includes a terrific turn from Dennis Hopper as the troubled heroes' even more troubled father, and gave Matt Dillon and Diane Lane another chance to play frustrated teenagers.

Rumble Fish was a noble effort at creating a true American art cinema—Francis called it his art-house film for kids. With its off-kilter impressionistic shots, its exaggerated sound effects, and its bleak portrait of a dying industrial city, the film took extraordinary risks that the art-house crowd appreciated but that never translated into commercial success. *Raiders of the Lost Ark* and *Star Wars* were the future, not *Rumble Fish* and *The Outsiders.* But Francis's groundbreaking work continues to influence U.S. movies to this day in the work of such directors as Jim Jarmusch, Gus Van Sant, and Quentin Tarantino.

The local casting for these films was fascinating. We set up a production office in the poorer part of Tulsa, where the beaten-down kids in both movies might have lived. Then we ran open calls—auditions that are basically open to anyone—from notices posted in community centers, churches, and grocery stores. Local people would come in and register, and we'd note their height, weight, size, age, race, address, and phone number. For the extras casting (which we never did again), I'd shoot Polaroids of everyone and file them by age and type.

We didn't need to audition the extras—a picture was enough—but we did need to hear people read for the speaking parts. Since we were mainly working with inexperienced actors, we took our time with the auditions, helping people learn to relax on camera.

With the extras, the key thing was to keep track of who'd already been used. If someone appeared at, say, the drive-in movie, you didn't necessarily want them showing up later in the bar. The goal was to populate an entire world, not to give the illusion that the same six guys were following the heroes all over town. I still think *Rumble Fish* is one of the most visually stunning movies ever to come out of Hollywood, and the reality of it—the look and feel of the working-class extras milling about in the background—was a central part of that success.

I really enjoyed getting to know the Tulsa community, which responded to both movies with warmth and an extraordinary spirit of cooperation. Still, working with the extras was extremely difficult.

Think for a moment how a movie schedule works. The assistant director calls you up and says, "We're doing scene 22A tomorrow at 4 p.m. Francis wants 150 extras to be at the drive-in movie." You get on the phone and start making calls—except maybe some of your extras don't have phones (it was a very poor community), aren't home (those were the days before answering machines and cell phones), or simply aren't picking up when you call (folks who work the night shift often take their phones off the hook if they're sleeping during the day). People sign up for a movie as a lark, but when it actually comes to rearranging their lives to accommodate a director's vision or a shooting schedule's logistics, well, that's another story. (These days, cell phones do help, but while L.A. and New York have a whole cadre of professional extras, most location extras still have day jobs and families, and they still have trouble accommodating a long-term shooting schedule.)

But let's say you do get 150 commitments for your 4 p.m. scene, and you breathe a sigh of relief. Then the A.D. calls again. "Sorry, Francis has changed his mind." (Or, We're running late. Or, One of the stars has a sore throat. Or, The owner of the drive-in has changed *his* mind. Or—well, you get the idea.) "So forget the 150 teenagers at the drive-in until next week. Now we need 50 adults for the barroom."

And the calling starts all over again—both to the folks you don't want to come in (yet), and to those you do.

Sometimes Francis would get a brilliant idea, and I just didn't know how I was going to make it work. One key scene in *Rumble Fish,* for example, was set in a poolroom, which we were shooting in a town close to Tulsa. Francis decided it would be great to have a band in the scene. Since the poolroom was supposed to be on the "black side of town," we needed an African American band, one that specialized in the bluesy Kansas City sound that seemed to fit the location.

"Oh, my God," I remember whispering to myself. "Francis wants a band."

Luckily one of the local guys standing near me happened to overhear. "I got a band," he offered.

"Thank you!" I said, praying that his band would work out. Indeed it did, and of course Francis was right—having the band in the poolroom added life and color to the scene. (I don't know what I would have done if Francis hadn't liked the band I found. Those are the questions you learn not to ask.)

Another centerpiece of *Rumble Fish* was a long sequence in which the hero and his brother spend the evening "on the wrong side of the tracks." It was a huge scene, involving three hundred extras for two solid weeks of night shooting. Many of our extras would work all day at their regular jobs, then come to our location and shoot all night. We had local cops doing security—and, as it happens, some local hookers playing hookers. I'm pretty sure some trade was being plied on the side as well. (If you watch the movie, notice the hooker who asks the hero's friend for a date. She's played by S. E. Hinton, the author of the source novel and co-author of the screenplay, as well as the author of the novel *The Outsiders*.)

Hookers notwithstanding, after three days it became exceedingly difficult to get more than about one hundred of our three hundred extras to show up. People had discovered how hard it is to be on a set—how much standing around you have to do, how much time it takes—and they simply didn't want to keep on with it. Sure they were getting paid, but not enough to make it worth turning their lives upside down. You'd try to convince someone that he or she had been "established"—that they were already in a shot and had to be there for the next time the camera found that part of the scene—but why was that *their* problem? They just wanted to go back to getting eight hours of sleep each night.

So we got creative. We'd put someone who looked like the missing person in the same clothes and hope that nobody would notice.

Throughout it all, our great inspiration was our director. The wonderful thing about working with Francis is that everyone—even the most obscure extra or the lowliest production assistant—always feels like part of the team. No one is a peon on Francis's set; everyone has a job to do, and everyone feels appreciated.

As a result, we had a lot of enthusiastic classmates at the University of Zoetrope, including the budding young actors that Francis eventually hired to stand in for the more experienced people—literally taking their places as Francis and his crew worked out lighting and camera shots. On most sets, the stand-ins aren't even actors. At Zoetrope, this non-acting job became a valuable apprenticeship. For example, on *One from the Heart* a then-Unknown Rebecca De Mornay stood in for Nastassja Kinski.

The people behind the cameras were also learning an enormous amount. "Video Ranger" Michael Lehmann—one of the guys in Zoetrope's pioneering video department—went on to direct *Heathers, The Truth About Cats and Dogs,* and *40 Days and 40 Nights.* One of the assistant directors on *The Outsiders* was David Valdes, who went on to become Clint Eastwood's producer—he came with Clint on *In the Line of Fire.* Daniel Attias, the second assistant director on *One from the Heart* and *Hammett* (a Zoetrope film directed by German wunderkind Wim Wenders) went on to work on *Beverly Hills, 90210;* he's currently doing *Entourage* and *House.* That was Zoetrope—a wonderful protected environment where Francis gave us the chance to learn, to take chances, even to make mistakes.

Not everyone was so generous. I remember casting a nice local actress to play the nurse in *The Outsiders.* She had several lines and was in a very, very complicated shot involving several camera angles and a series of moves. She had no trouble with the acting, but she hadn't done much film, and she had quite a bit of difficulty hitting her marks (taking the specific positions on the set that would enable her to be lit, framed, and miked as the director wished).

On a production of any size, there's always a first AD, who runs the set, and a second AD, who wrangles the extras and the smaller parts. The second AD on that movie was, to put it politely, a bit taken with his own power, and when I happened to show up on the set, he made the most of it. "Oooh, are you gonna be in trouble," he whispered. "That nurse you found isn't working out *at all.*"

My stomach was in knots until Francis came over. I could see the glee in the second AD's eyes as he anticipated the tongue-lashing I was sure to get.

"So this nurse," Francis said to me, "was she somebody's friend?"

"No," I said as calmly as I could. "She was the best actress we saw for the role."

"Oh. Okay," Francis said, and walked away.

The second AD looked at me in bewilderment. We both knew that some directors would have blamed me for the difficulty—Jane and I always have to keep in mind the possibility that an actor, especially one in a minor role, might end up costing a production way too much time and trouble. But most of the directors we work with aren't interested in laying blame, and certainly Francis wasn't. He just assumed that everyone was doing their best.

That second AD alienated a lot of people, as it happened. One day, my husband, Michael, visited me on the set around dinnertime. Patrick Swayze's wife happened to be there, too, and we all got into the line for the catering truck.

"Those other people can't be on this line," the second AD said, indicating my husband and Patrick's wife. "This food is just for people who are actually working on the movie."

Patrick laid into the guy—as well he should have. We all have a lot of sympathy for how difficult both the first and second AD jobs are—you're constantly mediating between the director, the D.P. (the director of photography, or cinematographer), the actors, and the crew. But that's no excuse for being a petty tyrant.

If I learned anything from Francis, it was the importance of finding the joy in what you're doing. There are miserable parts to any job, including Jane's and mine—but then you step back and say, "My God, look what I'm doing!" Francis's attitude was always, "Hey, kids, let's put on a show!" Sure, you tried hard to do good work—superb work, if you could manage it—but however much you struggled, it was no excuse for ignoring those magical times when it all comes together, or for allowing yourself to miss the intense joy that can be part of filmmaking at its best. My time at Zoetrope reminded me always to look for those joyous moments, and I'll always be grateful to Francis for that.

JANE

Meanwhile, back in Saigon, the rest of us were doing what we could to keep the studio afloat. For some time, the casting department—Jennifer, Janet, and I—had been one of the few elements of the studio that was still profitable, because we could so easily be "loaned out" to other producers. So for several months, Zoetrope paid us (or failed to pay us) our regular salaries, while using the casting fees we earned in its desperate attempt to stay afloat. We worked on *Yes, Giorgio* and *Frances* (the film that turned Jessica Lange from the *King Kong* girl into a respected actress), and even did some casting for *Reds*.

Still, we could no longer deny that Zoetrope had long ago ceased to be a viable employer. Jennifer, Janet, and I were planning to start our own company when Jennifer was offered a job at Columbia. Out of loyalty to us, she considered turning it down, but Janet and I urged her to make the most of the opportunity. "At least *one* of us should be working!" we joked.

So as the age of Zoetrope staggered to a close, Janet wrapped up *Rumble Fish* while Michael and I found a little office. Within two years, Michael would be the vice president who negotiated our deals, hired and fired our staff, coordinated our big searches, and kept us up-to-date on the latest video and computer technology. With Michael taking care of business, Janet and I are free to operate as "the artistes."

In those days, of course, there was precious little business to take care of. I ran up some curtains out of remnants while my second husband cobbled together some desks and shelves out of scrap lumber. When Janet got back from Oklahoma, we hung up our shingle—literally; we actually have a picture of the two of us grinning and pointing to it. Our apprenticeship was over: The Casting Company had begun.

JANET

Going out on our own was exhilarating—but nerveracking. Before, we'd always been on salary somewhere. Now we were responsible for our own incomes. Luckily, our reputations from Zoetrope, plus Fred Roos's and Jennifer's support, helped us get work pretty quickly.

One of my first post-Zoetrope movies was Brian De Palma's *Body Double,* a casting challenge from the very first scene. A beautiful woman is taking a shower, her body hidden by clouds of steam. She smiles provocatively as a handsome man starts to join her—

"Cut!" yells a director. We realize that we've been seeing not an actual event or even a porn movie but rather a scene about the *filming* of a porn movie. Out of the shower steps the actress, who's got a beautiful face but a flat chest. Into the shower steps the Body Double, who's got a homely face and magnificent breasts. "Action!" yells the director. And the steam rises again.

"Wow," I said to myself when I first read the script. "Great scene." But my stomach lurched just a little. I was the one who'd have to audition the breasts.

I loved working on *Body Double.* For one thing, I really liked the script, a noir-ish descent into the fascinating world of "adult" movies. I also had enormous respect for Brian,

who was terrific to work with—charming, low-key, and brilliant. I'll never forget going to meet him for the first time. He
put me at ease immediately, and I could see that he'd be a lot
of fun. As always, he wore his trademark safari jacket, a uni-
form that I soon came to see spared him the trouble of having to give up even a few minutes to think about clothing
instead of making movies. He has always been a great champion of women in the business, giving many women opportunities at the kinds of production jobs that, in the 1980s,
were still largely the province of men.

Body Double posed a set of casting challenges I've never
encountered before or since. The movie's main character was
a porn star, and for a while, there was some talk that Brian
was going to cast an actual porn star in the role. In the end,
he went with the legitimate (if uninhibited) actress Melanie
Griffith, mainly because he needed a terrific actress more
than he needed the reality factor or the shock value. However, a few of the smaller parts in the film were set aside for
X-rated talent, women who'd be comfortable with the partial
nudity and sexual explicitness that the film required. *Body
Double* was an R-rated film, a rating even less racy in 1984
than it is today. But Brian had to know that the actors could
do—or hint at—whatever he needed, from the suggestion
of two women kissing to the implication of an orgy in the
bathroom. My job was to find actors who'd take those di-
rections and run with them, who wouldn't hold up an
expensive, high-pressure shooting day by raising objections
or suddenly becoming shy. As with *Octopussy* and *Rebound,*
the movie would evolve somewhat in response to the casting:
what Brian decided to do in a particular scene would be determined at least partly by who was on the set and how they
inspired him.

So while I relied on the usual agency submissions for most of the larger parts, I also had to venture into the world of the "adult agencies" for actors who could create the pornographic atmosphere that Brian sought. This was new casting territory, and I was fascinated. I pored over the sexiest set of head shots I'd ever seen—okay, in this case, they were more like full-body shots—but almost immediately, it was just another casting job. I wasn't viewing pornography, I was doing what I always did: looking at actresses, trying to determine whether they had the qualities that a director needed.

When I visited one of the adult talent agencies to look at their books, I brought Michael with me, so I never felt personally threatened. I wouldn't have felt that way anyway, as it turned out. Adult agencies were a business like any other, and I was there simply to do a job. No one cared who I was; they were only interested in whom I wanted to hire.

Not that there weren't a few tough moments—but more in the auditions than anywhere else. This wasn't exactly the easiest film to read aloud: there was Brian watching from the sidelines, and there I was, wearing my usual loose turtleneck and jeans, sitting on the edge of a folding chair across from some hunky young guy or gorgeous young woman. "Oh, come on, baby, come on, baby, that's right, baby, give it to me good," I'd read, and the would-be porn star would moan and gasp in response. Most of the time, I got caught up in the process—I'd be picturing the actor in the scene, trying to see him or her through Brian's eyes, wondering if this one was sexier or more interesting than the beautiful creature we'd seen five minutes ago. But every so often, I'd see myself from the outside, and I'd be overcome by the surrealness of it all.

Then I'd look over at Brian, whose eyes were always twinkling. Despite the kinky atmosphere of the movie, Brian had a way of making it all seem normal and relaxed. He radiated calm—and maybe amusement, too—and that went a long way toward putting both me and the actors at ease.

"So," Jane would say as I'd pack up to leave for the evening. "Another day of casting boobies for Brian."

We weren't only casting women, of course. One day Jane happened to be doing the casting when James Woods came in to meet with Brian. At that point, Jimmy's career was definitely on the ascendant, although he was nothing like the Star he is today. Still, even then he had the manic, wired quality that we all associate with this brilliant actor, and he came in talking a mile a minute, his mind obviously working at top speed.

Jane happened to glance at his feet. She couldn't help noticing that Mr. Woods was wearing one brown sock and one black sock.

Jimmy picked up on her response immediately. Without missing a beat, he said, "I saw that, I just happened not to be paying attention when I put on my socks this morning," and went right back to continuing his conversation with Brian.

I also had to cast several actors to play porn stars—a far greater taboo in 1984 than it is today. As it happened, I ended up casting an actor who actually did gay porn. A reporter asked me later if I'd been aware of the man's background, clearly implying that I—and Brian, and the actor in question—should all be ashamed of ourselves.

"Nope, I had no idea," I said cheerfully, "but it was pretty good casting, wasn't it?" Later, the actor—a man living in a steady relationship and caring for an adopted daughter—called to thank me for not dumping on him. I still have trouble seeing what all the fuss was about.

Jane had a similar experience casting a stripper in *A Man Apart*. The character description read, "On a scale of 1 to 10, Assia was an 11," so Jane struggled for weeks to find an actress who was absolutely gorgeous, had a great body, and could also dance. The winner, Rachel Sterling, joined us at the pre-start party—and then Jane got a call. Someone had recognized Rachel from a porn film, where she'd gone by the name Angel Veil, and now the studio was wondering whether to keep this "questionable" performer in the film.

"We hired her to play a stripper, not a vestal virgin!" Jane fumed. "It took me a million girls to find someone fabulous enough to be an 11—and now they want me to go back down to a 9? What do they think, that porn viewers who recognize the poor girl will take out an ad to expose her?" In the end, Rachel kept her part, but the hypocrisy was striking.

It's ironic that Hollywood's reactions to Rachel and to the *Body Double* guy were so prudish, given how much the industry relies on beauty and sexuality. On the other hand, despite all the talk about Hollywood's wicked ways, we really haven't seen much misuse of sex per se. Every so often, a producer might ask us for a particular actress's phone number, but we simply remind him that we're a casting company, not a dating service. As in every walk of life, I'm sure some people do trade sex for favors—but honestly, movies cost way too much to let sex alone determine your casting. Even sexiness has its limits: while you often want hot, sexy actors on screen, plenty of Stars and even Superstars have personas that are warm, funny, and charming rather than "hot." Even looks aren't everything—to be consistently cast, you also need talent, determination, and a vision of the kind of work you want to do. Sexiness counts, sure—but it's not all that counts.

Still, ever since *Body Double,* we've had a soft spot for actresses with racy pasts. When former porn star Traci Lords came in to meet us, we made sure to treat her with the respect she deserved. And I'll never forget when we were casting a stripper for a Bond movie. Usually Michael does the preliminary casting of the strippers—women tend to feel much more comfortable stripping for a guy—and just sends us the callbacks. One of the dancers he chose was a very sweet woman who managed a strip club in L.A. and actually came from a stripping family in Kansas City. Her mom used to make the pasties for the girls in her dad's business; she thought they were little doll hats.

☆

Meanwhile, back on *Body Double,* I still had to find the perfect combination of homely face and beautiful breasts that would make that first scene work, so I lined up a few dozen actresses to come in to show me their mammary glands. I saw them privately—no need for Brian to watch the first round—and took Polaroids of the ones I thought were especially likely. I ended up taking Polaroids of everyone, in fact, because it was just too awkward to tell an actress that I didn't like her breasts. In those days, very few women had enhanced breasts, but the actress we hired did—and they looked perfect.

Throughout the whole process, I was as tactful as I could be, though the actresses didn't seem to care. No one answers a call for a bare-breasted role if she's not pretty comfortable displaying her anatomy, although I'm sure they'd have noticed if I'd treated them with lasciviousness or contempt. There are casting directors who seem to enjoy lording it over the "talent," even in less sexually charged situations, and actors from the smaller agencies are particularly vulnerable because they don't have powerful agents to go to bat for them. But Jane and I have always tried to treat every single auditioner just as we'd want to be treated—and as a result, agents will send their higher-status clients to audition for us when they might not allow them to read for many other casting directors. Kindness counts—in the casting business as in all others.

JANE

Kindness and courtesy are key ingredients in whatever success we've been fortunate enough to have. I don't understand why all casting directors don't work in the same spirit, but apparently there are some who don't. Although most of the casting directors *we* know are polite, professional, and willing to go the extra mile, we do hear horror stories from actors. Some casting directors keep people waiting for as long as two hours without so much as an apology. Others might summon an actor into their office and then say in disbelief, "What are *you* doing here? You're not *nearly* good-looking enough." And then there are the casting directors who behave just like the arrogant guy in a showbiz movie, cutting the actor off midway through his first sentence with a curt, "Okay, that's all we need."

Neither Janet nor I would ever treat an actor that way—and we've even had to fire assistants who did. Some of it, of course, is basic human decency. Who talks to *anyone* that way? So the actor is totally wrong for the part, or his reading wouldn't get him into the cast of a high-school play, or his head shot makes him look handsomer than he really is—so what? Let him read for two minutes and say goodbye. You have nothing to lose by being polite.

Beyond a basic belief in being nice, though, our courtesy is rooted in self-interest. Maybe that awkward actor will be perfect for some other role that doesn't require a gorgeous face or a beautiful body. Maybe he'll turn out to be the next Dustin Hoffman or Robert De Niro, neither of whom were considered beauties in their day. And maybe his poor reading is simply due to nervousness. If we can create a warm, comfortable atmosphere in our office, we're far more likely to see a performer's best work, especially if he or she is young and inexperienced. We've both seen many actors who turned out to be extraordinarily talented, charming, and charismatic— but you never would have known it from their first reading.

Take Julia Roberts, a young Unknown whom we cast in *Mystic Pizza*. The film was the story of three working-class girls struggling with love and romance. I wasn't worried about the first two: the luminous Annabeth Gish (granddaughter of screen legend Lillian) was to play the bookish dreamer, and I had two terrific new discoveries to choose from for the spunky fiancée whose sudden refusal to get married kicks off the picture—Lili Taylor (who went on to have a career in theater and independent film) and Laura San Giacomo (who later won fame for her supporting role in *Sex, Lies, and Videotape* and went on to star in the TV series *Just Shoot Me*).

I wasn't worried about most of the other parts, either, although I wasn't necessarily expecting to discover people like Vincent D'Onofrio, who played Lili's boyfriend, or Matt Damon. Janet and I always liked Matt, who at age fourteen was a really good kid actor doing theater in Boston with his pal Ben Affleck. Local casting director Carolyn Pickman, whom we later worked with on *The Perfect Storm,* recommended Matt and Ben to us. The guys were then studying with well-known acting teacher Paul Guilfoyle, whom we met through them and also went on to cast in *Air Force One* and other movies. We'd already cast a young man named Adam Storke as the rich kid, and as soon as we saw Matt's head shot, we thought he looked like Adam's brother. I honestly don't remember much more about Matt than that—though I'd love to say I always knew he'd be a Superstar. When he won his Oscar, a reporter called me, and I had to say, "Look, I'm not psychic. He was the cutest, rightest kid for the part—that's all I knew at the time."

Meanwhile, I had bigger problems on *Mystic Pizza:* I couldn't find Daisy, the apparently confident teen sexpot from the wrong side of the tracks whose heart is broken by a rich boy. So far, everyone I'd seen was either too sexual or too innocent. I needed someone who could flirt and tease and enjoy her sexual power—then wilt in shame at not knowing how to use the right fork.

I'd met Julia Roberts earlier that year while I was casting Ron Howard's *Willow.* I liked her spunk and wanted to get her on tape, but she could only come in on a Saturday. I was willing to give up an hour or two of my day off—until I found myself waiting in my office with no Julia. Finally her agent called to tell me that the actress's car had died. She never did make it in.

Now, almost a year later, I was in New York casting *Mystic Pizza* and Julia's agent called again. "Would you like to see Julia for Daisy?"

"Sure," I said cheerfully, "if you promise she won't have car problems."

At that point, Julia was nineteen years old and had only a few unremarkable films and an episode of *Miami Vice* under her belt. When she arrived for her audition, she confessed that the script had been delivered to her late the night before and she hadn't had time to read the whole thing. She didn't seem to understand the character, she felt unprepared, and she was dressed in the very un-Daisy-like outfit of baggy jeans and an oversize shirt.

What can I say? She was *Julia Roberts* even then, and somehow that shone through. Beneath the sloppy clothes and the uncertain attitude, I could sense an exuberance, a warmth, an unself-conscious sexuality that would make Daisy's clumsy forays into romance touching and even a bit humorous. Yes, I thought, watching the awkward girl fidget in her chair. Here was someone who could have a belching contest with her girlfriends at the bar and then turn on the teenage charm the moment a cute boy walked in the door. Someone who could show us a working-class girl reaching desperately for the glamour and elegance she knew she deserved but didn't quite know how to attain. Here was someone who could do what all movie stars do—make us identify with the character, rooting for her as though she was our own daughter, sister, girlfriend, as though she were somehow standing in for us.

To this day I couldn't tell you how I knew Roberts had that special quality, but it was definitely there. *You can do this,* I thought, looking at the uncomfortable Roberts, who was clearly not sure she could. *I know you can.*

"Look," I said, "do us both a favor. Read the script and come back tomorrow. Not just your scenes: all of it. For a part this size, that's really something you should always do. And though I am not usually a big believer in actors dressing for a part, why don't you put on a miniskirt and tank top? I just think wearing those clothes will help you feel more like Daisy."

The next day, Julia showed up in her sexy clothes—and there was Daisy, standing in our office. And when the now-prepared actress read the audition scene, she simply knocked it out of the ballpark.

The rest, as they say, is history. Julia went on to make a big splash in *Mystic Pizza,* along with Annabeth and Lili. Although Laura San Giacomo was also a terrific actress, she had, frankly, a far sexier body than Julia Roberts, who had a relatively small chest, as opposed to Laura, with her curvy figure and full breasts. As actresses, both Laura and Lili were strong contenders. But once we cast Julia as the femme fatale, Lili emerged as the righter choice for her best friend; Laura was, to put it bluntly, too hot.

Obviously, Julia Roberts had plenty of other charms. After getting her Oscar nomination for *Steel Magnolias,* she went on to play the lead in *Pretty Woman,* the role that made her a Superstar. We didn't cast that movie, so Janet and I went to see it with the rest of the general public, trooping out on our lunch hour to a local shopping mall. We knew how good Julia was, but even we were astonished at the huge waves of love from the audience that simply washed over the screen. Julia had gotten her first real break in our office. But *Pretty Woman* was where the Star was born. It was another example of the actress being in the right place at the right time, walking into the perfect part to show off her stellar qualities.

☆

Sometimes, you know an Unknown will turn into box-office gold, but you still have to convince the director. When Janet and I first met John Cusack, he was a lanky sixteen-year-old kid doing theater in Chicago. Right away we saw that he had a special intensity and drive that marked him as a future powerhouse. Even as a teenager, he was really smart, really funny, and just adorable. He was also a very well-trained serious performer who had studied at a Chicago acting school run by the parents of actor Jeremy Piven. Even when John was playing comedy, you felt that the stakes were extremely high, that you were watching a real person whose life was on the line. He could play a lovesick teenager in a way that made you take that young man's emotions very seriously, rather than writing them off as "puppy love." And he had a sense of himself—an idea about the kinds of meaningful movies and challenging roles he wanted to do—that instantly drew our attention.

He ended up coming to L.A. just as I was casting Rob Reiner's movie *The Sure Thing,* a charming film about a college boy who travels cross-country in search of the glamorous young woman who his friend tells him is a "sure thing." Meanwhile, of course, he falls in love with the bookish, earnest girl who's been traveling with him to see *her* boyfriend, the two of them constantly fighting in true romantic-comedy style.

The Sure Thing herself was to be played by Nicollette Sheridan, neatly solving the "Where do we find a sexual woman?" problem: Nicollette's on-screen presence simply oozed sexuality. Janet had first met Nicollette on the *Outsiders* set, where Nicollette used to hang out with her then boyfriend, cast member Leif Garrett. Janet and Nicollette bonded when they were both visiting Leif in the hospital during his attack of appendicitis. I'll never forget the day that Nicollette came in to read for the part of The Sure Thing. Our reception area was full of teenage guys waiting to read for the male roles in the movie, and all eyes were on Nicollette as she strode through the room on her long legs, bent over the reception desk in her short skirt, and signed in. She understood that her audition had already begun, and she knew exactly how to work the crowd.

The rest of the cast was in place, too. We'd tapped a then-unknown Daphne Zuniga for the studious girl who fights with, then falls for, our hero. And a very young Tim Robbins and Lisa Jane Persky were on deck for the exuberant show-tune-singing couple who become so annoyed with the leads' constant quarrels that they leave the soon-to-be-lovers by the side of the highway. (Tim was a very sweet, quirky guy whom I continued to think of for comic parts. A year later, when I was casting *Tough Guys,* a movie in which Kirk Douglas and Burt Lancaster starred as two elderly bank robbers, I had to find a funny young man for the third main role. My first two choices were Dana Carvey and Tim Robbins. Unfortunately for him, Tim was already committed to *Howard the Duck,* an unusual blip in an otherwise glowing career.)

Meanwhile Rob had just about settled on an unknown Anthony Edwards (later the star of the TV series *ER*) as the movie's hero when I suggested that he see John Cusack.

"Nope," Rob said when he learned that John was still seventeen. "Union rules for an underage kid are just too restrictive—I don't wanna get into it."

Unlike adults, teen actors aren't allowed to work overtime. During the school year, they can only work six hours a day, from a total of nine hours on the set (they can work eight out of nine hours during the non-school year), and you have to make sure they've got a tutor/welfare worker with them at all times. Also during the school year, they need a certain amount of hours studying with the tutor. Because there are so many kids in show business, the California labor laws are the strictest in the world, and a first-time director has enough to worry about without keeping a time clock on his leading man. So Rob didn't want to hire a leading man whose age would add any further complications to the schedule. In fact, it's standard in the movie world to hire an eighteen-year-old to play a sixteen-year-old. Some teenage actors even try to emancipate themselves so they can avoid the trough that usually plagues sixteen- and seventeen-year-olds in the business.

But I'd hired John before, and I knew he was smart, funny, and talented. I also knew Rob would never forgive himself if he didn't at least take a look. "Come on," I pleaded. "One little audition—what can it hurt? If you don't like him, you'll use Anthony Edwards."

Reluctantly, Rob gave in. As I'd expected, John gave a powerhouse audition—soulful, funny, intense. You could see how smart he was, and how miserable. You could feel his charm even when he acted like the world's biggest jerk. He was instantly recognizable as a budding romantic hero, the kind whose comic quarrels with the heroine would read as the most delicious foreplay, something you could laugh at and take seriously at the same time.

"Oh, thanks a lot, Jane," Rob said gloomily after John had left. "Now I'm stuck with a seventeen-year-old actor."

Luckily, John had the grades for an early graduation and turned eighteen while the movie was being shot, so Rob's labor problems evaporated. *The Sure Thing* helped establish Rob's reputation—and it launched John Cusack toward stardom. Today, it's striking to realize that almost no movies get made the way *The Outsiders, Mystic Pizza,* and *The Sure Thing* did—without a single recognizable name among the cast. When you look at the treasure trove of talent that came out of those films, it's hard not to wish that today's Unknowns had similar opportunities.

☆

Besides kindness, casting requires patience. After all, you've got more than fifty parts to cast. After riffling through thousands of head shots and calling in hundreds of actors, you tend to want results. So when an actor doesn't shine from the moment he walks through the door, both of us are strongly tempted to say, "Next!"

We resist the temptation, though, because we genuinely enjoy helping actors do their best work. There's something thrilling about watching a performance grow, even the extremely brief performance that you see during an audition. Nothing compares to the excitement of working with an ugly-duckling performer who suddenly turns into a swan.

One of our favorite "ugly duckling" stories involved a movie called *School Ties,* the story of a Jewish kid in the 1950s passing as non-Jewish so he could attend a fancy prep school. Other casting directors had filled every other part in the picture, but no one could find the young man they needed to anchor the movie.

We took the job with a certain amount of confidence, but when Janet and I looked at the audition lists, our hearts sank. They truly seemed to have seen *everybody.* They'd even come very close to casting Kevin Dillon, who unlike his brother Matt really has the map of Ireland written on his face. Finally, though, they decided that they needed someone whom the audience would be more likely to accept as Jewish but who could still "pass" as not Jewish.

"You know," I remarked, "there was this charming kid who came into our office the other day—he just got to town, so nobody's seen him yet. His name is Brendan Fraser."

"Oh, no," said the producer, shaking his head. "We've seen him. He wasn't any good."

There was another actor at the time with a similar name, and I was sure they meant him. They surely couldn't have meant *my* Brendan. Even after our brief meeting, I could see he was terrific—a solid actor with a fresh, eager quality and boyish charm by the truckloads. Who *wouldn't* like him at first sight?

Apparently not these people, who pointed to the appointment list. Sure enough, there it was: Brendan Fraser. How could he have failed? You only had to be in the room with him for five minutes to know how good he was.

"Can we give him another chance?" I asked. "I think he's got something." Reluctantly, they agreed.

I called Brendan's agent and asked if the young actor would be willing to come in and work with me. We read through the scene a number of times and talked about what was going on with the character, not so much because Brendan needed the acting lesson as because he simply needed to feel that someone believed in him. When his second-chance audition came up, Janet and I both walked him through the door, so he knew he could count on at least two people in the room being fans. I made sure I read with him, too, and with me to focus on, he managed to get his initial nervousness at bay. Once he relaxed, his charm shone through unmistakably, and he walked away with the part.

That's the kind of story that keeps Janet and me soldiering on through the bad auditions and the mediocre auditions and the auditions of talented people who aren't right—just for that one-in-a-million chance that the awkward kid who's too nervous to do his best work will, with a little encouragement, turn out to be another Brendan Fraser.

4 ☆ NAMES AND STARS

JANE

It's always a thrill to discover hidden talent in the ranks of the Unknowns. But for most of a film's larger parts, we're working with known quantities, actors who have a body of work to their credit and some kind of recognizable Name, if not actual Stardom. Especially in these cost-conscious days, with huge film budgets and enormous financial pressures on studios, the actors considered for major roles will usually be actors we already know about.

In fact, the casting process for any sizable role begins with a list of Names and Stars, including our ideas, the director's thoughts, the studio's suggestions, and top agents' submissions. These early lists cast a much wider net than we're ever going to use, to make absolutely sure that no stone is left unturned. If a disgruntled agent or studio head or even a frustrated director says, "Why didn't we ever talk about So-and-so?" you want to be able to say, "Remember, she was on the list, and then we decided she didn't have the chops," or

"We considered him, remember? But his bottom line is two million and we only had half a mill."

The Hollywood Hierarchy shapes our choices for every list: Are we looking at Stars, Names, or some of both? If the movie revolves around a young, handsome leading man, we probably need a Star—not least because no other Star is likely to play second fiddle to someone lower down on the hierarchy, and at least one Star is needed to anchor a film. However, if a script includes two major male roles of equal size, we might be able to get away with a Star for one and a Name for the other, especially if the Name is younger and seems to have Star potential.

For two major male roles of unequal size, we've got even more leeway. The biggest role must still be a Star, but while the other one might also be a Star, he could easily be a significant Name, especially if that Name has just won an Oscar, gotten a lot of buzz, or is known as an outstanding actor.

When a film revolves around a woman—well then, my friend, you've got trouble. You need a female Star for the lead, of course, but who do you get for the guy? Most big male Stars don't like to play second fiddle to a woman, but very few female Stars have the clout it takes to anchor a movie. Actresses like Reese Witherspoon, Cameron Diaz, and Renée Zellweger may be able to star in a "woman's film" paired with a cute young Name or lower-level Star, but usually it's the guy who sells the picture. (Again, the axiom is that women will go to a guy movie, but most guys won't go to a chick flick—and films are budgeted accordingly.)

Sometimes a movie gets green-lit without a Star, but casting still affects the way a movie is made. Ron Howard got *Ransom* green-lit before it was cast, for example, and he started talking to Alec Baldwin about playing the lead. Then suddenly Mel Gibson became available. Ron and the producers said an extremely polite "Goodbye and ever so sorry" to Alec and went on to make a much more prestigious movie with Mel. With an A-list Superstar like Mel attached, *Ransom* became a different type of movie.

Sometimes the green light waits on other factors. On *The Perfect Storm,* Wolfgang Petersen couldn't move forward until the storm technology was in place. As recently as five years ago, computer-generated effects were still hard to guarantee, so having the storm technology was paramount. For *The Da Vinci Code,* on the other hand, getting rights to the book assured a green light, and the cast was the icing on the cake.

☆

As soon as we'd cast Russell Crowe in *A Beautiful Mind,* we moved on to the mysterious Mr. Parcher, the intelligence agent who draws Nash into espionage. Though this character turns out to be merely a paranoid fantasy, the first two-thirds of the film hinges on our belief that he's real. We all felt that we needed a recognizable Star for this role, someone whose authoritative presence would make us believe in Nash's bizarre delusions. There was also a practical reason to cast Parcher next: Stars are expensive, and we wanted to know how much money we'd have left for the rest of the cast.

As usual, I brought Ron a list of candidates, but I honestly don't remember who was on it other than Ed Harris. He just seemed perfect. He has such strength and presence, and he only gets better with age—I consider him one of the great American actors. I remember when he was doing local theater in L.A., trying so hard to break into the business. His agent wasn't from one of the big agencies, but he believed passionately in Ed and worked extremely hard to get him a shot. Ed isn't a personal friend—I haven't even cast him all that often—but I know how hard he's worked. You almost have the sense that he made himself a Star through sheer will-power, because he's one of the few who've done it on acting talent alone, rather than on fabulous looks or some special kind of charisma—although he has plenty of both, plus sex appeal!

Maybe it's his years of struggle that give Ed such a sense of authority. Certainly that authority helps the film, because you are ready to believe every word he says. When you discover that he's one of Nash's hallucinations, you feel almost as ready to doubt your own sanity as Nash is.

Ron agreed that Ed was the perfect choice. Since we didn't have a lot of money, he called Ed directly, drawing on the warm relationship they'd developed during *Apollo 13*. The studio ended up paying Ed a fairly sizable sum, but whatever it cost, it was worth it. Without an actor like Ed to make you believe that the fantasy is real, the espionage scenes would all have been just so much hokum. Ed anchored the movie in an extraordinary way—and isn't that what Stars are for?

☆

For the role of Alicia Nash, on the other hand, we weren't really looking for a Star. All we wanted was a good, strong Name.

Part of that was budget. Because male stars are so important in bringing in audience, they're fairly expensive (female Stars—always excepting Julia Roberts—are somewhat less so). *A Beautiful Mind* was being made for only $40 million, a relatively small amount of money by commercial standards, and Ron had already spent the lion's share of the casting budget on Russell and Ed.

Even if we'd had more money, though, we could never have gotten a Star for Nash's wife—the part was simply too small. Size isn't only a matter of lines or screen time. Mr. Parcher was, in a sense, Nash's nemesis, and Ed Harris in that part came off almost as a cameo, a Star turn in a serious role. Alicia, while a juicy part for a talented actress, didn't have the same weight—basically, it was a "wife part." If someone at the level of Julia Roberts, Meg Ryan, or Nicole Kidman had signed on, people might have started wondering why she was suddenly doing supporting roles. There's a point at which every female Star has to decide if she's going to quit the business or age gracefully into the mother, aunt, or inspiring neighbor—but no Star who was the right age for Nash's wife would be ready to make that decision. So off we went to the ranks of the Names.

Our first thought was to find someone we could cast against Russell. That's fairly common: we almost always cast from the top down. If Tom Cruise is playing the leading man, we'll offer one set of ideas for his wife, best friend, and boss—if it's Harrison Ford, we might make different choices. Among other factors, we consider a Star's age, style, coloring, height, and personal preferences. After all, you don't want two redheads in a scene, a best friend who's sexier than the Star, or a loving couple who in real life can't stand each other. It's as though the Star emits a kind of force field, shaping the world of the movie.

Casting around Russell presented an additional challenge, because he was as demanding as Ron when it came to requiring top acting talent. A true craftsman, Russell looked for solid training in every single actor he worked with. So we'd need an Alicia who had what we call a great set of chops—the acting ability to keep up with Russell.

Because the real-life Alicia Nash is actually Latin American, we also wanted to find out if she had to be cast as a Latina. Ms. Nash said no: she cherished her heritage but didn't mind being played by an Anglo. So here, in no particular order, are the genuine suggestions, second choices, and never-gonna-use-'ems who were on our first list for Alicia Nash:

Charlize Theron
Rachel Griffiths
Elizabeth Hurley
Mary-Louise Parker
Catherine Zeta-Jones
Lili Taylor (whom we had met working on *Labyrinth,* in which we had cast Jennifer Connelly)
Calista Flockhart
Jennifer Jason Leigh
Amanda Peet (whom we later cast in *Something's Gotta Give*)
Robin Wright Penn (another one of our discoveries, in *The Princess Bride*)
Emily Watson
Penélope Cruz (a nod to the Latin American angle)
Julianna Margulies
Rhona Mitra
Catherine McCormack
Famke Janssen
Frances O'Connor
Julia Ormond
Mía Maestro (another Latina)
Ashley Judd

Rachel Weisz

Hilary Swank

Mira Sorvino

Magali Amadei (Italian—but perhaps someone who
    evoked Alicia's heritage)

Claire Forlani

Bridget Moynahan

Robin Tunney

Mary McCormack

We'd also included Elizabeth McGovern, who, years ago, had starred in *Once Upon a Time in America,* in which her childhood self had been played by a twelve-year-old Jennifer Connelly. And then, of course, there was Jennifer herself, whom Ron knew from co-producing *Inventing the Abbotts,* a small film in which she'd had a starring role.

Most of the candidates on a first list will never be serious contenders. In this case, we'd included actresses like Charlize Theron, who was then beginning to draw a certain amount of attention but was not yet considered a serious actress. (*Monster* changed all that—now she's too big to play Alicia.) Emily Watson and Catherine McCormack were British, and the Australian Russell didn't want a cast of actors all "doing American accents," distracting him from his own efforts to master Nash's Virginia speech. (By the time Ron cast British actor Paul Bettany as Charles, Nash's best friend, this no longer mattered to anyone, least of all Russell.) Still other candidates were good actresses but just not "right." We'd put them on the list to make sure we'd covered all our bases— but now we could move on.

So, out of these first thirty women, we called in fourteen to meet with Ron:

Famke Janssen
Frances O'Connor
Julia Ormond
Rhona Mitra
Mía Maestro
Ashley Judd
Rachel Weisz
Hilary Swank
Mira Sorvino
Magali Amadei
Claire Forlani
Bridget Moynahan
Mary McCormack

And, of course, Jennifer Connelly.

Jennifer was an especially serious contender because she'd just done *Requiem for a Dream,* a not-yet-released independent film about which there was already a great deal of buzz. Jennifer's agent—the same Risa Shapiro who later brought us Paul Bettany (see Chapter 8)—had sent us a tape before the film came out, and we were stunned by Jennifer's charisma, as well as by her daring performance. So Jennifer, along with all the other Names on the list except Claire Forlani, Ashley Judd, and Mary McCormack, made it to the next level: a real-life audition with Russell.

This audition served two purposes. First, it gave Russell a chance to weigh in. (If the Star isn't happy, nobody's happy.) But Ron also wanted to make sure his two romantic leads had good chemistry. Every actress who came in to read with Russell was good—they wouldn't have been asked otherwise— but of that select group, Jennifer and Russell had far and away the best chemistry. There was just something that happened when they looked at each other that made you care about them as a couple, made you wonder how her love might comfort this lonely man, or how his awkward genius might intrigue this cool, sophisticated, yet passionate woman.

Moreover, Jennifer and Russell were both extraordinarily skilled performers. So there was no danger that the highly trained Russell would become impatient with an actress of limited range, someone who couldn't reliably repeat a take or switch into character at a moment's notice, someone whose choices were pedestrian or predictable rather than on the level of his own risky, unexpected performance.

And indeed, beyond the chemistry, Jennifer brought her own extraordinary intensity to what could have been a minor part, endowing Alicia with so much feeling that she made the role seem bigger than it was. Kathleen Quinlan had done much the same thing in *Apollo 13,* for which she'd also won a Best Supporting Actress Oscar nomination. Although Quinlan had had very few lines of dialogue, her suffering face and quietly impassioned performance made her the touchstone for all the families left behind on earth. When you saw her listening to the radio, wondering whether her husband would ever come back, you didn't need to hear her speak. The forlorn, determined, slightly angry look on her face told you all you needed to know.

In that film, too, chemistry had been an important factor in casting Quinlan, who had a terrific rapport with Tom Hanks. The other strong contender for the wife role was Frances McDormand, an extraordinary actress who'd gotten an Oscar nomination a few years earlier for her work in *Mississippi Burning.* When we made *Apollo 13,* McDormand was far better known than Quinlan and would have seemed to be the more logical choice. But when you saw Quinlan and

Hanks together, they just felt like a couple. It didn't hurt that Quinlan also bore a strong resemblance to the real-life woman she portrayed, though in the end, that wouldn't have been a deciding factor. More important was the fact that Mc-Dormand was almost too strong for the part. You couldn't quite believe her entire life was riding on whether her husband made it back, especially in a part with very little dialogue that depended almost entirely on "quality"—the image that the actress projected. McDormand's strength, wonderful as it's been in other roles, made her less right for this film than the vulnerable Quinlan.

Jennifer was clearly poised for Stardom and obviously destined for more than "wife parts." But like *Apollo 13, A Beautiful Mind* was a prestige project, and even before the film started shooting, there was kind of an Oscar buzz around it. Despite the fact that *Requiem* was making Jennifer an ever-hotter commodity, we thought she'd say "yes" to this high-profile film whose Star and director were both on Hollywood's A-list. Happily, she did.

JANET

Chemistry is often the deciding factor in how a film gets cast, even though nobody can quite define that word. We think it grows out of what happens when two actors play together. If they inspire each other to ever-greater heights of creativity; if they generate mounting sexual excitement, a delicious sense of fun, or a deep feeling of affection; if they challenge each other like two good tennis players, pushing each other on to ever-more skillful and risky acting—well then, there's chemistry.

Chemistry isn't only for sexual partners. It's just as important between two best friends, or two guys in a buddy movie, or sometimes even between family members. Think Robert De Niro and Joe Pesci as the brothers in *Raging Bull*—chemistry. Or Samuel L. Jackson and John Travolta as the bantering gangsters in *Pulp Fiction*—more chemistry. Even Judy Garland, the Tin Man, the Lion, and the Scarecrow had chemistry. In every single one of these cases, you believe that a relationship existed before you ever walked into the theater, or you marvel at the bond you see forming before your eyes.

JANE

Sometimes, of course, chemistry fails, and then an otherwise promising movie may fall short. Jennifer Jason Leigh and Billy Baldwin didn't work particularly well as a romantic couple in *Backdraft,* for example. Much as I like Jennifer as an actress, if I had that movie to cast over again, I would have done it differently. Part of the problem was logistics—Jennifer had rushed straight off another movie set to join us. You just never thought that she and Billy were a match made in heaven. Instead, they seemed like one of those couples who, in real life, always had you wondering about exactly why they were together.

JANET

In *Air Force One,* on the other hand, I thought Harrison Ford had a terrific rapport with screen wife Wendy Crewson. *Air Force One* revolves around Harrison as the president whose family is kidnapped by terrorists, so you really need to feel that the wife is the love of his life. You don't take up Harrison's time by having him read with twenty people, so we invited only two First Lady candidates and Wendy was the clear winner. She and Harrison hit it off right away, laughing and joking together even during the audition, and you could see the potential for a deep affection. On-screen, there's a delightful sense of them enjoying each other in their sexy and affectionate banter.

JANE

Another high-octane presidential couple was Michael Douglas and Annette Bening in Rob Reiner's *The American President*. In that classic romantic comedy, the two leads have to be very much equals, with both parties coming off as smart and sexy and fun. You really need to root for the two of them to get together, otherwise there's no picture. Michael and Annette found a way to convey the deep mutual appreciation between two strong people surprised by the depth of their passion.

One of my favorite examples of chemistry came in *A Few Good Men,* between Tom Cruise and Demi Moore. Here we needed sparks to fly as the characters fight their way through the picture. But we also needed to keep the chemistry relentlessly asexual, since Rob Reiner didn't want any sense that the quarrels would end up in bed. This was a battle of ideas—political passion, not the sexual kind.

As soon as Tom read with Demi, we knew we could stop looking. Both Tom and Demi were sexy, beautiful, and impassioned, yet you never felt you were watching a romance. As Rob put it, Demi's mind wasn't on sex but on her legal briefs. Just think of Michelle Pfeiffer in the same role, and you can see why Demi was such a good choice—there would be no way on earth not to fall in love with the lovely, vulnerable Michelle. But Demi, while attractive and sexual in her own way, managed to be feisty, passionate—and all business.

We also saw terrific chemistry between Tom Cruise and Jack Nicholson. With an actor as powerful as Tom, it takes a pretty strong performer to silence him, even with a power-house line like "You can't handle the truth!" Only an actor at Jack's level could top Tom. So when Rob heard that Jack was interested—I think Jack had seen the Broadway play on which the film was based—he immediately offered him the part. I'll never forget our first read through, when we'd assembled Tom, Demi, and our fabulous supporting cast—Kevin Bacon, Kiefer Sutherland, Kevin Pollak, J. T. Walsh. Everyone gave a powerful first reading, but when Jack started in on the courtroom scene, the rest of us were absolutely in awe. After all, here was a genuine Hollywood icon—some of the younger guys had practically grown up watching his movies—and now he was giving That Speech. Rob just sat there grinning.

Jack also had terrific chemistry with Diane Keaton, his co-star in Nancy Meyers's *Something's Gotta Give.* The two hadn't seen each other since they'd played illicit lovers in *Reds,* but when they read together now, you could practically see them sparkle. Of course, both Jack and Diane are extraordinarily gracious and generous. Nancy always requires numerous auditions, so Jack had to read with several candidates for his young girlfriend, just as Diane read with several potential boyfriends. Both Stars were unfailingly professional and gave 150 percent in each audition, inviting every auditioner to do his or her best. It's never cheap to hire Jack, but if you get him on board, you've got a brilliant actor who commits fully, body and soul.

JANET

Sometimes, as in *A Beautiful Mind,* we cast the film around the "force field" of a Star. At other times, the force field comes less from the Star than from the setting.

Take a movie like Wolfgang Petersen's *The Perfect Storm,* set in the fishing village of Gloucester, Massachusetts. The real stars of Wolfgang's movie are the Gloucester fishing community and the Perfect Storm itself—a freak collision of two hurricanes and a cold front.

Undoubtedly, the movie needed a strong Star presence in the central role of Captain Billy Tyne, a part that we eventually filled with the wonderful George Clooney. But although Clooney was key to the film's success, I wasn't so much thinking of him as of Gloucester itself when I envisioned the supporting players.

John C. Reilly is one of my favorite actors, and he was clearly at the top of my private list. He's an exciting performer on many levels. Not only did he have an authentic, grounded, regular-guy quality and a strong set of chops, but he'd also developed his career in a particularly thoughtful way. Look at John's résumé and you see a series of seriously important films: *Casualties of War, State of Grace, Shadows and Fog, What's Eating Gilbert Grape, Magnolia.* Clearly, he's a very smart guy who's always surrounded himself with good people. He'll never have the remarkable good looks that cry out for a leading man role—no matter how much we liked him, we couldn't have cast him as Captain Billy or even as the cute rookie played by Mark Wahlberg—but he's got a very interesting physical quality and an incredible range: from the sweet, schlubby husband in *Chicago* (plus he can sing and dance!) to the imposing bad guy in *Gangs of New York.*

Thus, in the world of Names, John is one who teeters on the brink of being a Star, particularly since his work on *The Good Girl* with Jennifer Aniston. That movie didn't quite make John a household name, but it definitely boosted his stock in the industry. He's at the point where he doesn't have to audition—you know his work, and you offer him the part—and he was one of the more difficult deals we made on *The Perfect Storm.* But everyone thought he was so good and so right that they weren't willing to lose him over money.

I'm glad it all worked out. Watch John as the wistful Murph, longing for the wife who's left him and the son who still adores him, and before you opens up not just a whole life but a whole world of Gloucester fishermen who go on one fishing trip after another, always getting less pay than they bargained for, always having to return to sea too soon. It's a way of life that wears men out, destroys families, and ultimately brings Murph to his death. John isn't on-screen all that often, but whenever you see him, you feel this history, and the movie benefits accordingly.

William Fichtner was another strong Name and a great addition to our ensemble. He's good-looking, interesting, and, like John, he's got a terrific range—he can play a hero, a villain, and pretty much anything in between. With the right part, he could make it up to Stardom. Meanwhile, he's a solid Name who's been working a lot in television and who had one of the major roles in *Crash.*

John Hawkes became a Name by virtue of appearing in *The Perfect Storm,* from which he went on to draw mega-attention for his work in the HBO series *Deadwood.* Although you probably wouldn't cast him as the romantic lead in most films, he's also drawn raves for his work in a fabulous low-budget movie by independent filmmaker Miranda July, *Me and You and Everyone We Know.* He doesn't have the classic good looks that make for a more conventional star, but he's got the acting chops to do just about everything, plus the intensity and "size" to carry a film. He can tell quite a story with those eyes, and his essence stays with you even when he's off the screen.

One of the key scenes for John's character is where he makes a connection in the bar with a lonely woman. Both characters are looking for love, and you get the feeling that they might find it with each other. When we read the script, we immediately thought of Working Actress Rusty Schwimmer for the part—and later found out that it had been written with her in mind. We brought her and John in to tape the scene where they begin to make their tentative connection. Somehow, though, the audition didn't quite come off, and Wolfgang wasn't convinced.

"But Wolfgang," I said, "you *know* these are the people."

Upon consideration, he agreed. Although Jane and I hadn't directed the audition the way Wolfgang would have, our director was able to see past our work to the actors, who were indeed fabulous in his version of the scene.

The last crew member was Allen Payne, who played the somewhat mysterious West Indian fisherman. Allen had the least to do, but he made the most of it. I'd say that he, like Rusty, is a classic Working Actor who's always doing something—he'd been on *The Cosby Show* as a kid and hasn't stopped working since—but who hasn't yet won Name recognition.

By the way, actors, Fichtner was forty-four when he did *The Perfect Storm,* and he's just now becoming a Name. Sometimes it takes a while before you find the part that pushes you up to the next level.

JANE

Janet and I must always keep the big picture in mind, but actors, agents, and managers often have a narrower focus:

getting the actor a job. As a result, they sometimes assume that if a performer is good-looking or talented enough, that's going to trump every other consideration.

Sometimes, of course, it does—but usually only at the Star level. Yes, they rewrote a few lines in *Octopussy* to cast Maud Adams, and I suppose after telling that story, I'll never again have any credibility when I insist on ethnic-appropriate casting. But that film was very much the exception. When I was casting *A House Divided,* a movie about a Palestinian-Israeli romance, I really needed Middle Eastern–looking actors for both the Israeli and the Arab characters. It didn't matter what ethnicity they *were,* but it did matter how they appeared. Yet despite breakdowns that specified a Middle Eastern appearance, many agents insisted on pitching me their blond-haired, fair-skinned clients—gorgeous men and women, to be sure, but you couldn't imagine them in the Middle East.

Different films require you to create different worlds. Ethnicity, as in *A House Divided,* may be one component of your movie world; class, as in *The Perfect Storm,* is another. *A Few Good Men* called for a bunch of guys who looked like Marines. And when I was casting *Apollo 13,* I needed to staff a NASA control room.

Although the control-room personnel in that movie are all relatively small and undistinguished parts, pretty much every guy in town longed to be on that set. I guess they all wanted to be astronauts when they grew up, and they saw this as their big chance, especially since the actual cast would attend NASA's control-room school. Talk about an embarrassment of riches: I had agents calling me, begging me to give even nonspeaking parts to actors who would normally command significant costarring roles. On the short list of guys that Ron really liked were such Names as Gary Cole, John Corbett, John Hawkes, Zeljko Ivanek, Ray McKinnon, Will Patton, Jeremy Piven, Alan Ruck, Richard Schiff, Jamey Sheridan, Dylan Walsh, and Bradley Whitford. The guys who finally made it—including Joseph Culp, Andy Milder, and Joe Spano—weren't necessarily better, they just helped create a stronger, more diverse ensemble. The challenge was to get lots of interesting faces so that when Ron brought the camera back into the control room, we'd be looking at people we recognize. Yet because NASA of that era was overwhelmingly white, male, and WASP—I think there was one guy playing "the Jew"—they all had to look ethnically similar.

Somehow we managed to get a wide range of mobile, expressive faces that we could distinguish at a glance by age, shape, and personality. It was sort of like assembling a giant puzzle, making sure that all the pieces fit but didn't blend into one indistinguishable mass. The group we put together ended up bonding so deeply that a bunch of them still meet every Thursday for lunch.

We faced a similar challenge with *A Beautiful Mind,* which had four speaking parts for Nash's Princeton classmates: Sol, Bender, Hansen, and Ainsley. They all had to look upper class and to appear relatively Anglo-Saxon except for Sol—again, the only Jew. (Like NASA in the sixties, postwar Princeton wasn't all that diverse.) Whereas all the NASA guys had to be pocket-protector-wearing nerds, the Princeton kids had to look like math students—no football-player types or budding comedians.

Okay, but how would the audience ever tell them apart? How were we going to create a lively, bantering group—one that functioned enough as a unit to make Nash feel left out, but which had enough internal diversity to keep the sparks flying?

I ended up filling the part of Sol with Adam Goldberg, whom we'd cast before in Ron's *Edtv*. Here his mournful, wry delivery and dark curly hair marked him indeed as the token Jew. Josh Lucas, who jumped to Name status with that movie and who, with his roles in *Glory Road* and *Poseidon*, has become a Star, played Hansen, who begins as Nash's nemesis and ends as a major supporter. Josh has a classically handsome face and in contrast to Adam, he seemed fair. Anthony Rapp as Bender was also fair, but ginger-haired, and he had a square face and a wonderful solidity that contrasted with Josh's restlessness. And Jason Gray-Stanford, who played Ainsley, was sort of halfway between Anthony and Josh— blondish-brown hair and a kind of wide-eyed look that could mutate instantly into playful disdain. (Jason went on to work on the *Monk* series on TV.) All four guys were terrific actors, and all firmly in the Name category. They'd all been working for years, and Anthony had a solid career in the musical theater, having starred in the Broadway musical *Rent;* we'd hired him years earlier for *Adventures in Baby-sitting*. They looked like they belonged together, but you could still tell them apart.

Someone once asked me how, in a situation like that, I know which actor should get which part. "I don't," I replied. "I just pick out a bunch of actors who all seem right and watch the director try them out in different groups and combinations." It's almost a tactile decision: A and B feel right together; A and C don't. B and D are too similar, so we can't use them both, but E brings a new note into the group. A, B, and E together feel like a tight unit—say, a group of entitled Princeton students that will make Nash's outsider status clear at a glance. But introduce actor F, and suddenly, the group is too diverse, too undefined; the tight community feeling has somehow gotten lost. Sometimes there's no way to predict or explain how the combinations will work: you just get the actors together and feel your way through.

Usually we don't bring actors in to read with each other when a relatively small part is involved. But sometimes you need to see what the combination is going to look like, especially when casting family relationships. When we were doing Rob Reiner's *The American President,* for example, we needed to find someone to play Annette Bening's sister. So we brought in a handful of actresses to audition with Annette and ended up choosing Nina Siemaszko. She and Annette looked as though they could be sisters, and there was a nice rapport between them when they read together. Seeing the two women, you could believe there was some kind of biological connection. By the same token, we'll sometimes bring in potential parents and kids. Once again, we're not only looking for the "best actor," but for the actor who feels the most right.

This can be tough on actors, though, especially when they *know* they've done a good job. For an actor trying to break into the business, or for one trying to rise through the ranks of the Working Actors, it can be hard to remember that we're more interested in the movie as a whole than in the work—good, bad, or excellent—of any one actor. This harsh reality can seem especially painful when an actor faces the agonizing round of "almost-got-it's" that haunts the career of even the most successful performer.

Take Dustin Hoffman, who was attached to *Outbreak* and *Hook* when we cast them. He actually came in to our office to make sure we were qualified to do the casting—he wanted to know that we'd be kind to actors! By then, he was a major Star, but when he and I did summer stock together back in 1963, he was just a talented guy with a big nose. The ethnic look was not yet in, and "Dusty" was struggling— even though *we* all knew that he was far and away the best actor in our little company.

Then Dustin got what he thought was his big break. He landed an understudy gig for Martin Sheen, who had the lead in a Broadway production—and Martin was about to leave the show. As understudy, Dustin was poised to step in for a few nights, except that suddenly, while boiling water on the hot plate in his tiny kitchenless apartment, he scalded his arm and had to go to the hospital. Someone else went on for Martin, and Dustin came within an inch of chucking show-biz altogether.

Somehow, though, he kept at it, doing a series of obscure, low-paying off-Broadway plays. Finally he got the lead in Ronald Ribman's *Journey of the Fifth Horse* at the American Playhouse Theater—a somewhat less obscure but still off-Broadway house. Mike Nichols, who was making his first film (*Who's Afraid of Virginia Woolf?*, starring Richard Burton and Elizabeth Taylor), happened to attend—and when he went on to make *The Graduate* a few years later, he remem-bered Dustin.

Even then, though, history might *not* have been made. Charles Grodin was the first choice for the part of Benjamin Braddock, so Dustin Hoffman only got the part that made him a Star after Charles Grodin turned it down.

JANET

Jane and I witnessed a similar saga with Dylan McDer-mott, who was one of our favorite actors from the first time we met him. He'd just gotten out of Juilliard—one of the country's top acting conservatories—when his agent asked Jane to read him for Montoya in *The Princess Bride.*

Montoya was the fiery Spanish aristocrat bent on avenging himself against the six-fingered man who had destroyed his life. So Dylan decided that every time he said "the six-fingered man," he'd spit—the ultimate gesture of contempt. It was a funny and brilliant idea, and you could see he'd been well trained. But eventually the choice started to wear a little thin. Somewhere into the third or fourth "six-fingered man (*ptui!*)," you could see Dylan thinking, "Why in God's name did I start this—and how do I stop?"

Committed actor that he was, Dylan kept spitting to the end of the scene and somehow mustered the resolve to make it work. Jane was so impressed that she called him back to read for director Rob Reiner. "Maaaaaaaaaybe not the spitting this time," she suggested gently. Dylan spit only the first time he said the name, and we all thought he was terrific. Then Rob hired Mandy Patinkin.

We remembered Dylan, though, so when he moved to California, Jane brought him in for *Willow.* Again, he ended up meeting with the director—Ron Howard this time—and again, he didn't get the part.

Dylan was gorgeous, charming, well-trained, and talented, but he just couldn't seem to get a foot in the door. One part after another kept eluding him, often by a hair's breadth. In 1992 we finally cast him as the lead in *Jersey Girl,* a charming low-budget film co-starring Jami Gertz. (Jami, a relatively well-known Name in those days, had won the part over Sandra Bullock, who at that point was at the bottom of the Name heap.) Jami and Dylan were actually in the car on the way to a press junket—and, they thought, Stardom— when the car phone rang. The event was canceled, a studio flack informed them. The studio had looked at the movie and realized that, hey, it really was a great script. So they were going to remake it—with bigger stars.

When I cast *Jurassic Park,* I taped a lot of people to show director Steven Spielberg—that was another time when we didn't have a script and were just using dialogue right from Michael Crichton's book. Dylan gave yet another powerful audition, and I put him up for one of the leads, but he didn't get that part, either.

By this point, Dylan was on the verge of quitting the business. He must have thought he was cursed—and he *knew* he hadn't worked for a year and a half. Then one day he got a call from his agent, telling him he'd been hired to play Clint Eastwood's partner in *In the Line of Fire.*

"What's *In the Line of Fire?*" Dylan wondered. "Did I even audition for that?"

Well, yes. And no. We had taped Dylan doing one of his trademark fabulous auditions for *Jersey Girl*—charming, sexy, adorable—so when we were casting *In the Line of Fire,* I showed Wolfgang the old tape.

True, the character Dylan was reading in the *Jersey Girl* audition was nothing like the one he'd be playing in Wolfgang's movie. *Jersey Girl* was the story of an uptight, arrogant yuppie who falls, romantic comedy–style, for a sweet working-class girl. Dylan made a charming yuppie—but for *In the Line of Fire,* he was up for a dedicated young federal agent, a man who risks his life to save the president. Most directors would have wanted to meet Dylan or at least see him read for the part. But looking at the *Jersey Girl* tape, Wolfgang could tell that here was a good, strong actor who knew how to establish sympathy for a character very quickly. The *Line of Fire* character isn't on-screen all that long. He drops his kid off at school, he's late to work—and then he gets killed (in the line of fire). Wolfgang needed someone who could win the audience's sympathy swiftly and surely, so that when the character gets killed, we really feel the loss.

"He's perfect," Wolfgang said when he saw Dylan's tape. "Hire him." And so we did. On the same day, Dylan met the woman who was to become his wife, so I guess you'd count that as a good day.

JANE

One of the most poignant "almost-cast" stories I know was the decision not to use John Belushi in *Night Shift*—though in that case, the decision was John's alone. Before casting Michael Keaton in the part that made him a Star, we'd offered the wacky, manic role of Bill Blazejowski to John Belushi, then riding high on *Saturday Night Live* and *Blues Brothers* fame. But the movie was to be shot in Los Angeles, and John didn't want to leave New York.

Then while we were shooting the movie, John died of an overdose—in Los Angeles. I've often wondered whether he might somehow have muddled through if he'd had *Night Shift* to absorb him during those troubled times. Or maybe he knew better than we did that he was already too far gone.

Virginia Madsen's story is another example of how erratic an actor's career can be, even when the actor is talented, professional, and gorgeous. We met Virginia when we were casting *Dune,* David Lynch's first Hollywood movie. The love interest in that film was the breathtakingly lovely Princess Irulan, a character whose beauty had to go beyond mere good looks into the realm of the iconic. As we'd be reminded years later when we worked on *The Princess Bride,* it's harder to cast beautiful women than it sounds. Pretty girls may be a dime a dozen in Hollywood, but someone whose beauty makes you gasp with surprise *and* who can act is tough to find. Sure, beauty is only skin deep, but whatever is *under* the skin has to shine through; otherwise you're just looking at a pretty canvas with no life to it. It's why many models, lovely as they are, never quite make it as actors.

Then one day someone from William Morris called and asked us to meet a young girl who'd just come in from Chicago. (As it happened, she'd attended Winnetka High School with her best friend, the actress Rusty Schwimmer.)

As soon as we saw her, we knew we'd found our princess. Virginia had gorgeous, glowing blond hair and an unusual combination of innocence and intelligence, as though she'd come from another world. Her beauty had that same old-fashioned quality; she wasn't a Valley Girl but a Raphael painting. Virginia wouldn't have been right for, say, an Alicia Silverstone movie—you wouldn't have wanted to see her in a mall—but for *Dune,* she was perfect.

Before the meeting had even ended, Jane called producer Raffaella De Laurentiis, who, with David, was already on location in Mexico. "You have to see this girl," Jane told Raffaella. "She's just what we've been looking for." It was actually easier, faster, and cheaper to put Virginia on a plane than to get tape to the director and producer. And sure enough, David and Raffaella found Virginia just as enchanting as we did.

Virginia never stopped working for more than a couple of years after that. But her personal life had its ups and downs—she married and divorced and found a new boyfriend and had a child—and somehow, she seemed to make one bad career choice after another. After a super-strong start, she made a string of mediocre movies and from being a very desirable Star, she fell to the status of a kind of has-been/Name. She took on the tarnish that our industry associates with failure—or with anything less than stellar success—and producers and directors began to resist bringing her in for A-list projects.

Often we'll fight for people whom we think are good, even if the industry has turned against them—and many of our directors will fight as well. We did manage to get Virginia seen for *Ghosts of Mississippi,* in which she had a brief but fabulous turn as Dixie, the hero's first wife—a woman so embedded in conservative Southern culture that she leaves her husband over his crusade against Medgar Evers's murderer. It was a bit of a struggle to get the studio to accept her, but she'd done a terrific audition, and director Rob Reiner felt she was worth the extra effort. I agree. Just as John C. Reilly makes you see three centuries of Gloucester fisherman in *The Perfect Storm,* Virginia evokes generations of white privilege in *Ghosts of Mississippi.* You watch her performance and you understand what her husband is up against.

We once tried to get Virginia on a little movie called *My Life,* starring Michael Keaton as a dying man. She gave an extraordinary set of auditions as Keaton's wife, and we thought she would be great. But that's one fight we lost. The studio must have thought Virginia was last year's gorgeous blond starlet—and they preferred *this* year's gorgeous blond starlet, who in those days was a young Nicole Kidman. Virginia, it seemed, had had her shot and failed.

A few years ago, Virginia's agent called and asked if Virginia could come in to catch up. She knew we'd always been her champions, and I think she saw our office as kind of a safe harbor. When she walked through our door, she looked fabulous. She'd gained some weight over the years, but by this point, she'd lost it again, and by anyone's standards was a beautiful woman. We knew how good she was—and she knew we knew. So we sat around for a while, chatting.

"Look," she told us. "I'm forty, my kid has grown up, I'm just looking to do a tasty little part in a tasty little movie. Some kind of quality picture. I don't need to be the star—I just need a choice little part."

Jane and I did our best. I suggested Virginia for the coach's wife in Peter Berg's *Friday Night Lights*—a fairly small role with almost no dialogue, but requiring a strong sense of a woman who stands by her man. I think Virginia would have been wonderful, but there were a few days' conflict between our schedule and some movie she was doing in Canada, and there was not enough interest to try and work out the dates. We ended up going with Connie Britton, who did a terrific job (and who went on to play the same part in the TV version of the movie). But I was sorry that we hadn't been able to use Virginia.

Then came *Sideways*. Virginia has told the story of how this was a part so fabulous that she just had to do it. Somehow she found a way of getting seen—since we didn't cast that movie, we don't know the details—and somehow she got cast. I couldn't help seeing the parallels between the wounded, earthy woman in the movie and Virginia herself. Like the character she played, I'm sure she was just looking for a little peace. Instead, she found a renewed Stardom.

Ironically, now that she's done *Sideways,* she couldn't even consider a part as small as the one in *Friday Night Lights*. Virginia got one of Hollywood's very rare second acts—even rarer for women over forty—and Jane and I couldn't be happier for her. It's nice when the good guys win.

JANE

When I think about life for actresses over forty, I'm enormously grateful to be a casting director. Even beautiful
women like Michelle Pfeiffer or highly acclaimed actresses
like Meryl Streep have to watch a younger generation of
women take over—often paired romantically with older guys.
Sally Field, whose love interest was the somewhat younger
Tom Hanks in *Punchline,* when she was all of forty-two,
went on to play Tom's mother in *Forrest Gump,* a mere six
years later. I think that pretty much says it all. Hollywood
isn't kind to anyone who ages, but older women find it increasingly hard to get major roles, while guys like Harrison
Ford, Mel Gibson, and Bruce Willis go on their sexy, starring
way throughout their fifties and sixties.

Janet and I met Bruce Willis just as he was getting his
start. Our first office was in a building owned by two incredibly nice agents, Nicole David and Arnold Rifkin, who ran
the Rifkin-David Agency. One advantage of renting there
was that we got to know their clients, including Raul Julia,
Amy Irving, and Patrick Swayze, whom Janet had cast in his
first two movies, *Skatetown, U.S.A.* and *The Outsiders.* They
also represented Bruce Willis, who'd just left the world of
New York City's off-off-Broadway theater to take a small part
on the TV show *Miami Vice.* My friend Jodie Tillen designed
costumes for that show, and one day she called me long-
distance. "I just put clothes on this guy who was really something," she told me. "If he ever gets out to Hollywood, you
should definitely meet him." When she gave me his agent's
name, I strolled across the courtyard to speak to my land-
lords. "Who is this guy, Bruce?" I asked them. (Jodie later
tipped us off to Benicio Del Toro as well.)

Janet was still doing *Rumble Fish* in Tulsa when I moved us into the Rifkin-David building, where I soon got one of the most exciting Calls of our career. Would I be interested in casting *Dune*? Not only was Raffaella producing it, but her father, the famous Dino De Laurentiis, was executive producer.

Raffaella was just starting her career as producer in those days, though she'd already done the enormously successful *Conan the Barbarian* and *Conan the Destroyer.* Her father, of course, had produced such classic Italian films as Federico Fellini's *La Strada* and *Nights of Cabiria,* as well as executive producing *Serpico, Death Wish,* and *Three Days of the Condor.* He'd also been involved with *Dead Zone,* which I'd cast for Raffaella while still at Zoetrope, and—in an ironic twist for me—*King of the Gypsies,* where my desire to cast had been born. To cast a film for the De Laurentiis family felt like getting Hollywood's Royal Seal of Approval, and it reassured both Janet and me that maybe this venture could work after all. Not to mention that the fee paid for the lumber that we used to make our desk.

So off I went to meet with Raffaella and David Lynch, who at that point was best known for a cult hit called *Eraserhead* and the brilliant *Elephant Man.* David's training had been as a visual artist, and his filmmaking thus far had been within a very independent world. *Dune,* adapted from the beloved sci-fi novel by Frank Herbert, would be his first big commercial project—a transition I'm not sure he was wholly prepared for. For example, David wanted to make *Dune* in black and white—an artistic decision if there ever was one.

"No!" Dino said in his thick Italian accent. "Nobody wants to see a black and white! We make this film in color!"

Later David would learn more about how to preserve his own artistic vision while keeping the commercial interests happy. He needed the kinds of big budgets that studios could offer him, so he'd have to learn how to work with the money men, not against them. *Dune,* however, was his first foray into big-budget movies, and it took him a while to get his bearings.

I had admired David enormously ever since I'd first encountered his work at Zoetrope. Since David was a very Zoetrope-y sort of person, Francis Ford Coppola had planned to do some kind of project with him, though it had never gotten very far. David had submitted a very odd script called *Ronny Rocket*—a movie that I believe he still wants to make. The film was a kind of dream about a weird little pus-filled guy, sort of a midget rock and roller who was part human and part robot and had to be plugged in to function. Then he takes over the world. Somehow there were a lot of subways involved—subways and pus. I never quite got it; in fact, when I read it, I called Janet and asked her if she thought it was a test. Maybe Francis was just waiting to see whether any of us had the courage to say, "*This* emperor has no clothes." But no: David believed in that film, even though it seemed highly unlikely that anyone—even Francis—would ever be willing to make it.

I found *Eraserhead* a very strange film as well, and I'll admit that I never quite got it, but I was blown away by *Elephant Man.* I'd seen the play on Broadway, and I was so entranced by David's version that I watched it four or five times in a row. And when I met with David and Raffaella, I could see that David was an infinitely intelligent human being who, like his work, never quite conformed to expectations. He wore the same outfit every day: khaki pants, a white shirt, a bolo tie, and a black jacket. You'd go into his office and see this eclectic bunch of objects that only an artist would have collected: rocks with strings attached to them, the strings pinned up on the wall; a dozen Woody Woodpecker dolls; a collection of drawings based on dissected chicken parts that he had assembled. He was fond of making very specific and intriguing pen-and-ink line drawings to illustrate his ideas, although casting human beings who could live up to his visual imagination was something of a challenge.

I was eager to get started on our post-Zoetrope career, and I was honored that both Raffaella and David wanted to bring me onto their movie. But I must admit, I felt a bit daunted. Once again, there wasn't a finished script, so it was up to me to plod my way through the pages of a dense, complicated novel. I'm not much of a sci-fi fan, and I couldn't imagine casting these bizarre characters. A giant snake? A man covered with pustules who was so fat, he floated? A three-year-old who speaks in long, complicated sentences as she foretells the future? Turning Frank Herbert's—and David Lynch's—vision into an actual film began to seem like a monumental task.

The job wasn't made any easier by the fact that David, artist that he was, wanted to cast the entire film simply by looking at photographs of the actors' faces. I think he felt he could divine who was right simply by how they looked— which of course was important, but hardly the whole story.

"Don't you think we should actually meet some of these people?" I said one day.

David looked at me as though I'd made the most radical suggestion in the world, although we did eventually start meeting people. It must have been Raffaella who convinced him.

In any case, many of our candidates were Europeans whom we had to cast based on their body of work—we couldn't afford to bring them from Europe unless we knew we were going to use them. Jurgen Prochnow, for example, had just done Wolfgang Petersen's extraordinary German film *Das Boot.* For David and Raffaella, that was all they needed to make a deal with Jurgen's agent. We also cast Siân Phillips, who'd done the icy, magnificent Livia in the BBC series *I, Claudius.* I blush to admit I'd never heard of her, but Janet—now back from Tulsa—came into the office one day, saying, "Do you know who'd be good for the Reverend Mother?" (We'd been trying to get Glenn Close for the role, but she wasn't interested.)

A particularly hard part was Alia, the three-year-old child who foretells the future. The role called for a kid who could speak long, complicated sentences, and I couldn't imagine finding a child who could handle it. Then one day I met with a stunning five-year-old who was small enough to look two years younger. She not only articulated the complicated dialogue, she actually sounded as though she understood it. We'd discovered this beautiful, brilliant child on an episode of *That's Incredible,* where she and her brother recited Shakespeare sonnets. That little girl was Alicia Witt, who went on to play Cybill Shepherd's younger daughter on the sitcom *Cybill,* followed by a movie career.

One of my favorite *Dune* actors was Sting, who in 1982 was still part of the Police. Sting has made several movies since then, but he was barely an actor at that point, though he had done a bit in the rock movie *Quadrophenia.* Janet and I had met Sting at Zoetrope, where Martha Coolidge, one of Hollywood's few female directors, was also putting together a rock-and-roll movie. The film never got made, but Sting did an extraordinary test, with his rock-star presence and his unbelievably gorgeous face. When we screened his test, every woman at Zoetrope, from age twenty to fifty, went, "Oh, my God." It was a pleasure to hire him for *Dune.*

But the centerpiece of the movie was the young hero, Paul Atreides, charged with saving the world through his profound connection with his planet's ecology. Herbert's book was even more popular in 1982 than it is now, and when we announced that we were looking for someone to play Paul, every hot young kid in town wanted to be considered. Out of this search, we decided to cast Val Kilmer— whom we'd later go on to use in *Real Genius* and *Willow,* and who'd become a Star doing such movies as *Top Gun* and *The Doors.*

At that point, though, Val was still an Unknown. But he was also a very exciting up-and-coming young actor with a strong sexual presence. As soon as we cast him, the makeup team set about trying to change his brown eyes into Paul Atreides' famous all-blue eyes, in which the whites and pupils as well as the irises were blue. That's the problem with filming a cult novel—there are some details you simply can't avoid. So we sent Val down to Mexico to prepare for shooting, where the various coloring efforts promptly gave him an eye infection.

Just before we were about to break for the Christmas holidays, Raffaella became concerned. "I don't know," she said in her lilting Italian accent. "Something's missing. I just think there's something else we need for Paul. Maybe you should go and look again."

I resisted the temptation to remind her that we'd already looked at just about everyone there was—and that Val had already gotten sick in the service of this movie. Instead, I sent

our associate Elisabeth Leustig off to Seattle and San Francisco while I braved the post-Christmas snowstorms en route
to Chicago and New York.

Soon Elisabeth called me from Seattle. "Well," she said,
"there's one guy up here that everybody keeps talking about.
I've met him—he's kind of a nice guy, but he's got this funny
chin. I don't know."

"Neither do I," I replied. "But get him on tape and see
what happens."

Elisabeth and I met back in L.A., where we handed the
tape over to David and Raffaella. The kid was a local actor,
Elisabeth explained, and though he didn't even have an
agent, everybody thought the world of him at the Seattle
Repertory Theatre. His name was Kyle MacLachlan.

We all liked his tape, so we brought him to L.A. to meet
David. It turned out that Kyle was a huge fan of the entire
Dune series, so the meeting quickly took a belligerent turn.
Eager to safeguard the purity of his beloved novels, Kyle in-
terrogated David for several minutes. What were his inten-
tions here? Was he making this movie for the right reasons?
Would he treat this extraordinary work with the respect that
it deserved? Because if not, Kyle declared proudly, he wanted
nothing to do with the project.

David assured the young actor that he did indeed have
the best interests of the book at heart. We tested Kyle, and
David decided to go with him. Something about Kyle's
heartfelt defense of the book, his blend of passion and entitle-
ment, persuaded David that he could indeed play a valiant
young prince wholly dedicated to saving his planet.

Now we needed someone to negotiate a deal for the
agentless Kyle. (No Hollywood production will negotiate directly with an actor; it's too easy to get into legal and logisti-

cal difficulties.) Having discovered Kyle, Elisabeth felt rather protective of him. She thought that she and her husband, Jack, should manage Kyle's career, which enraged Raffaella, who quite rightly considered it a conflict of interest for someone who was helping to cast the movie to also represent someone in the cast. So Elisabeth dropped out of the picture and eventually started her own casting company. Jack and Kyle had formed a bond, and worked together for many years. And Elisabeth went on to a successful career that included casting *Dances with Wolves* (she'd met Kevin Costner when I'd given him a bit part in *Frances* so he could get his SAG card). Tragically, she was killed by a hit-and-run driver in Russia while working on *The Saint*—which ironically enough starred Val Kilmer.

As a result of *Dune,* Kyle went on to form an amazing artistic relationship with David Lynch, who used him in *Blue Velvet* and the TV series *Twin Peaks.* Clearly Kyle was an actor who fit right into David's world. Although *Dune* never completely came together as a movie—I think David's independent focus and Dino's commercial sensibilities never quite meshed—Janet and I are both proud of having helped one of Hollywood's most interesting directors find one of his key collaborators.

Val, meanwhile, was off the picture, in one of those devastating reversals that seem so common in actors' lives. Ron had to make a similar decision while casting *The Da Vinci Code.* That book, too, is full of fascinating characters who don't necessarily resemble ordinary human beings, including Silas, the villainous albino, who was originally to be played by a very interesting young Danish actor named Thure Lindhardt.

But when we brought Thure over to do a screen test with wardrobe and makeup, he just didn't look right. He had to play a scene in a loincloth, and when you looked at Thure's small, thin, boyish body, you just couldn't believe he had the power to kill all those people. So with great pain and reluctance, we decided to recast.

We weren't expecting to get a real albino, of course, but we did feel that we needed someone fair. There's only so much you can do with makeup, and it would be very difficult to turn an olive-skinned Italian or Greek into an albino without making him look like a Kabuki actor. We had seen some bigger, brawnier Scandinavian performers, but in the end Ron went with the pale-skinned Englishman Paul Bettany.

Paul already had a complicated relationship to *The Da Vinci Code*. Ron had considered him for the film, but decided that Paul was just one British actor too many; at that point, Ron was more concerned about giving the film a truly international flavor. Paul, meanwhile, wasn't really available. He had two children with his wife, Jennifer Connelly (yes, they met on *A Beautiful Mind*), and since they both wanted something that resembled a normal family life, only one of them was supposed to be making a movie at any time. Now it was Jennifer's turn, and she was finishing a picture in Canada. But because Paul, Ron, and Jennifer had all bonded on *A Beautiful Mind*, the Bettany-Connelly family agreed to break their rule. Paul went to Paris for a couple of weeks to play Silas—and we'll hope to use Thure some other time.

☆

On *The Da Vinci Code*, we had to say "no" to an actor we liked. Sometimes, we have the opposite problem: an actor who keeps saying "no" to us.

When we were making *Beetle Juice*, for example, we literally had to beg Michael Keaton to take the title role. *Beetle*

Juice was the second feature film by director Tim Burton, then best known for animation and someone whose quirky vision seemed to make a lot of people nervous. Not me—I thought he was brilliant. But *Beetle Juice*—the story of a dead couple who hire an obnoxious ghost to scare a live couple out of their house—seemed to break a lot of taboos even while presenting itself as family entertainment.

Now the movie seems almost tame. But it happened to be the first of its kind—a gross-out movie about death, which had previously seemed such a solemn subject—and Tim's movie seemed to scare away actors even faster than Beetlejuice the ghost scared off people.

We not only knew Michael, we'd given him his start in *Night Shift*. But like so many of the other actors who'd turned down parts in Tim's film, Michael's first reaction was to be offended by the despicable Beetlejuice, especially once he'd read the scene in which the ghost gropes a young girl's breasts.

I'd met Tim Burton by this point, and I could see that he knew exactly what he was doing. I also understood that the offending scene would be toned down by the time that shooting began. But Michael was genuinely disgusted by the role, with its rotting body and lecherous gestures, and he wanted nothing to do with it.

Nor did anybody else. For Beetlejuice, we'd been rejected by Tim's other choice, Sammy Davis Jr. For the punky kid, we'd gotten a "no" from sixteen-year-old Winona Ryder. Catherine O'Hara had passed on another role. The venerable Sylvia Sidney—star of such Hollywood gems as the 1936 Alfred Hitchcock film *Sabotage* and the 1937 classic gangster movie *Dead End*—told us that the script was the most disgusting thing she'd ever read. After five desperate weeks, the only performer willing to be in the picture was Geena Davis, who was then a Name (she's now a Star), and we couldn't commit to her because she was too tall. Until we found Geena a six-foot husband, we were a film without a cast.

We kept going back to Michael, but his manager, Harry Columby, kept saying no. After five or six failed phone calls, I found myself at a production meeting with Tim and producer David Geffen.

"Look," I had to say, "I've pulled out all the stops, but I can't even get Michael to meet with Tim. I think we've got to move on."

There was a dispirited silence around the table. Maybe we shouldn't have been surprised. Michael was a Star by then, and he'd gone on from *Night Shift* to do the well-received *Mr. Mom*—while even mere Names like Sidney and O'Hara had refused to be in this movie. Nobody knew who Tim Burton was (yet). Nobody got his sense of humor or his weird genius. And everybody was too grossed out by his movie to even meet with him.

"Fine," said David, breaking the silence. "Get me Harry Columby on the phone."

Everyone watched in stunned silence as I hurriedly dialed Harry's number and passed the phone to David. "Harry!" David began in his expansive, jovial voice. Then he launched into a sales pitch that could have convinced Mother Teresa to star in the remake of *Basic Instinct.*

"You just don't get it, Harry," David said hypnotically into the phone. "This is the kind of part that's going to get Michael an Academy Award for Best Supporting Actor. I mean, he will be brilliant, absolutely brilliant—there isn't an actor working today who could play this part the way Michael could, and if you don't convince him to at least meet with Tim, you'll never forgive yourself, Harry, and Michael will never forgive you. What's the last picture he did—*Mr. Mom*? Yeah, it was okay, but it's not the kind of movie that's going to win him an Oscar, is it? You want him playing househusbands and pimps the rest of his life? This is the kind of part that can make a career, Harry, and if you let Michael look the other way, you'll be missing the biggest opportunity of his life."

David's pitch went on and on, the rest of us watching in mesmerized silence, until finally, unbelievably, Harry said yes. Of course he couldn't promise anything, but yes, his client would give up a precious hour of his busy life to meet with Tim Burton. David put down the phone.

"We got him," he announced. And so we did. As soon as Michael met the inimitable Tim, he too was won over to the director's unique vision.

I've never seen anyone do what David Geffen did—not on any other movie I've ever worked on, and not even a second time on *Beetle Juice*. Tim himself had to convince the other actors, which he managed to do in a variety of ways. Our assistant director had just worked on a movie with Sylvia Sidney and he was still able to get her on the phone. Once he'd made contact, he passed the phone to Tim, who explained his vision for the film and, frankly, begged. I don't know if it was Tim's artistic integrity or his willingness to plead that persuaded her, but finally she said yes. Catherine O'Hara was somewhere out of town—maybe in Minnesota—so Tim flew out to meet with her. I, meanwhile, was more or less continually on the phone with Winona Ryder's parents, trying to convince the teenager that although "gross," *Beetle Juice* was a movie she'd be glad to be in.

And, indeed, *Beetle Juice* was shockingly successful. It solidified Michael Keaton's Stardom, it set Tim Burton off on his own bizarre and brilliant path, and it didn't do so badly for any of the other actors, either. Despite our faith in the film, we were all completely surprised—except, of course, for David Geffen. I guess that's *why* he's David Geffen. He played Harry Columby like a Stradivarius—I've never seen anything like it.

5 ☆ STARS AND SUPERSTARS

JANE

Although I helped cast most of the roles in *A Beautiful Mind,* there were two actors I never saw: Russell Crowe and Ed Harris. That's because Stars at their level rarely have to audition: given their previous body of work, producers and directors usually just offer them parts. Between auditions and offers there is also a kind of midway stage known as a meeting—literally, when a director and/or producer sits down with an actor to discuss the possibility of working together.

Depending on the relative power of actor and director/ producer, there are three possible reasons for a meeting: the actor knows he can have the part and is checking out the director; the director knows he can have the actor and is trying to decide whether he wants him; or both parties are trying to figure out whether they want to work together. Sometimes these possibilities are spelled out explicitly; sometimes they're simply understood. It's all part of the elaborate dance of power that takes place among Hollywood's top ranks—a dance that changes depending on the dancers, the level of funding, and the latest reports from the box office.

To take a random example, comedian Steve Carell was probably auditioning for parts right up until his hit movie, *The 40-Year-Old Virgin,* started to make big bucks. (In fact, we cast him in his first film role, in John Hughes's 1991 film *Curly Sue.*) After his extraordinary success, Carell graduated from auditions to meetings virtually overnight. And who knows what his status will be a year or two from now?

Daniel Craig, whom we cast as James Bond, is another breakout success story. Before he was chosen to play 007, he was relatively unknown—definitely the kind of actor who expected to audition. Even after doing a significant role in Steven Spielberg's *Munich,* his status didn't change much; the film didn't do well and never won Craig the kind of industry recognition that, say, Jennifer Connelly netted from the much smaller film *Requiem for a Dream.* After Daniel makes his first Bond flick, though, everybody in Middle America will know his face, and everyone in the business will be clamoring to work with him. Unless he wants to be seen for something way out of his type, he'll never have to audition again.

Looking back on the people we've cast, it's striking to notice when their careers took off—when they jumped from auditions to meetings. For Julia Roberts, *Mystic Pizza* was the film that got her noticed, but *Pretty Woman* was the movie that made her a Star. Likewise, George Clooney was recognized for his TV work and many of his films, but *The Perfect Storm* bumped him up to a whole new level. And Michael Keaton? The movie that solidified his Star status was the film he never even wanted to do—*Beetle Juice.* He can thank David Geffen for that one.

JANET

To anyone outside Hollywood, the difference between audition and meeting may sound trivial, but to insiders, the distinction is crucial. For an audition, you actually read a scene for a casting director, or, as you move up the ladder, for a director. Either way, though, you have to prove yourself. Auditioning indicates that some people, at least, aren't familiar with your work or aren't sure that you can handle a particular part.

To some extent, an actor is *always* auditioning—as is everyone in this business. Even directors may find themselves auditioning to attract studio interest, producers, Stars, or, if they're making independent films, financing. But if you are an actor with dreams of Stardom, you may long for the day when you're no longer dancing attendance upon some willful filmmaker, trotting out your wares like some kid in *Forty-second Street*. Instead, you imagine, you'll be sitting with the director like an equal, sipping San Pellegrino and chatting about the movie in a civilized fashion. This fantasy director already knows your work (if only because he's just reviewed the reel that your agent sent over last week). You're not performing for the director; the two of you, artists together, are conferring about a project of mutual interest.

Well, sometimes it happens like that. Sometimes you alternate between meetings and auditions, depending on the director's preferences, status, and style—and upon the ups and downs of your own career.

True, when an actor has really reached the A-list, he or she may not even be willing to meet at a director's office— that feels too much like an audition. Meetings at this level have to be arranged on neutral turf—at a restaurant, or maybe a bar, ideally halfway between the actor's home and the director's office. Even then, an actor entitled to turn up his nose at reading for some young indie filmmaker will gladly go in to audition for, say, Steven Spielberg.

☆

When we were casting *Jurassic Park*, we taped several auditions for the part of scientist Ellie Sattler, but we also arranged a few meetings, including one with Oscar-nominated actress Laura Dern, who from early on had been a big favorite both of ours and of producer Kathleen Kennedy. We liked Laura because she was smart and interesting and you could believe she was a scientist. (It's surprising how many Hollywood actresses of whom that isn't true.) We also liked her because she was a character actress.

Now here's where the terminology can really get us into trouble, and yet it's impossible to talk about casting without it. The industry's basic vocabulary recognizes two major categories: leading man/lady, and character actor/actress.

Leading men/ladies are the heroic types with a certain amount of dignity, grandeur, or glamour. Think Julianne Moore, Diane Lane, George Clooney, Brad Pitt. They have that commanding presence that fairly shouts, "This movie is all about me," and every single one of them is larger than life.

Character actors are pretty much everybody else. They're the quirky actors who tend to be more about the acting than the stardom—so usually, but not always, they're Names instead of Stars. Russell Crowe is one of the few performers who can go either way: his roles in *Gladiator* and *Master and Commander* showed he could be a leading man, but his parts in *The Insider* and *A Beautiful Mind* were classic character roles—not heroes, but men written on a smaller, more human scale. Jennifer Jason Leigh, Philip Seymour Hoffman, Laura Linney, and Dustin Hoffman, on the other hand, are all straight-out character actors, even when they're playing the biggest part in the movie. They have neither the "movie star" good looks nor the leading player's heroic (male) or grande dame (female) quality—they're too down-to-earth, too quirky, too life-size.

Most Working Actors are character actors—after all, a movie has only a few parts for genuine Stars. Imagine a film in which everyone—from the cop on the corner to the waitress at the coffee shop—is absolutely gorgeous and bigger than life. It might make a pretty picture, but it wouldn't be a believable movie.

Sometimes, of course, a highly significant role is more of a character part: the crazed sea captain in *Pirates of the Caribbean,* the crippled man in *My Left Foot,* the former mental patient in *Twelve Monkeys.* It's one of the sad ironies of the movie business that leading men and ladies can, and often do, get cast in character roles, whereas character actors can't always do the leads. To some extent this is a question of looks. Johnny Depp, Daniel Day-Lewis, and Brad Pitt have always been gorgeous enough to play leads; they just prefer the quirkier roles. Likewise, Julianne Moore has the beauty to become a leading lady, but she seems to prefer more offbeat choices. Most characters actors, on the other hand, don't have the looks or the presence (or the name recognition) to play leading men or women.

As a character actress with a respectable body of work, Laura Dern was an interesting choice for *Jurassic Park.* She had the intelligence and acting chops to make what might have been a thin part interesting and fresh. Some roles are written so specifically that they're tough to cast. You need an actor who can bring just the right quality to make the story work. Other roles, like the one Laura eventually played in *Jurassic Park,* can go any number of ways, as the list of actresses who came in to audition makes clear:

Embeth Davidtz
Helen Hunt
Marisa Tomei
Gwyneth Paltrow (Steven's godchild; and her first job
    was in *Hook* as young Wendy)
Kristin Davis
Jeanne Tripplehorn
Robin Wright (long before she'd married Sean Penn;
    actually, she had a meeting)
Laura Linney
Jennifer Grey
Kyra Sedgwick
Dana Delaney
Lara Flynn Boyle
Marg Helgenberger

Any of these fine actresses could have made the part work. They just didn't happen to be choices that excited the director as much as Laura Dern, who brought to the part her own special quality: her vivid intelligence, her unusual sense of timing (she always seems to wait half a beat longer than you'd expect), her feistiness, her sudden charm. And, unlike some leading ladies or ingenues, she'd be willing to run through the brambles getting dirty and disheveled. So when the picture she was shooting in Canada finally wrapped, I was happy to set up a meeting.

☆

Steven went all out to make his guests feel comfortable, especially the children, so the offices where he met actors included a game room complete with pinball machines and video games, as well as a kind of meeting room furnished Southwestern style—those comfortable burlap couches, little wooden end tables graced with Indian artifacts, everything organized in soothing tones of ocher and orange and rust. You really felt as though you were in someone's living room—the perfect atmosphere to put a nervous actor at ease.

The day Laura came in for her meeting, Steven and I were already there, urging her to be seated, inviting her to help herself to the sodas, fruit, and little candies that had been set out on the low coffee table. Often, though, I'll be waiting with an actor for several minutes before the director joins us or asks us to join him. Although the whole image of a meeting is that it's a social occasion, everyone knows that it's really a job interview, which makes some actors understandably nervous. So I'll do everything I can to help them relax: chat about a past or current role, or maybe talk about anything *but* the business—hobbies, family, vacation. Sometimes I sense that the actor would just prefer to be left alone, a quiet moment before turning on the charm for a director.

Laura's was the only meeting we'd scheduled that day, so we were able to avoid the farce of trying to keep well-known actors from running into one another—Kevin Bacon coming in one door just as Kevin Spacey is going out another. We always try to make every actor feel that he or she is the only one we're meeting, though of course everybody knows better.

Some directors are awkward or abrupt at these meetings, making it difficult for the actor to relax. But with Steven, the actor was always the center of attention. He'd make it clear that he was familiar with her work, and nothing puts an actor at ease faster than that. He was friendly and gracious, and when he asked an actor about her thoughts, he seemed genuinely interested.

True, he is *Steven Spielberg,* a larger-than-life figure even when you're hanging out in what feels like his living room. But with Steven, it's all about the work, and actors—who have a finely honed ability to divine what a director truly wants—can tell right away that he's not looking for flattery. He's just trying to find out whether they've got enough personal chemistry to make it through the long months of shooting a movie.

Francis Ford Coppola, another larger-than-life figure, would sometimes break the ice by asking an actor which room his family ate dinner in. As the actor thought back to the circumstances surrounding this childhood meal, he relaxed—clearly, there was no right or wrong answer to this question!—and before he knew it, there he was, chatting with Coppola, for heaven's sake, as though they were just two people having a conversation.

Steven tended to focus more on the work, but actors like talking about that, too. "So tell me, how do you see the part?" Steven might ask, and when the actress answered, he listened attentively, as though her answer really mattered.

"I do have sort of a clear idea, but I'm happy to take direction," an actress might answer, or, "Actually, I was kind of confused. If she's such a fireball in Act I, why does she fall apart so quickly in Act II?" (Although movies aren't formally divided into acts, Robert McKee's and Syd Field's screenwriting classes have ensured that just about everybody in Hollywood uses that term.) A truly self-confident actress might even say, "Would it be okay if I just *showed* you?" and the meeting turns into an audition anyway.

At Laura's meeting, the actress made a point of saying that she thought it would be fun to be an action hero. With that positive, eager comment, Laura was signaling that she was no art-house snob who'd complain about the lack of character depth; instead, she'd be a trouper about running through those brambles, always ready to yield the spotlight to her costars—the dinosaurs. I cheered silently for what I considered a smart move on Laura's part, grateful that she hadn't done some of the foolish things I'd seen other actors do. I cringe just thinking about the many actors who've told the director, "Oh, I haven't had time to read the script. Why don't you tell me about it?" Or the actors who are overly chummy with the director, as though they really were old friends. Or, of course, the actors who are actually *late* to a meeting or audition, or who come in looking as though they haven't slept in weeks, or wearing jeans and a T-shirt for what's supposed to be a glamorous part. And let's not even talk about the actor who has done a beautiful job reading for us—and then brings in a completely different interpretation of the character for the director.

Jane's pet peeve is the actor whom she extensively prepares for either a meeting or an audition—describing the script, the situation, the demands of the part. Then, when the director asks, "Do you know what I'm looking for?" the actor will say, "Oh, I have no idea," instead of saying "Well, Jane told me—but I'd love to hear your take on it."

I tend to get annoyed when actors make wholesale changes in the script while reading for the director—simply improvising their own dialogue, changing the rhythm that the writer has carefully constructed. This is especially problematic—not to mention insulting—when the director is also the writer. Of course sometimes you ask an actor to use their own words or even to improvise. But directors like John Hughes and Rob Reiner have labored over every word, and they don't appreciate an actor ignoring their careful choices. (Note to actors: If you *must* change something, at least ask first!)

Another thing I find frustrating is when a director takes the time to talk with the actor about another way to do the scene. The actor nods—he understands—and then proceeds to give the exact same reading. Clearly this is an actor who doesn't know the meaning of "take direction."

Happily, Steven liked Laura as much as we all hoped he would. The next day, we called Laura's agent to say that her client had the part.

According to an interview I happened to catch on the Independent Film Channel, Laura also knew the meeting had gone well. But she was surprised, she admitted, that she'd had a meeting in the first place. For someone as big as Steven Spielberg, she would have been satisfied with an audition.

JANE

The questions of who counts as a Star, when they actually became a Star, and how long they've got before they're no longer a Star are of paramount importance in show business. Politics, personality, the fashions of the moment, and a thousand other factors go into this calculus. But after having worked in the industry for twenty-five years, Janet and I have spent a fair amount of time thinking about the part of the equation that concerns the actor's own star quality. Although we've made our mistakes like everybody else, we have come to know what it's like to be in the room with a Star—even before they've achieved their Stardom.

The first time we met Bruce Willis, for example, he was a mostly unemployed actor referred to us by a costume-designer friend who'd dressed him for a guest spot on *Miami Vice*. We tried to cast him in a little low-budget movie we were working on, but he told us that he'd just done a pilot for a series called *Moonlighting*.

Before *Moonlighting* and *Miami Vice*, Bruce had been doing low-budget theater and working as a bartender in New York City, and if we'd happened to meet him behind the bar, who knows? But when he came into our office, we could tell: there was something special about him. He had lively eyes, a killer smile, and a powerful personality. You could see at a glance that he was strong and good-looking and sexy and funny. But it wasn't just that. He had some kind of extra intensity, a sort of expansiveness in his work, so that when he was reading for a part, his energy suddenly filled the room and you couldn't take your eyes off him.

We had the same sense of *Aha!* when we met Charlize Theron on a general—and again, neither Janet nor I could take our eyes off her. It was as though she sparkled, as though a special kind of light surrounded her.

Of course, Charlize was a lovely young woman, but we weren't only, or even mainly, responding to her looks. As a plain ordinary woman who works in the film industry and lives in Los Angeles, I meet breathtakingly beautiful women every day—in my office, on the set, at the corner Starbucks— and, that infamous shampoo commercial notwithstanding, sometimes I *do* "hate them because they're beautiful"! But some beautiful women are simply terrific human beings, and somehow they manage to project their beauty and their sensuality from some place that isn't threatening to those of us who are plainer. You like them as human beings, *and* their beauty takes your breath away. Charlize certainly has that quality—her beauty seems to be part of her likability, almost as though she's sharing it with you.

Julia Roberts is another actress who has that likability in spades. She may not be "the most beautiful woman in the world," but she has something better than beauty: charisma. When she read for Daisy, even in her sloppy shirt and loose jeans, she exuded something very special. She was only nineteen years old, but you could still see the beginnings of Julia Roberts the Star; in fact, you almost had to be blind to miss it. Forget the unflattering clothes: you could have put a paper bag on her head, and the star quality would have come through.

Julia still auditioned for directors after *Mystic Pizza*—it took several years for her to achieve the kind of Superstardom she has today—and she was always friendly, genuine, even self-deprecating. After she got her Oscar nomination for *Steel Magnolias,* she came in to read for *Ghost,* though director Jerry Zucker decided she was still a little young for the role. (That was the part that eventually went to Demi Moore.) Julia couldn't have been nicer about it, and she made no bones about saying, "Oh, remember that time on *Mystic Pizza* when Jane sent me home and made me read the script again?" She had that humility, that inherent decency, that you can still sense whenever you see her on a talk show or at a press event. Sure, she's got millions now, but she grew up in a working-class family in Georgia, where her mother taught city-sponsored acting classes in public parks, and you feel that she's never forgotten where she comes from. Despite her extraordinary success, she hasn't set herself apart from the public who's helped make her who she is, and that public responds by identifying with her, liking her, loving her. To them, she's just the girl down the street who got really, really lucky, but who remembers your name and says hello when you run into her.

Of course not all Stars are so charming when you meet them in person. Some of them are quite shy—as I was—and they just want to act. Consider the extremely talented David Strathairn, who dazzled on-screen as Edward R. Murrow in *Good Night, and Good Luck*. When he came in to meet with Janet and me, I don't know if he said two words, and he certainly didn't dazzle the room. It was only when he started acting that you saw what was special about this performer, and maybe some part of him that couldn't emerge any other time became visible when he was playing someone else.

Likewise, there are some Stars who are terrible human beings, and whatever charm or likability they manage to project is just a function of their ability to keep the mask up. Janet and I tend to meet actors when they've got a stake in being nice—we're usually their first stop on the way to being hired, so why would they alienate us? If they're big enough to mistreat us, they're probably too big to meet with us in the first place.

While I'd be the last person to invite sympathy for the poor little badly behaved Stars, I must admit that I *do* feel sympathy for them, partly because I've had a tiny taste myself of how disorienting and invaded a Star's life can be. Back when I was living with Ralph Waite, the mammoth popularity of *The Waltons* affected not only his life but mine: suddenly,

everybody wanted to get close to "Pa Walton"—and to anyone who had access to him. I'd go to a party with Ralph and
find my picture in a fan magazine as the "unknown woman"
who'd shown up as his date. The next week I'd be shopping
at the local grocery store and some total stranger would ask
me to sign her box of cornflakes. If that's what I got for being
the anonymous companion of a relatively minor celebrity, I
can only imagine how overwhelming and relentless that kind
of attention must be if you're actually a Star, let alone a major
one. You want to have a quiet dinner, but people who recognize you get annoyed if you won't give up your private time
to answer their questions or sign their napkins. You're going
through a tough breakup—but every time you show your
face, someone's monitoring you for wrinkles, extra pounds,
or a sour expression. You make a casual remark to a reporter
or to someone who has access to a reporter, and suddenly a
flippant or ironic comment comes back to haunt you in ways
you can't control.

The contrast between the public's godlike adoration
and the demands of your working life is also crazy-making.
When you're making a movie, you can't drink, smoke, or
even miss a few hours sleep—every bag and wrinkle will be
magnified by the camera, and your looks will be criticized
with relentless glee by the press and public. On the days
you're called to shoot, you show up for makeup at 5 a.m. and
stagger over to the set by 6, ready to pour your heart and soul
into the character you've created. You're working long hours,
often separated from your family, and you have the nagging
sense that everybody's job is riding on yours; if you turn in a
lousy performance, the whole movie suffers. But take one
step outside the set to where the public is waiting, and you've
got thousands of strangers ready to overwhelm you with

demands, gifts, offers of sex—all their own frustrations and fantasies.

Withstanding any of this requires a remarkably centered, strong-minded human being, and that's not necessarily a job requirement for becoming an actor! You trained to take on the facial expressions and body language of *someone else*— now, in the midst of all this adulation and invasion, how do you now keep a sense of who *you* are? The problem is compounded by the feeling that you'll never again meet anyone who doesn't somehow want to take advantage of you. The only person in the world who doesn't need your help is, perhaps, another Star.

One of the jobs I had before becoming casting director was a personal assistant to Barbra Streisand and Jon Peters. I'll never forget the night we were driving home and Barbra decided she had a craving for some Chinese food. We were just passing her favorite restaurant, and I offered to jump out and pick up an order.

"No," said Barbra. "I'll do it. Nobody will ever recognize me with this hat."

Sure enough, she came back to the car fifteen minutes later, carrying a carton of egg rolls and absolutely glowing. "Mission accomplished!" she said with delight. I couldn't help feeling grateful that despite all the strains of being a single mother with no career prospects I, at least, could always pick up an egg roll.

So if Stars behave badly in private, there may be good reason for it, unpleasant as they may make the lives of everyone around them. And whatever they're "really" like in intimate situations, it's remarkable how powerful their presence can be when they're "on," whether that means acting or simply working the room. Over the years, I've learned to respond to that quality in a very instinctive, almost physical way. If I find myself paying intense attention, if I realize I can't look away, if the hairs on the back of my neck stand up and a shiver goes through me—then okay. I'm with a Star.

JANET

Julia Roberts and Charlize Theron certainly had Star quality from their teen years, and guys like Harrison Ford and Clint Eastwood seem to have it into their sixties, seventies, and beyond. But Star quality isn't the only quality you need to become a Star, much less to remain one. So, always bearing in mind that there are dozens of exceptions for every rule, what do you need to become a Star?

Well, okay, it usually begins with looks. Yes, there are the guys like Steve Carell, Philip Seymour Hoffman, and Gene Hackman, who somehow became movie stars even though they (basically) never got to kiss the girl. With comedians like Adam Sandler or Mike Myers or Will Ferrell, part of their appeal is their goofy appearance. And, as you can see from the examples I've used, it's extremely rare for a woman who's not beautiful to become a Superstar, or even a Star.

The next factor, predictably, is age. It's very difficult to remain an A-list Star past the age of fifty if you're a woman, or sixty if you're a man. As we've seen throughout this book, there are always exceptions. But by and large, the peak of a Star's appeal is over by the time he or she reaches middle age, even if the actor in question is still gorgeous, talented, and charismatic. I'm not saying that they don't get the leads or even the big salaries. But they're no longer the ones whose mere presence in the cast guarantees funding or a decent opening weekend.

Of course, there are lots of actors who don't particularly want to play by these rules. John Cusack, for example, was always very careful about the roles he'd take because he had a strong artistic vision about the kinds of movies he believed in. He didn't particularly want to be a movie star; he wanted to be an actor, and he shaped his career accordingly, although, like everyone else, he's probably made some choices he regrets. Sometimes you look at a script and it seems as though it will be a wonderful movie—and then, well, it isn't. So many factors go into making a great picture, it's not surprising that you can't always tell ahead of time what's going to work and what won't. But at least John has always tried to make substantial, risky choices.

Benicio Del Toro is a similar case. He had an extraordinary intensity, intelligence, and sharpness of judgment, along with a kind of sexual charisma that depended less on good looks than on his confidence and drive. He had an aura that simply flashed "Danger!" and probably the greatest sense of unpredictability of any actor we've ever known. Plus a great smile. His agent must have been in despair for years, because we'd keep trying to cast Benicio in some big commercial movie, and he'd go off and do a tiny independent film instead. Thanks to his work in *The Usual Suspects, Traffic,* and *21 Grams,* the public now knows his name, but Benicio is still charting his own course, less concerned with stardom than with crafting a body of work that expresses his inner vision. Johnny Depp, Philip Seymour Hoffman, Kevin Kline, Daniel Day-Lewis, Kevin Spacey—all of them have made choices that have, at least to some extent, taken them out of the mainstream industry into independent film, theater, or other pursuits entirely.

George Clooney is a fascinating and perhaps a unique combination of A-plus-Star and maverick. He does the big commercial roles and the independent films—and he also creates his own films, large and small. At age forty-four, he gave an interview expressing his concern that he only had a few more years of true stardom. After you turn fifty, he wondered, who wants to see you kiss the girl? Meanwhile, though, he seems to be on the verge of achieving greatness behind the camera as writer, director, and producer.

JANE

One of the reasons that actors like Depp, Cusack, and Del Toro have relentlessly avoided traditional Stardom is because Stars are often typecast—required to play the same sort of character again and again and again. When I was casting *The Holiday* for Nancy Meyers, we tried desperately to get Hugh Grant to play the romantic comedy's leading man, a part that had been written with him in mind. But Hugh wouldn't bite—he simply couldn't bear to do yet another charming, slightly hapless, self-deprecating, boyishly sexy hero.

A Star who is self-confident and determined enough may simply demand to be seen for a part that he wouldn't normally be cast for. This happened when Rob Reiner was making *Ghosts of Mississippi,* the story of Mississippi assistant district attorney Bobby DeLaughter's years-long crusade to reopen the trial of Byron De La Beckwith, the accused killer of Medgar Evers. Two previous attempts to try Beckwith in the mid-1960s had both ended in mistrial, and when De-Laughter wanted to reopen the case, Beckwith was already in his seventies.

I started making a List of "old guy" actors for Beckwith

as we brought in James Woods to audition for DeLaughter's boss. But Jimmy had other ideas.

"I know I'm supposed to be reading for this other part," he told Rob, "but I really want to give Beckwith a shot. Will you just let me read it?"

Well, how are you going to say no to James Woods? I happened to know the request would be forthcoming, because Jimmy's agent had called and told me about it. I felt it was Jimmy's thing, so let him try it, as long as it wasn't going to create an uncomfortable situation or embarrass our director. And I knew Rob well enough to know that he'd take it in the right spirit, whether it turned out that Jimmy was right for the part or not.

So when Rob agreed, Jimmy took charge. "I need you to sit right here," he told Rob, and he staged the entire audition in such a way that Rob could only see a portion of his face— but could hear his accent and feel his attitude.

Beckwith was a man who'd hated black people and Jews all his life. He'd gunned down a major civil rights leader right in the man's own driveway, and gotten away with it—hell, he'd been admired for it, speaking for years at Klan rallies and other white supremacist events on the strength of his notoriety. According to an FBI informant, he'd even bragged about getting away with the murder. Everyone who knew him, including the informant, considered him a very, very scary guy.

Well, Jimmy gave a very, very scary reading. At the end of it, Rob just sat there for a few minutes. Then he said, "Okay" and offered Jimmy the part on condition that the makeup test worked out. As Rob put it, "We don't want to look like a bunch of schmucks with too much makeup on our faces."

The makeup worked fine—in fact, it was pretty amazing—and even in retrospect, I can't imagine anyone else making that part work so well. Who but James Woods could present such an evil man, dripping with venom, sizzling with hatred, so that—no matter what his age—you understood just how dangerous he was? Most Hollywood actors try to play younger rather than decades older, but Jimmy made a courageous move, and his effort was rewarded with an Oscar nomination.

JANET

It's wonderful when an actor comes to inhabit a part so fully that you feel as though it had been written for him. That's how I felt about Billy Bob Thornton's portrayal of Gary Gaines, the real-life coach of the Permian Panthers. Gaines, his team, and his community were the subject of the renowned sports book *Friday Night Lights,* and when director Peter Berg set out to make a movie based on that book, he needed a Gaines who could embody the real man's qualities: toughness, kindness, a profound sense of honor that nonetheless allowed him to put extraordinary amounts of pressure on his high-school players. Like *The Perfect Storm, Friday Night Lights* is the story of a community, even if it's anchored by a hero. Whoever played Gaines had to seem not like a movie star descending into the battered West Texas landscape but rather like an organic part of that landscape, a genuine member of his football-mad community.

Billy Bob came immediately to everybody's mind. We knew he'd fit right into the Texas milieu, and that his laid-back yet intense acting style would fit right into a cast that would be composed of up-and-coming young actors, local performers, and some real-life college and minor-league foot-ball players. He has that Star presence that fills up a screen, but he also looks as though he's right out of working-class Texas—and his father was a high-school sports coach. We were all thrilled when he said "yes."

We were similarly lucky to get Derek Luke to play Boo-bie Miles, the charismatic African American player laid low by a knee injury at a crucial point in the season. Luke had won renown as the lead in *Antwone Fisher,* and he had the sparkle and bravura to play the young hotshot. But he also seemed to fit right into the rural community of Odessa, Texas, where the movie was set. A Star who doesn't seem like a Star isn't always so easy to find.

By contrast, when we were casting *The Perfect Storm,* we wanted a bit of Star quality in our two leads. Yes, we needed guys whom the audience would buy as working class, and both George Clooney and Mark Wahlberg had a kind of rough-and-ready quality that kept them from looking incon-gruous on a working sword boat. But *The Perfect Storm* pits these two guys against the largest storm anyone had ever seen—a conflict of almost mythic dimensions. We wanted heroes who were larger than life, who expressed great men's ability to rise above their circumstances, whereas *Friday Night Lights* is at least partly a story of people who were beaten down by theirs. The guys in *The Perfect Storm* were leading men; the coach and Boobie Miles were character parts.

Another reason we were so happy to get George for *The Perfect Storm* was, frankly, because we could afford him. Now we probably couldn't—as we've seen, he's risen to the A-plus list. But when we were shooting *The Perfect Storm,* he was still "only" on the A-list—big enough to help get the movie made, but not so big that we couldn't spend the lion's share of the budget on the special effects.

☆

Finding a Star for *Poseidon* was an adventure in itself. In fact, the entire casting process of this picture was a saga of scheduling nightmares and script rewrites. Yet somehow, as with all of Wolfgang's movies, we always had fun. Wolfgang is the kind of director who makes sure that there are always two kinds of soup on the set every day. He knows his actors will end up getting soaked, banged around, and otherwise put through their paces. When they come off the boat sets, cold and dripping, they're always greeted with a warm blanket and a cup of hot soup.

But before we could get to the soup for *Poseidon,* we had to get to the script. As with so many of our big films, we began with only a partial screenplay—some 65 pages out of a potential 120. The film was to be a retelling of *The Poseidon Adventure,* the 1972 disaster/adventure movie that was one of the pioneers of the genre, about a luxury liner that is overturned in mid-ocean. For a harrowing two hours, we watch passengers and crew scramble through the giant upside-down ship, trying to reach safety. The new version was also very exciting, with the proverbial cast of thousands (a type of film also pioneered by the original), including about ten main roles.

The story turned upon the character of John Dylan, the mysterious, reluctant leader of the intrepid group of survivors whom we follow on their journey through the overturned ship. Early in the process, Wolfgang met with Clive Owen, whose agent soon received an offer.

A few weeks later, I got one of my least favorite kinds of calls. The morning after the Academy Awards, Wolfgang called me to say, "Clive has dropped out." My blood ran cold—had I heard right? I had. Clive told Wolfgang how much he'd wanted want to work with him, but this was simply not the kind of movie he wanted to do right then.

I immediately started checking availabilities of the other likely candidates. It was slim pickings since Stars and even Names are usually booked well in advance, and with an offer out to Clive, we hadn't made any others. I was also working madly to keep track of the availability of the actors on our lists for the other roles. Although we had a start date, we might end up pushing it a bit, or someone who hadn't been available might fall out of a film. All the agents involved— several dozen at least, to cover multiple choices for the lead and nine supporting parts—were asked to keep me posted about any changes in their clients' schedules.

Josh Lucas was on our list for Dylan—the same Josh Lucas we'd discovered when I was casting *The Outsiders* TV series and whose performance in *A Beautiful Mind* bumped him up to Name status. More people heard of him when he did *Sweet Home Alabama* with Reese Witherspoon, and now he was starring in *The Glass Menagerie* on Broadway opposite Jessica Lange. Sorry, Josh's agent told us. The Broadway commitment meant that Josh just wasn't available for *Poseidon*.

By this point, we were holding off on casting Dylan until a full script was ready to go out with an offer. Even the agents didn't have a script. With the rewrites, the movie was becoming more of an ensemble cast, with the role of Robert Ramsey emerging as co-leader of the group. Other roles were evolving, too—so we kept making new lists, looking at new actor reels and DVDs, and auditioning new actors, which meant asking still more agents and managers to keep me posted on their clients' availability. We didn't know exactly who we wanted or who would be available, but I was doing my best to keep all our options open.

At one point, we started thinking about casting Topher Grace, the charming young star of the TV series *That Seventies Show* and Dennis Quaid's costar in *In Good Company.* To be honest, it seemed like one of those wacky, out-of-the-box ideas that probably wouldn't work—but what if . . . ? The problem was that Topher was way too young for the part, which called for a man in his early thirties. Until recently, Topher had been playing a teenager, and he still looked like the twenty-six-year-old he was.

On the other hand, Wolfgang had been very impressed with Topher's work on *In Good Company,* and Topher was a huge fan of Wolfgang's. His father was a great admirer of Wolfgang's *Das Boot,* so Topher had grown up seeing that film not once but several times. Was there any way, his agent wondered, that Topher could be considered?

There still wasn't a script to read, so Topher couldn't audition. But we brought him in to Wolfgang's office at Warner Brothers, where the two men basically hung out for half an hour or so.

Topher had a real maturity to him, no question about that. He definitely knew how to handle himself, and we'd all found him a very interesting actor. But in the end, we just couldn't get past the age thing. There was another character, Christian, who was in his early twenties—and Topher's age read as too close. Plus, the movie's romantic plot involved our hero meeting a young woman with a nine-year-old son. Both the woman and the kid are supposed to fall in love with the hero, and he with them, so that at the end of their ordeal, you feel they're going to become a family. At age twenty-six, Topher seemed too young to take on that kind of fatherly role. So with regret, we said "no" to Topher and continued on our search.

One of the guys we looked at was Josh Hartnett. But he was shooting in Romania, and we were never able to set up a meeting.

Then one day I got a call from Chris Andrews, Josh Lucas's agent. *Menagerie* wasn't doing very well, and if it didn't get any Tony nominations, it might close early. By this time our start date had pushed back a bit, making Josh's "availability gap" much smaller. Hmmm . . .

By the time we had a shooting script, guess what? Josh's schedule had somehow become much closer to ours. Now instead of a three-month gap, the conflict was only a matter of weeks. So Josh's agent asked us to take a look at *Stealth,* the action movie that Josh had recently completed, still being edited at SONY. I trooped over there to watch it, and then a week later, we all went—Wolfgang, the studio executive assigned to the picture, Jane, and me. By this point, no one but Jane and me had even met Josh, who was still in New York doing his play. But the footage we saw looked terrific. Josh had always been a handsome guy, but here he was absolutely gorgeous. More important, he looked *big.* He'd gone from being an actor who disappeared inside the role to a heroic leading man of real stature. That may not be the kind of part he always wants to play—interviews he's given suggest it's not—but on *Stealth,* director Rob Cohen told us, he'd really "put Josh through hero school," and you could see that Josh had passed with flying colors. There were a lot of scenes where he had to stare off into space, worrying about the safety of his crew, and the action movie featured a lot of blue- and green-screen work, in which the actor is shot in front of a blank screen that's later filled with special effects. It takes a special kind of acting skill to react to something that isn't there, to convey that sense of being larger than life without seeming arrogant or corny, to play the fact that you're the handsomest, strongest, and most commanding presence in the room. George Clooney brings that kind of heroism to *Oceans Eleven* and *Oceans Twelve;* Russell Crowe brought it to *Master and Commander* and *Gladiator.* Although both actors can play ordinary, even flawed, men, they've both learned how to convey that superhero quality that makes an action film work—and in *Stealth,* Josh had learned that, too.

My sense is that Josh never set out to be a Star. He always wanted to be an actor, someone who could make people forget who he was as they concentrated on who he was portraying. With looks like that, I'm sorry, you've *got* to be a movie star. But Josh is a very grounded, dedicated guy, and I'm sure he'll be one of the Stars who makes his own way, rather than letting the p.r. machine have its way with him.

☆

With Josh cast, we could zero in on Wolfgang's top choices for the other roles: Kurt Russell would play Robert Ramsey, a man who, after the rewrites, had become the co-leader of our valiant group. Emmy Rossum would be Kurt's daughter, Jennifer. And the role of Christian, Emmy's fiancé, would be played by Mike Vogel, a gorgeous and talented young actor whom we'd discovered for *Supercross,* a motocross film. Then there was the wonderful Richard Dreyfuss for Richard Nelson, a gay man who had recently been dumped by his partner of many years; Mía Maestro (who'd been on our wife list for *A Beautiful Mind*) as Elena, the stowaway; Andre Braugher (best known to audiences from his stellar work on *Homicide*) for Captain Bradford, the ship's captain who insists that staying in the ballroom is the only way to be saved; and one of my favorite kid actors, Jimmy Bennett, to play nine-year-old Conor. Rounding out the group was Jacinda Barrett to play Maggie James, Conor's mother. Jacinda had made a splash in *Ladder 49* and *Bridget Jones: The Edge of Reason,* where she plays Bridget Jones's apparent rival, who turns out to be in love with Bridget.

Unfortunately, Josh wasn't the only actor with scheduling issues. Jacinda was on a film in Canada and Michigan that was finishing right when we were starting, with one day in particular that was a real problem for our schedule. Since every shooting day of a huge film involves dozens of actors, as well as location logistics, changing even a single day is no easy matter. But the producers on Jacinda's other film were crazy about her and went to incredible lengths to work with us on the problem date, so the matter was eventually resolved.

Much to my relief, the dozens of small roles from the original script got whittled down to a mere handful, but as shooting approached, we still hadn't cast two of the pivotal roles: Valentin, the waiter who was stowing away Elena, and Lucky Larry, a loud, drunk gambler. Eventually, we got Freddy Rodríguez (best known from the HBO series *Six Feet Under*) to play Valentin, and Kevin Dillon, whom I'd met years ago through his brother Matt, for Lucky Larry.

In the end, we were all pleased with the way we'd assembled a mixture of Stars and Names, creating a strong ensemble. Since *Poseidon* was shooting in L.A., I was able to go to the read through, the ritual in which as many of the main actors as possible are assembled to sit around a table and read through the script. (An assistant or two reads the smaller parts.) Everyone has been cast, they all know they've got the part, so no one has anything to prove—it's just a chance for the team to get a vision of the film. Wolfgang and one of the producers, Akiva Goldsman (who had met Josh when they both did *A Beautiful Mind*), sat at the head of the table, smiling as they heard their movie. And yes, the cast was delicious. Thank you, casting gods!

6 ☆ MAKING SURE

JANET

Bringing an actor in for a second, third, or fourth audition is known as a "callback," and for both us and the actors, this can be a harrowing experience. A callback means the actor has gotten that much closer to landing the part, making it that much more disappointing if the role eventually goes to someone else. A callback also indicates that someone on our side of the table—us, the director, or a studio person—hasn't yet made up his or her mind.

As with the audition process, there's a fine art to doing callbacks. First, you're usually joined by other authorities—the director, certainly; perhaps also a producer or two. (Occasionally, one or more studio representatives will come along, but this is rare.) Your goal is for these other decision makers to see in the actor what you saw. As in a meeting, you're a kind of hostess, trying to make sure everyone is comfortable.

Another significant feature of callbacks is that you're no longer comparing the actor to your ideal image of the

role—or at least, that's not all you're doing. You're also mea-
suring each actor against all the others whom you've called
back. Depending on the situation, you might call back as few
as two or as many as a dozen actors—a small enough number that you can keep all or most of them firmly in mind. So
you watch Actor A, thinking, "Well, he's got the sleazy charm
we're looking for, but isn't he a little young? If we go with
Actor B, we'll get the sense that this guy has been a traveling
salesman for a long, long time—that's kind of good, isn't it?"
Then Actor B comes in, and you think, "Wow, Actor B is
good, but Actor A is *so* much cuter. For sure, any woman
would buy what he's selling! So which is more important
here: Actor A's cute, fresh, adorable look, or Actor B's suggestion that the guy's been doing this for years?"

As you try to figure out which actor has what you want,
you might ask actors to vary what they're delivering. Perhaps
you suggest that cute young Actor A play the scene as though
he's exhausted; or maybe you ask world-weary Actor B to in-
ject more sexual charm and liveliness into his reading. You
learn more about how far an actor can stretch—and you also
learn that some things just aren't going to change. Perhaps
Actor A will look young and boyish no matter what he does,
whereas when you ask Actor B to turn on the charm, suddenly he looks ten years younger. Sometimes the actor you
liked on first viewing just keeps giving you the same performance; other times, an actor turns out to have hidden depths
or an incredible range or for whatever reason just does a better job on the callback than he did first time out. You made
one set of judgments at the first audition—now you've got a
chance to look at them more deeply. The actor who was your
first choice drops to fifth place; an actor you almost didn't
call back becomes your favorite.

Often, of course, the director is the one to work with the actor, but sometimes that task falls to us, especially if the director isn't there. Always, though, we're watching with the director's eyes, imagining what he's going to look for and making sure he gets a chance to see it. When we submit the tapes from the callbacks, we don't want anyone to wonder what might have happened if we'd asked the actor to be sexier, funnier, more intense. We want to be sure that the director has seen exactly what he needs to make his choice, or at least to narrow the field.

JANE

The callbacks on *A Beautiful Mind* were relatively straightforward, though the Sexy Coed callbacks were not completely without incident. Remember, I'd brought in fifty for a first look, and then I'd called back a dozen of those to work with Ron Howard. Ron had in turn selected three finalists to read the scene with Russell Crowe.

The day this second callback was scheduled, Russell happened to be doing makeup tests for one of the movie's later scenes, and his face was tender and sore from all the old-age makeup. "Don't really smack him," Ron suggested to the first woman who read. "Just, you know, pantomime it." Obediently, the first auditioner gave the scene her all, perched on her barstool, cool and insouciant.

Then Russell came to the climactic line of the scene: "So, could we go right to the sex?"

The actress paused, allowing the shock and disgust to register on her lovely face, and drew back her arm for an enormous slap. Just as her fingers reached Russell's cheek, she stopped, suggesting the climactic blow.

"That was great," Ron said, courteous as always. "Thanks

so much." Russell, too, thanked the excited actress—at least she'd gotten to work with the Star for a few minutes—and off she went.

In came the second woman, but this time, Ron forgot to tell her to pull her punches, and it slipped my mind as well.

"So, could we go right to the sex?" Russell asked again. As with the first auditioner, he was acting full out, drawing the young woman into the scene, giving her every chance to match his performance.

The second actress, too, took a moment to register shock and revulsion. Then she hauled off and smacked poor Russell with all her might.

Already tired from a long day in the studio, Russell was somewhat less than amused. You could see him thinking that even without the director's instruction, a professional actress should have known how to fake the blow. After all, when they were actually making the movie, the scene would have to be rehearsed, then shot. How would Russell survive a full-out slap for take after take after take?

As it happened, Ms. Karate Kid didn't get the part. I swear it wasn't because she hit Russell—she just wasn't as interesting as winning candidate, Tanya Clarke—but of course, *she'll* never believe that. Till the day she dies or leaves the business, she'll be convinced that slugging the star cost her three minutes of screen time in an Oscar-winning movie— the very three minutes that might have been her big break.

JANET

So our first advice to actors who get called back is: *Don't slug the Star.* Beyond that, though, we can offer a few more helpful suggestions.

First, try to be calm. That's not the most original advice—
we know you've heard it before—but it's even more important in a callback, where the tendency is to feel that the stakes
have suddenly been raised another hundred notches or so.

Well, they have—and they haven't. Yes, you're that much
closer to being cast. Yes, doing a good job and making a good
impression are definitely preferable to the alternative. Yes,
your performance and behavior during a callback *might* help
determine whether or not you get the part.

But there are still dozens of reasons why you might not
get cast—reasons that have nothing to do with you, your talent, or anything you can control. Maybe the lead just decided to dye her hair blond—and you've suddenly become
one blond too many. Sure, we could ask you to dye your hair,
too, but maybe we now need a Mediterranean type in your
part, and you're just too Scandinavian. If you've made a good
impression, we'll file you away as an actress we'd love to see
again, but even if you're the next Julia Roberts, we may not
cast you for this.

Or, if you *are* the next Julia Roberts, perhaps that's why
we don't want you. We've already got a Star in the leading
role, and secretly, we think you're more magnetic, more
sparkling than she is. Casting you as the best friend or the
jealous sister is going to make her look bad, and we don't
want that. (Even when this isn't strictly true, it's a great thing
to tell yourself after an unsuccessful audition!)

In some cases, the director, producer, or studio is simply
going to want a more experienced actor, or someone with
more name recognition. Again, if Jane and I have liked you,
we'll file you away for future reference, and you're entitled to
hope that the director, producer, or studio exec will do the

same. Nevertheless, you may not be able to get *this* part, even if we all agree that you're prettier, more interesting, or a better actor than the person who does get it.

Of course, sometimes personal considerations come into play. The producer has a sister, and yours is the part she'd be right for. You're both good, but tie goes to the sister. Or the girlfriend. Or the actress the director has worked with before. He knows he can count on her—he just doesn't know that about you, yet.

Having said this, I hope you can see how much good you can do yourself by coming into every callback—indeed, every audition, every meeting, every occasion for contact with anyone in the industry—with a willing, cheerful, professional attitude. Maybe you're only at the callback because Jane or I like you so much—we know you're a long shot, that the director probably wants to go another way. So before you've even walked through the door, you've lost the part, but you do have the chance to make a favorable impression on people who might call you again. The less personally you can take everything, the better off you'll be.

As pretty much every story in this book makes clear, you never know what's going to lead where, so investing an enormous amount of hope or anxiety in any audition, meeting, or callback is never a good idea. In fact, if we leave budding actors with only one piece of advice—hard as it is to take— it would be to look at callbacks (and auditions in general) as nothing more than the opportunity to make a good impression and practice your craft. Enjoy the moments you get to spend acting, and then let the whole experience go, knowing that if we liked what we saw, we'll do everything we can to make sure you get called again.

JANE

Certainly the "you never know" slogan applies to the marathon series of auditions, meetings, and callbacks that were involved in casting *Ghost*. The story began when I read the script, which at first glance looked like an ordinary, though very passionate, romance between banker Sam Wheat and potter Molly Jensen. Sam loves Molly but can never come right out and say, "I love you." The best he can do when she says, "I love you," is to answer, "Ditto."

Then Sam is killed in a seemingly random mugging, and Molly must face life without her beloved. Here's where the twist comes in: Sam loves Molly so much that he can't cross over to the other side until she's taken care of. He remains on earth as a ghost, only to discover that his murder wasn't random after all: the mugger was hired by Sam's trusted colleague to get some bank codes from Sam's wallet, so that the evil colleague could proceed with a money-laundering scheme. Molly still has the codes—and now her life is in danger.

Desperate for a way to communicate with Molly, Sam discovers Oda Mae Brown, who claims to be able to talk to the dead. The joke is that she's a clever fraud, a total con artist—until Sam makes contact with her. Suddenly her Harlem apartment is full of spirits seeking to communicate with their loved ones, even as Sam frantically insists that she help save Molly.

Ghost was an effective blend of comedy, thrills, and romance, with the wisecracking Oda Mae providing the comedy. As soon as I read her lines, I could hear Whoopi Goldberg's voice in my head, pronouncing the words in her distinctive deadpan rhythm. It didn't even feel like a choice to me; I simply assumed the part had been written for Whoopi.

Mind you, this doesn't happen to me very often. Usually when I read a script, I'm wide open. In fact, I don't want to get married to any one choice, in case that person's not available or not of interest to the director. Sure, a well-drawn character or detailed character description might conjure thoughts of specific actors, but I usually try to come up with several choices, especially at the first-reading stage.

Not this time. I heard Whoopi's voice speaking the lines the way Oda Mae hears Sam's voice asking for help.

It wasn't as though I had any particular attachment to Ms. Goldberg, though I'll admit I was a big fan. I'd seen her one-woman show on TV, and I'd caught her in a couple of other movies. We all knew she had a terrific sense of humor, but I also saw her as a woman of great heart and humanity. That's the quality that really endears her to the public, and I thought that quality would work beautifully for the passionate romantic side of *Ghost.*

Still, Whoopi seemed less my choice than the script-writer's. In fact, I assumed this so unconsciously that at my first meeting with director Jerry Zucker, I simply asked, "So, have you hired Whoopi Goldberg yet?"

Jerry was a bit taken aback. "Well," he replied, "we've thought about her and she's a possibility, of course. But we'd like to see who else is out there."

Now it was my turn to be taken aback. I couldn't quite believe that Whoopi wasn't as obvious a choice to everyone as she was to me. But I'd learned by now that there are many directors who can't ever quite go with a first choice, no matter how good it might seem. A few years earlier, when I was casting *Tough Guys,* we'd needed a young funny guy to play against the superlative Burt Lancaster and Kirk Douglas. I came up with this terrifically talented comic actor whom nobody knew much about—Dana Carvey. Dana had done small bits in a few films, but he hadn't yet made a name for himself on *Saturday Night Live*. I was sure he was the perfect choice, and I made the mistake of bringing him in first, before the producers and director had seen anybody else. Silly me: instead of realizing that I'd started with the best, they naturally assumed that there were plenty more Danas out there. It took many, many auditions in both New York and Los Angeles before they finally cast Mr. Carvey. (These days, I make very sure not to bring my first choice in first—unless I have a long-standing working relationship with someone who I know will grab the best when he sees it.)

So perhaps, I thought, it would be the same with Whoopi. I didn't see why we needed to look at anyone else, but you couldn't blame Jerry for not wanting to commit. After all, Whoopi's career wasn't exactly at its zenith. Although she'd made a big splash in *The Color Purple,* none of her films since then had done very well. In the days when she *was* the "next big thing," a couple of movies had changed the sex of the main character just so she could play the leading role. Those movies hadn't done well, though, and as is the way of the industry, Whoopi got the blame. While she wasn't exactly box-office poison, she wasn't the hottest thing in town, either.

Meanwhile, Jerry was far more concerned about who was going to play his male lead. Although he was pretty sure he wanted the "lesser Name" Demi Moore for the female lead—either her or a young Nicole Kidman, who'd sent her demo tape from Australia—we weren't making any moves toward either woman until we had the guy problem settled.

It's a cardinal rule in Hollywood that you don't cast the girl until you've got the guy. That's partly because the male actors are more expensive and more powerful, so they're often granted a say in the choice of co-star. And it's partly because women will go to a movie that their boyfriends or husbands want to see, but men won't necessarily go to a movie that their girlfriends or wives want to see. So unless you're making a straight-out chick flick, you start with the guy. (And if you *are* making a chick flick, forget about getting an A-list guy—or an A-list budget.)

Jerry was an A-list director, and he was making the film at Paramount, which was a big studio. That alone should have guaranteed him an A-list hero, not to mention that *Ghost* had a terrific script—thrills, fights, murders, and what was to become a near-legendary scene of the leads making love in Molly's pottery room, their bare skin streaked with clay. In theory, Jerry should have been able to get any guy he wanted.

But Jerry was being very picky. He wanted one of Hollywood's top ten action heroes—Stars at the level of Mel Gibson, Harrison Ford, and Bruce Willis. And so far, none of those guys would bite.

In retrospect, given how successful *Ghost* eventually became, that seems hard to believe. But this was the late 1980s, and special effects were still a matter of stop-action shots and other techniques that look primitive by today's computer-generated standards. To Jerry's top picks, *Ghost* was a special-effects movie. Worse, for most of the movie, the woman is alive while the guy is dead—what kind of part was that? Poor Jerry was getting one "no" after another.

The last name on Jerry's List was Patrick Swayze, whose career at that point was a little bit in the doldrums. Patrick had been very big right after *Dirty Dancing,* but then he'd made a couple of movies that hadn't done well. So it was going to take a while before Jerry worked his way down to Patrick.

While Jerry went after the guy, I was still worrying about Oda Mae. I saw just about every African American actress of a certain age then working in America. Because the male lead literally materializes through Oda Mae's body, our only restriction was that the actress shouldn't be too obviously sexual or drop-dead gorgeous. That left us a fairly wide field, and we saw 150 actresses in three months.

It began to take on the proportions of a comedy routine. Nell Carter would come in. She'd give a great audition. "No," Jerry would say after she'd left. "That's not it."

"Fine," I'd say. "*Now* can we hire Whoopi?"

"Not yet."

Loretta Devine would come in. She'd give a great audition. "No," Jerry would say after she'd left. "That's not it."

"Fine," I'd say. "*Now* can we hire Whoopi?"

"Not yet."

Jennifer Holliday. Patti LaBelle. Alfre Woodard. Great audition. "That's not it." "*Now* can we hire Whoopi?" "Not yet."

Of course, Jerry wasn't ignoring Whoopi. In fact, early in the process, he'd dispensed with auditions and scheduled an actual meeting with her. Coming to Hollywood after a career as a bawdy stand-up comic, the free-spirited, no-nonsense Whoopi had developed a reputation for being "difficult," but she was all humility at that meeting. She freely acknowledged the rumors that had spread about her conduct on other sets and calmly offered Jerry an explanation for every problem.

"I'd really love to play this part," she told him, "and I'll do whatever it takes." She knew this was the part that might resurrect her career, and she let Jerry know she knew. She didn't exactly say she'd work like a dog, but the implication was there.

Jerry wasn't opposed to Whoopi, but he still wasn't ready to commit. One day he came in with a new idea. "What about Tina Turner?"

"What about Tina Turner?" I said to myself. "What about those lips, those eyes, those *legs*?" How in the world could Sam materialize through the body of Tina Turner without it seeming—well, perverse?

But if Jerry wanted to see tape on Tina, it was my job to get it for him, especially after Tina heard about his interest and expressed some interest of her own. We'd already done one New York casting trip for Oda Mae, and we didn't have any casting people out there, but the New York City Paramount offices were willing to provide space and a video camera. So I asked an actress friend to do me a favor (or maybe I did her one) by running the camera and reading the lines with Tina.

My friend was thrilled to have met Tina, but Jerry was less enthusiastic. "No," he sighed, after seeing the tape. "That's not it, either."

"*Now* can we—"

"Not yet."

☆

While I was lobbying for Whoopi, Jerry was getting the cold shoulder from every guy in town. Finally, we got to Patrick.

So Patrick and Jerry had a meeting. Jerry thought Patrick was a really nice guy—everybody did. But he wasn't sure if Patrick was The One. After all, Sam was supposed to be an investment banker. Still, he was from Texas, which gave him more of a down-home than a Yuppie quality, and you never actually saw him at his job. As I saw it, the banker aspect of Sam's character was the least important thing about him. What matters is how much we care about his romance with Molly and how painful we find his death. But Jerry still thought of Sam as a young professional, and Patrick didn't quite fit that image.

Then Jerry found out that Patrick had a new movie coming out, *Road House.* "Come on, Jane," Jerry said. "Let's go see *Road House.*"

I'd already seen an early screening of *Road House,* a violent little film in which Patrick plays a kickboxer, and I was pretty sure that it wouldn't do Patrick's chances any good. "Oh, please, Jerry," I begged, "please do not go to see that movie. It won't convince you to hire Patrick. In fact, it will do exactly the opposite."

Undaunted, Jerry set up a screening. "Are you coming?" he asked me.

"No, I am not," I told him. "As soon as you see that movie, I already know what you're going to say."

Sure enough, Jerry walked out of the theater vowing, "Patrick Swayze will never be in *Ghost!*"

As it happened, Patrick's agent was Nicole David, the person who'd rented Janet and me our first offices, not to mention signing for our phone and lending us her photocopier. She was a terrific agent and a very old friend of ours, so of course we'd sent her a copy of the script, which she had duly shared with Patrick. Usually an agent won't even let an actor know she's got a script unless she's fairly certain she can get him an audition—otherwise, it makes her look weak. But Nicole had given Patrick a copy of *Ghost,* maybe because at that point, it was the kind of project she wanted for him. Patrick read it and loved it, so Nicole started begging me to get him an audition.

"I know he and Jerry have had a meeting," she'd say. "But Patrick is willing—eager—to audition. All he wants is for Jerry to see him read."

I thought having Patrick audition for Jerry was a terrific idea. Maybe if Jerry actually saw Patrick read, he'd realize how romantic the guy could be and forget about that banker thing. Meanwhile, I was also working on Kevin Kline, who had also said "no" to what he saw as a special-effects movie. Jerry and Kevin both had the same agent at CAA, so I went through him.

"Come on," I pleaded. "You owe it to your client Jerry to set up a meeting with your client Kevin! Jerry is your *very own client*—how can you hold out on him?"

Finally the CAA guy set up a conference call between Jerry and Kevin, who was shooting a movie in Seattle. And finally I convinced Jerry to let Patrick come in and read. Jerry didn't want to be in the position of rejecting Patrick, whom he liked very much as a human being, even if he wasn't so sure about him as Sam the Banker. So I promised that if Jerry hated Patrick, I would take the blame.

Okay, so we've got Patrick coming in to audition for Jerry and producer Lisa Weinstein—not the biggest Patrick Swayze fan on the planet, I have to say. Then, one hour later, we've got Kevin calling from Seattle for a phone meeting. Terrific. Maybe we'll get a male lead for this picture after all.

In comes Patrick, ready to read. He knew exactly what the circumstances were, and to his credit, he didn't let it get to him. He just worked his way through every one of the script's big romantic scenes. In one of the great moments of my acting career, I read with him. When we got to the climactic moment—the one where Sam finally says, "I love you," and Molly says, "Ditto"—I looked up, and Lisa, who had been one of the biggest voices opposed to casting Patrick, had tears running down her cheeks.

"Wow," said Jerry, leaping out of his seat. "That was beautiful. Patrick, you have the job."

And I, still locked into a passionate embrace with Patrick Swayze, thought, "But Jerry, you've got a conference call with Kevin Kline in five minutes!"

Jerry offered Patrick the role on the spot. Then he called his agent and canceled the call with Kevin.

☆

We'd cast Patrick, we'd cast Demi, now we were down to Oda Mae. I was gearing up for another Whoopi campaign when Jerry came into the office, all excited. Some well-meaning industry friends had just given him a new list of seven possible Oda Maes. "What about one of these?" he asked, waving the list in the air.

I took a look at it. "Jerry," I said as tactfully as I could, "you've already seen every single one."

Jerry looked crestfallen.

"So," I said. "*Now* can we hire Whoopi?"

"Well," Jerry said. "Maybe we should meet with her again."

By this time, Whoopi was in Wilmington, North Carolina, filming *The Long Ride Home* with Sissy Spacek. So Jerry and Patrick flew to Wilmington and met with Whoopi in the first-class lounge at the airport.

Meanwhile, Janet and I were on our way to London for the premiere of the new James Bond film, *License to Kill*, in which we'd finally gotten to cast Benicio Del Toro. When we got to the hotel, there was a cable waiting for me:

"*NOW* CAN WE HIRE WHOOPI?" . . . YES! GIVE MY REGARDS TO THE QUEEN. LOVE, JERRY.

"You know," I told Jerry when I got back, "Whoopi was born to play this part. She will win an Academy Award, and we will look like geniuses."

And so it came to pass. *Ghost* became one of the highest-grossing movies of all time, Whoopi got her Oscar, and Patrick, Demi, and Jerry didn't do so badly either. As for Janet and me, we felt as though we'd gotten a refresher course in one of the cardinal lessons of casting: *If you find what you want, stop looking.* For those of us sure that a better actor, a better job, a better lover is always over the next horizon, it can be a hard lesson to learn.

JANET

Auditions and callbacks are part of a working actor's life. Although sometimes actors need a little extra support or coaching, we can assume that they generally know how to handle the audition-callback process.

But when you're casting real-life people to play themselves or people like them, that's something else again. You've got to work with these untrained actors in a different way, looking not for a professional performance but for what these "ordinary folks" can reveal about the characters you want them to play. Untrained actors can enrich a movie considerably, bringing an extraordinary depth, a heartfelt quality, and a sense of reality that you can't get any other way. But working with them definitely poses some special challenges.

On *Friday Night Lights,* we relied heavily on both untrained actors and local professionals to portray football players, coaches, and community residents. The movie was based on the book of the same name—a sports book so beloved that every kid in the movie had read it—about the 1988 football season in Odessa, Texas.

Both the book and the movie tell a complicated story. In the 1980s, Odessa, like the rest of West Texas, was devastated by the oil bust and the subsequent depression. Its champion high school, Permian, was comprised of mostly poor students, though the school's athletic department was lavishly supported by wealthy alumni. The book is as much a portrait of a community riven by racial and economic fault lines as it is a conventional sports narrative.

Despite or perhaps because of the book's success, the town of Odessa had a real love-hate relationship with *Friday Night Lights.* Partly because of the controversy, it took nearly fifteen years to bring this project to the screen. Director Alan Pakula had tried unsuccessfully to turn the complex, multilayered book into a script, but he died before he could finish. (The film is dedicated to him.) Director Peter Berg—cousin of the book's author, H. G. Bissinger—was the one who finally succeeded in presenting a powerful portrait of a town that both loved its high-school football heroes and subjected them to extraordinary pressure. Race and class still exert a significant influence in the world of the movie, but the larger intention is less to portray social problems than to explore the importance of a team like the Panthers to the Odessa community.

Luckily for us, the community loved the movie, as did the sports world in general. We were glad to get such a warm welcome, because we relied on the community's support at every stage of the process. Without the townspeople's coop-eration—without their permission to shoot at their high school and their Dairy Queen and the other Odessa loca-tions; without local residents' participation as extras and in small speaking parts—we wouldn't have had the authentic-ity that the movie needed.

It helped that we brought on the real-life coach Gary Gaines as a consultant. His only request was that his charac-ter never swear, since he himself never did.

Casting Billy Bob was easy—he'd been everybody's first choice. Likewise, we were delighted to go with Derek Luke as Boobie Miles. We also brought Lucas Black to Texas to play Mike Winchell, the quarterback. Lucas was the little boy who played opposite Billy Bob in *Sling Blade,* though that had nothing to do with him getting this part. In fact, since Mike was one of the bigger roles in the film, the studio was considering a Name, a possibility we explored even as we au-ditioned Lucas.

Lucas gave a terrific audition, and both Pete and I loved him. Moreover, Lucas really wanted this role—he had played high-school football in Arkansas, and he understood the world of small-town sports very well.

I was totally honest with his agent (agents in this town know everything that is going on anyway), and told him we were exploring Names but to keep in touch with me. Lucas even passed on a project so he could remain available if we came to him, which happily we did. In the end, we didn't need another Name, and Lucas's low-key, understated ap-proach to the role made a striking contrast to the theatrics that Derek brought to the more flamboyant Boobie.

Many of the other major parts on the team came from

Los Angeles as well. For Chavez, the son of an attorney who eventually goes to Harvard and becomes an attorney, too, we brought in Jay Hernandez, who had done *Crazy/Beautiful* with Kirsten Dunst. For Don Billingsley, the hotshot star player whose father pressures him unmercifully, we brought in newcomer Garrett Hedlund, who gave a memorable performance in what was only his second film. As it happened, we knew him from *Troy.* Lee Thompson Young came in to play Chris Comer, the young running back who replaces Boobie after his injury.

That was five of the six core players to be cast from L.A.—so we almost had our home team. The sixth core team member, Ivory Christian, would be cast out of Austin.

Now, what about our opponents? *Friday Night Lights* covers eight different football games, requiring eight opposing teams and eight sets of coaches—guys who could get on-screen and simply deliver. So I looked at local coaches while second-unit director and football consultant Allan Graf went out to find real players in Austin.

A second-unit director shoots material that doesn't involve speaking parts or major players—crowd shots, weather, establishing shots that show what a location looks like. On this film, Allan's job also involved shooting lots of football plays.

I've got to say, I was impressed at how well the real-life coaches could function on camera. They took direction beautifully, and they all looked relaxed and natural on-screen. Or rather, they looked tense and keyed up—just the way they would for a real game. When you consider the kind of pressure they're under when they coach—the way all eyes are upon them, and all their players are looking to them for leadership under the most difficult conditions—maybe it's not so surprising that they could repeatedly come through for Pete, take after take after take.

Although Allan was casting most of the football players, it was my job to cast all the speaking parts, which included the one remaining core team member, Ivory Christian, the team's spiritual center. I started by going through Allan's files, which included hundreds of pictures that people had brought in with them or Polaroids that Allan had taken. I pulled shots of any African American guy who looked like a linebacker and seemed young enough to play a high-school senior and called them all in for auditions, working just as I would have done with any head shots.

Luckily, I wasn't working alone: I had the enormous help of Jo Edna Boldin, local casting director extraordinaire and a talented acting teacher to boot. "Try it again," Jo Edna would say to one nervous auditioner after another. We knew the kids who were reading could play football, and they definitely had the right look. But could they act? If it was up to Jo Edna, they could. "No, don't look at anything else in the room—just look at me. Relax, honey. That's right. Take a deep breath. Don't try to *do* anything—just read the lines. That's right. Good. Now try it again."

Often when inexperienced—or even experienced—actors come in to read, anxiety can push them over the top. They feel that so much is riding on them getting the part, they start exaggerating their emotions, straining their voices, and generally giving first readings that are way too big, especially for a movie camera, which tends to catch the subtlest shades of expression. With either a pro or a new actor, you often have to say, "Terrific, that was a great start. Now let's try another take—and keep it simple." Or in some cases, "Stop acting so hard!"

My goal with these guys was to get them to stop doing what they thought of as acting and just to rely on their own natural instincts. It might take two or three or twenty takes before the boys could get the words out. But I was willing to take the time if I sensed that someone might have something special once he had calmed down. "That's right," I'd say, over and over again. "Just look at me—breathe deep— and let's do it one more time." I was willing to go through as many as thirty read throughs, if that's what it took to get it right.

When a young man named Lee Jackson came in and read, Jo Edna and I looked at each other with hope in our eyes. Lee's reading was simple, real, heartfelt, and as we worked with him that day he got better and better. Lee had been a star player at the University of Texas, Austin, and he happened to be exactly like the character for which he was auditioning—a quiet, polite, and deeply religious person. Early in the film, Boobie teases Ivory for wearing white sneakers instead of the much cooler black Nikes. Ivory says it doesn't matter what color your shoes are, but then we see him coloring his sneakers with black Magic Marker.

Lee wasn't expecting to do any acting. He thought he'd just been brought on to play football. When I asked him if he wanted to audition for a speaking role, he was thrilled. At age twenty-four, he was still playing professional ball, but luckily for us, he was available for our schedule.

Although he'd never acted before, he knew the right questions. "What am I supposed to be?" he asked me before the audition began.

"Ivory is sort of a quiet kid," I explained. "He's the religious one. He doesn't say much, just sort of looks quietly at everyone, taking everything in. But he's strong—the others have to know that they can count on him in a crunch. In the book, he's sort of torn between his religion and his football. In the movie, that doesn't happen so much. But his faith is still a big part of him."

Lee nodded attentively. "Yes, ma'am," he said when he saw I had finished. Ivory's persona was enough like his own that he felt comfortable with the challenge.

Of course we still had to work with him a bit. Together we went over his few lines, and he definitely got better. But he still wasn't giving the performance that we thought he was capable of.

"Look," Jo Edna said finally. We were reading the scene where Boobie makes fun of Ivory's shoes. "What would you say, yourself, if someone talked to you like that?"

Ivory began to answer, but Jo Edna cut him off.

"No," she said. "Show us."

We started the camera rolling again, and one of the assistants fed him the lines. Lee came out with a few words—not defiant, exactly. Not defensive, either. Just sort of holding his ground.

"Terrific!" Jo Edna said. "Did you feel it? That's the guy—see, he's like you! Now try it again, the way you would in real life."

Lee kept getting better, but we still felt there was further he could go. Then I had an idea. I'd remembered that Lee had told me that, like Ivory, he was also very religious. In fact, on his own team, he was sort of the moral center, the guy who always came out with a little prayer before the game while the rest of his team joined hands and listened.

"Why don't you give us a little prayer?" I suggested. "Like you'd do in your own locker room, before a game starts."

Lee took a deep breath, and we started the cameras rolling. "Oh, Father-Lord," he began. "Give us the strength today to do what needs to be done . . ."

Jo Edna and I looked at each other and smiled. Yes. This was our Ivory.

Later that day, I ran into Allan back at the production office.

"Hey, I found a great guy for Ivory," I told him.

Allan looked a little crestfallen. "Too bad," he said. "'Cause there's a guy I'd really like to use—this kid named Lee Jackson."

It's nice when everybody agrees. I thought Lee was going to fall through the floor when Pete said to him, after his callback, "You're hired." The studio quickly approved him, and Allan started running practices with our version of the Panthers. The team spirit began to build.

There was one sizable part in *Friday Night Lights* that went neither to a professional actor nor to a local resident. Instead it went to country-western singer Tim McGraw.

I'd actually met Tim when we were casting *The Perfect Storm*—he came in to see us when he was in L.A. for a country-western awards show. He'd read the book and loved it, and he kind of hoped to get in on the movie.

Tim wasn't at all right for *The Perfect Storm*—he was way too Southern for that New England setting. But we had a great meeting, and I promised him that if a part ever came up that he'd be right for, we'd definitely keep him in mind.

When we were casting *Friday Night Lights,* I was looking hard at the part of Charles Billingsley, the alcoholic, abusive father of star player Don Billingsley. In Charles, we see the downside of Odessa's football mania: a former state champion, Charles has never gotten over his lost glory, and he takes his frustration out on his son. I thought Patrick Swayze would be really good in the part, but we decided it would be more interesting to go with a strong but unconventional choice. Country singer Dwight Yoakam is a wonderful actor, and for a while we talked about using him. But once the idea of using a country singer had been broached, Tim's name rose to the top of the list.

Tim isn't the easiest guy to set up a meeting with. He's very busy—always on tour or in the recording studio—and it took a certain amount of work to get him and Peter in the same place. But he'd loved the book, so he ended up coming to Austin in his private jet and reading for Pete in the production office we'd set up there. I think Pete may even have run the camera himself for that very private reading, but afterward, he showed me the tape.

I was amazed. I'd thought Tim might be good: he had a relaxed kind of charm, a powerful presence, and even though he hadn't formally trained as an actor, he knew, as a singer, how to tell musical stories with heart. But he was hardly typecasting for this role. Tim is a very nice guy, and I wasn't at all sure how he'd do at portraying an angry SOB like Charles Billingsley. Plus, a lot of the time Billingsley is drunk, and that's a real trap for an actor. It's hard to play a convincing drunk without going over the top.

Still, Tim pulled it off—and beautifully. Pete happened to be passing through the lobby as I was coming out of the little room where we'd set up the VCR. "My God," I said to him, "Tim was amazing. We should push for this."

"I think so!" Pete agreed. Apparently the studio liked the tape, because they gave us their go-ahead, too.

Money might have been a problem. *Friday Night Lights* was always going to be made "for a price," as they say in Hollywood. Tim and his wife, Faith Hill, are pretty much country royalty, but luckily for us, he was willing to work for first-time actor money. His only demands were that we schedule his parts carefully, so he didn't have to sit around Austin waiting for his shooting days to come up, and that we make sure there was space at the airport for his private jet.

As it happened, Tim had a complicated relationship with his own father. He didn't find out until he was twelve years old that he was the son of baseball player Tug McGraw, who'd fathered him out of wedlock, and Tim didn't meet Tug until he was nineteen. In fact, Tug wasn't even sure that Tim was his son until the two men met. Then Tug said, "You're my kid," and the father-son relationship began.

The month before shooting began on *Friday Night Lights,* Tug McGraw died. (Tim later wrote a multi-award-winning song about it, "Live Like You Were Dying.") So Tim had quite a bit of emotion to work with in the painful father-son scenes. When I saw the movie at the premiere, I was struck by how emotional the part was, and by how much authenticity Tim brought to it. Even a more experienced actor might have gotten trapped into chewing the scenery—playing the part with the kind of self-indulgence where the focus was on how much the actor was feeling, not on how much pain the character was in. But Tim's performance, while full and deep, was very subtle. As with every true actor, you always felt that the character was not exaggerating his emotions but restraining them. No matter how much pain he expressed, you always sensed he was holding a little something back.

I didn't get to see Tim until the premiere—he just didn't happen to be in Austin while I was there. Someone once asked me if I didn't feel a lack of closure—if, after meeting him, seeing his tape, and then pushing to get him cast, I didn't want the payoff of seeing him work or at least hearing him thank me for my efforts on his behalf.

Not at all, I replied. My payoff for *Friday Night Lights* was that it was a terrific movie—and that I could see the contribution our casting efforts had made. Unlike the high-school heroes we'd helped cast, Jane and I weren't in it for the glory. If you do this kind of job at all, you do it for love.

7 ☆ THE LITTLEST STARS

JANE

From *Lord of the Flies* to *Harry Potter and the Sorcerer's Stone*, we have always found casting children a challenge. I'm a bit surprised when I realize how many movies we've worked on that revolved around children: besides *Lord* and *Harry,* Janet and I have cast *Stand by Me, Dennis the Menace, Home Alone* and *Home Alone 2, Baby's Day Out, North, Curly Sue, Hook, Miracle on 34th Street,* and *Parenthood,* not to mention all the movies that center on teenagers: *The Outsiders, Rumble Fish, Ferris Bueller's Day Off, Adventures in Babysitting, Mystic Pizza, Friday Night Lights.* Then there are the movies in which adults play the lead but at least one kid has a central role, and the movies where we needed a child for just a few minutes—but those minutes were crucial to making the movie pay off. Clearly no casting director can get very far without a good understanding of how to work with children.

While there are some ways in which casting kids is just like casting grown-ups, there are other ways in which you're talking apples and oranges. The techniques of film acting were not developed with children in mind, and it can be quite a challenge to find children who can function in the complicated world of a movie set.

An adult actor relies—or should rely—upon a combination of instinct and technique, but the technique is crucial. In film, you often have to jump right into the middle of an emotional scene, picking it up at a high point or a difficult moment. It's technique that enables you to generate the tears or the anger or the ecstatic joy of first love right at the moment that the sound guy and the gaffer (who does lights) and the camera operator and the D.P. (director of photography, or cinematographer) and the director are ready for you; and it's technique that enables you to repeat that emotional moment again and again and again. And then, when the director and crew have gotten the shots they need from the front, they set up the shot a second time from the side, or a third time from below, or a fourth time from the other side, and after another three- or four-hour wait, you have to jump back into the emotion a second, third, or fourth time, trying to generate a level of intensity and a kind of line reading that will match all the other work you've done, so that when everything is cut together in the editing room, several dozen takes, shot over several days, will meld seamlessly into a coherent scene. As you can see, it's a highly technical job as well as an artistic one, and while the best actors are often fueled with divine inspiration, they must also be able to rely upon their craft.

With kids, though, you're unlikely to find someone who at age five or ten or even fifteen has truly mastered the craft of acting to that extent, let alone someone who thinks consciously about who a character needs to be. True, you sometimes run across a Dakota Fanning (*War of the Worlds*) or a

Jimmy Bennett (*Poseidon*). Those kids know more at age eight about how to create a character than some actors learn in a lifetime. Most child actors, though, approach film acting in a spirit of play. Your job is to help them play in a way that will produce the performance you want. Once they can use their fertile little imaginations to enter into the spirit of the story, their "let's pretend" mind-set will, ideally, steer them toward genuine emotion and interesting choices.

"Suppose you were a very powerful prince, and you knew that any order you gave, someone would have to do it right away—or lose their heads. How would you speak to your servants? How would you speak to your friends? Show me. Pretend I'm the servant who has just told you that you can't have dessert."

Or, "What if you were very, very sad because your best friend is going away? You have to say goodbye to her now. Show me how sad you are."

When Janet and I select adult actors to show our directors, we're looking for performers with solid technique, people whom the director can count on to hit their marks, repeat takes, and take direction. But when we choose kids, we're usually looking to see which children can most easily and fully immerse themselves in a world of fantasy and play that suits the needs of the script.

While the child is exploring a fantasy world, we're looking for the kid's special "quality." In that way, casting kids and casting grown-ups is just the same. Every performer, of any age, projects a certain aura, a certain flavor. Our job is to find the performers whose flavors will best serve the film.

In *A Beautiful Mind*, for example, we needed a child for Charles's niece who seemed wistful and lonely. At first we believe her sorrow comes from the fact that her parents have died in an accident. Then Nash realizes that over all the years he's seen her, she's never gotten any older—which in turn leads him to understand that both the niece and Charles are delusions produced by his disease. So for this imaginary child we needed a wispy little person, waiflike and insubstantial, but with a knowing, haunted look in her eyes, a young person possessed of what Janet calls an "old soul." Since she had so little dialogue, we couldn't rely on what she said or even what she did to convey that quality: her very being had to exude a sense of otherworldliness.

This wasn't an easy set of requirements to fill. Most professional child actors are hearty creatures who make a living doing sitcoms and Kellogg's commercials. Their job is to be cute and funny and happy and charming. But we didn't want Kellogg's; we were looking for the anti-Kellogg. The anti-Kellogg who could act.

To find this miracle child, we saw hundreds of kids. Our first task was to filter out the kids who simply weren't comfortable on camera. You would think that no parent would bring in a child to audition if the child was painfully shy, afraid to leave her mother outside the door, or too timid to have a conversation with a relative stranger. Well, think again. All sorts of screen mothers (and fathers) shepherd their beautiful but frightened children to auditions of all types, so we've gotten used to spotting and gently dismissing the kids who don't really want to be there.

JANET

I must admit, even after twenty-five years of casting kids, I'm still surprised at all the ways screen parents—usually mothers—find to involve themselves in their kids' auditions. Although we never let parents in the audition room—any kid who can't manage without a parent at close range is probably a kid who can't function well on a set—there are always one or two moms who stand right by the audition-room door, hand cupped to ear, trying their damnedest to hear what's going on inside. We tell our assistants not to let them do that, but somehow they persist—and then, presumably, they're in a position to do a blow-by-blow review of every moment of the audition with their poor, beleaguered child.

Then there are the parents who make promises, otherwise known as bribes: "If you do a good audition, I'll take you to McDonald's." "If you get a callback, I'll buy you a toy." What's next, "If you don't get the part, off to bed without your dinner!"?

Less upsetting but still annoying are the parents who have given their children such careful coaching that we never hear the kid's own unique version of a part. Granted, a lot of the kids we see are too young to read, and they need their folks to teach them the words and explain the situation. But that doesn't mean we want a kid to come in with every single inflection in place. (In fact, we often tell kids to throw the script away and simply use their own words.)

Then there are the mothers who slick their kids' hair down with their own spit—never a pretty sight—and the moms who anxiously isolate their children from all the other kids in the waiting room. I don't know if they think the competition is making their child nervous or if they're afraid that some other actor will steal their child's line reading, but it's sad either way.

My favorite parents are the ones who express the key idea that this is supposed to be fun. Instead of asking, "How'd you do?" when they pick up their kids, they ask, "Did you have a good time?" Then, no matter what the answer is, they say something positive and supportive, and focus on the next activity at hand. They convey the message that no audition is that big a deal, that having fun is the main thing, and that they'll love the kid exactly the same no matter what happens with their career. If only adult actors had that kind of reassurance!

A fond memory of screen mothers came during auditions for a movie—I don't even remember which one—where for some reason we had to cast a twelve-year-old boy and a stripper. That day the waiting room was full of extremely sexy young women, prepubescent boys—and their mothers. Some of the moms had a sense of humor about it, but others took one look at these actresses—dressed to make the most of their assets—and did everything they could to keep their young sons from noticing the obvious. Nevertheless, my sense is that quite a few boys hit puberty that day!

JANE

Young or old, everyone's a bit intimidated at an audition, so you have to find a way to put your performers at ease. With kids, Janet and I usually work our way slowly into the scene, trying to play with the kids a bit and see if we can get them to have fun with the make-believe. We want to see who can relate to us rather than being completely focused on the camera.

We're also prepared to give children more direction than adults. Often, when actors of any age come in for a smaller part, they've gotten only the "sides"—the few pages with their audition scene. Rarely do they get the chance to read the whole script. As a result, they don't know the context for their scene, or even whether they're reading for a comedy or a drama.

Grown-up actors should find some way of doing their homework—asking their agents about the project, or, at the very least, coming in early for their audition and quizzing the receptionist. And if we know a grown-up actor has had access to the script but hasn't bothered to read it, we tend to get annoyed.

With kids, though, we take it for granted that we've got to set up the situation for them. When I was casting the main character's son in *Cinderella Man,* I had to explain to kids who (hopefully) had never missed a meal in their lives that the little boy in the scene had stolen a salami because his family was hungry. I wanted them to be nervous about confronting their angry father, and to convey the fear that if Daddy couldn't provide enough food, they might end up in an orphanage like the boys down the street. No five-year-old was going to read the entire script, so I had to make it come alive for each of them and then see how ready they were to "play" with me.

The little girl in *A Beautiful Mind* was in some ways even harder to cast because the haunted quality we were looking for is so rare among child actors. Still, we did wind up with a handful of little girls who I thought could do the job. As usual, Ron Howard met with my top choices and then picked five little girls to audition with Russell Crowe.

There was one girl in the bunch whom I especially liked— a very talented actress—but she was just a bit too solid-looking. You couldn't really believe such a sturdy kid was the figment of anybody's imagination. So we ended up with the ethereal Vivien Cardone, a wisp of a seven-year-old who was so thin and small that she could pass for the five-year-old specified in the script. That was a bonus: we got the two extra years of maturity and skill without having to sacrifice the character's extreme youth. Vivien—named for the equally ethereal Vivien Leigh—had done several commercials by the time we cast her, so she had a strong on-camera presence and a lot of practice hitting her marks, repeating takes, and doing all the other technical jobs that are part of film acting. She's gone on to several seasons in the TV show *Everwood,* where her tragic quality serves her well in the role of a girl who's lost her mother.

JANET

With kids—even fairly young kids—you can rely on a bit of coaching and play to get the performance you want. With babies, though, you take what you can get. In *Baby's Day Out,* I needed to find beautiful, happy, cooperative babies. There was just one catch: they couldn't start walking until after the film had wrapped.

Baby's Day Out was a kind of infant version of *Home Alone*: a baby somehow gets away from his parents and begins crawling unsupervised through Chicago. As the innocent child narrowly avoids one catastrophe after another, the audience gasps and the baby smiles.

Clearly, if the baby started walking while the picture was still being shot, we'd be in big trouble. You can't get a walking baby to go back to crawling, and because the movie had lots of close-ups, we wouldn't be able to substitute a new baby.

On the other hand, if we cast a baby who was too young, he wouldn't even be able to crawl. In fact, the babies we auditioned *were* too young to crawl, and we could only hope they'd still be right for us when shooting began five months later.

To make matters even more complicated, I needed twins, as everyone does whenever a baby has a major role: a single baby can't possibly give us all the shooting hours we require. When they're six to twenty-four months old, they can be on the set for four hours a day, and can work only two hours a day. (At least we needed a slightly older baby: babies aged fifteen days to six months can be on the set for only two hours a day, and they can only work for twenty minutes of that time.) In this case, the whole movie was based on close-ups of the baby's serene smile, so I also needed the cutest Gerber baby in the world.

This was something that the novice director found rather difficult to understand. He tended to want more offbeat-looking kids, babies who had interesting faces rather than classically cute ones. But a baby whom we might want to look at for a few minutes in a medium shot was not the same kind of child who could sustain close-up after close-up after close-up of a serenely smiling face. "We need leading-man babies, not character babies," I explained, and eventually he got it.

Our problem was further complicated by the fact that the babies had to be cast several months before we started shooting. As any parent knows, gorgeous infants often go through a less gorgeous stage, while placid, good-natured babies sometimes develop more temperamental personalities as they get older. But most serious of all was the fact that no babies come with a guarantee that they won't walk "too soon." Twins I could find, cute I could recognize. But how could I guarantee that the baby wouldn't start walking?

First things first. Besides the usual breakdown to agents (some identical twins have agents—commercials love them), I sent out a call to twins clubs across the country, asking parents to send me videotapes of their identical babies. I probably would have gotten a bonus if I'd found triplets—three chances to extend the shooting day!—but most triplets aren't identical, and as infants, they tend to be smaller than twins, depriving us of that chubby-cheeked "perfect baby" look. So after reviewing hundreds of videotapes and meeting a few dozen sets of twins, I settled on two boys from Delaware, who were good-natured, cooperative, and cute as the dickens.

Their parents were nice, too, which was of prime importance. You don't want to make a deal with a kid only to find that the parents are raising difficulties at every turn. Every child who works on a film is protected by an elaborate set of labor laws and social-service regulations, and any responsible parent wants to be sure that the rules are followed. But all too many "screen parents" seem to think that the more trouble they make, the more important they are. You try to spot those parents in the casting process, because they can make a director's life even more difficult than it already is.

Screen parents are like any other parents—they run the gamut from good to dreadful. The story of Macaulay Culkin's father is well known by now: how the father was a failed actor who lived vicariously through his performing children and then used his kids' success for his own empowerment. I actually met Mr. Culkin a couple of times, first when I cast Macaulay in *Home Alone* and later, when Macaulay came in to meet with Steven Spielberg for the kid in *Jurassic Park,* a role that eventually went to Joey Mazzello.

The Culkins were a theatrical family—Macaulay's aunt is the actress Bonnie Bedelia—and Macaulay was making a splash in off-Broadway productions before he turned eight. In fact, at the age of five, he turned in a heart-wrenching performance in *Rocket Gibraltar,* a Burt Lancaster movie about a troubled family. He went on to make *Uncle Buck* for director John Hughes, which put him right in line for John's *Home Alone.*

Macaulay was never as deep or instinctive an actor as Dakota Fanning, but he had a very special quality that you can see even in his earlier movies. Recently I caught a few minutes of *Uncle Buck,* and I was struck by how Macaulay's face seemed to radiate soulfulness, even when he was just hanging out at the bowling alley or watching his uncle do chores. He always seemed to have a sorrowful, knowing quality beneath those angelic little-boy looks—and in light of later revelations about his father, it's clear that he'd had a lot to deal with from a very young age.

Now here we were waiting for Steven Spielberg. Mr. Culkin gave me a smug smile, as if to say, "Well, we were nobodies when I met you before, but we're Stars now, Macaulay and I!" I remembered how, when we were doing the deal for *Home Alone,* Macaulay's agent would call us and say, "Okay, I have twenty pages of notes from the dad."

Despite the challenges of growing up with an exploitative father, Macaulay seemed to be a great kid. Parents never attend these director's meetings—again, if the kid can't function well without Mom or Dad in the room, this is not a kid you want to hire—but Macaulay was happy to chat with Steven and me. He spent half the meeting talking about what a great actor his little brother Kieran was. I couldn't help being struck by the contrast between Mr. Culkin's ego and Macaulay's lack thereof. This child Star seemed much more interested in convincing us that Kieran was a good actor than that he himself was.

Macaulay loved acting, of course, but sometimes we see kids who don't want to be acting, let alone auditioning.

Many an adult actor—Jane among them—has given up the business because the audition process is so brutal; the only reward is that you sometimes get to do the work you love. If you don't love it, auditions can be excruciating—there's just too much rejection. Of course, any kid who's cute enough will get auditions like crazy—for commercials, TV shows, movies—but if they don't want to be there, they won't do a good job and they're never going to get cast. Yet parents persist in dragging these terrible little actors, these sad little kids, to audition after audition. I once saw a little boy whose mom had driven him three hours to get to my audition—sadly, a common occurrence. He wasn't very good, but I had him do the scene three times, just so he wouldn't feel the trip had been wasted.

JANE

When I was casting *Table for Five,* I met a boy who came in for one of the family's three kids. "How did you decide to be an actor?" I asked brightly, hoping to put the child at ease.

"I didn't, actually," the boy replied. "My mom decided for me."

"Oh," I said, somewhat taken aback. "But do you have fun doing it?"

"No," he replied. "Actually, it embarrasses me."

I had the boy read the scene—what else could I do?—and in fact, he wasn't half bad. But I wasn't going to cast a kid who didn't want to be there. "Don't you want me to do the scene again?" he asked.

"No, you were terrific!" I told him.

The boy sighed. "My mom says, if I don't do it twice, it's 'cause I wasn't good."

"No," I said firmly. "You were good. You were so good, I

didn't need you to do it again." I wouldn't have cast that kid no matter how desperate I got—no way was I going to be responsible for his psychiatrist bills!

I ended up casting Robby Kiger in that part. Now there was a kid whose family had their priorities straight. If Robby had a Little League game that conflicted with a callback, guess what? He went to the game.

Likewise, Freddy Savage had great parents. They made sure he had to wash the dishes, take out the trash, and do all the regular chores that teach a kid how to be responsible. We cast him in *The Princess Bride* before he rose to fame on *The Wonder Years*. He's a grown-up actor now who's also branching out into producer/director work.

For the record, Cher—whose son, Elijah, came in to read for *Lord of the Flies*—seemed to be an excellent screen parent. She kept herself very much in the background and didn't expect any kind of special treatment for her kid. Although she was clearly enormously proud of him, she was also ready to let him find out for himself what a hard life an actor can have, even with a Superstar/Pop Star mom waiting in the wings.

Sometimes we'll get asked about child actors who seem to be under lots of pressure, even when they clearly love the work they do. Haley Joel Osment, for example, once burst into tears when he didn't win a Golden Globe. I can't speak specifically for Haley Joel, of course, but my own sense—as a kid who studied acting, an adult who works with child actors, and the parent of a child who never wanted to act—is that if a kid loves acting and has good, strong, supervisory parents, he or she doesn't face that much more pressure than any other kid who's passionate about something. Most childhoods include disappointments that can seem overwhelming, even if they're not as public as Haley Joel's. What kid hasn't cried when their team loses the big game, when they're passed over for cheerleader or ignored at a party or don't get the lead in the school play?

I always loved Freddy and Ben Savage's parents, because they gave their kids a sense of proportion and discipline. Those children lived off their father's salary, no matter how much money they made of their own, and you can be sure they went to bed on time whether they were starring in a hit TV series or not. As a result, both boys grew into happy, well-adjusted adults. Meanwhile, I'm sure there are lots of little prom queens and high-school heroes out there who have absorbed the message that their childhood victories are all-important, kids who get special privileges when they do well and who are punished—overtly or covertly—for doing badly. Showbiz kids are more on display than their "civilian" counterparts, but I'm not sure the parenting issues are all that different. There are lots of kids who collapse under the pressure of growing up, both in and out of show business, but I doubt they outnumber the Ron Howards and Jodie Fosters, the child Stars whose parents help them find healthy ways to cope.

Among my favorite screen parents of all time were Mara Wilson's mom and dad. Mara was only five when she came in for *Mrs. Doubtfire,* but she knew all about acting because her older brother was in the business, too. She had a husky little voice with a very slight lisp, and we fell in love with her. We had to fly a bunch of kids up to San Francisco to meet with Robin Williams, and at first, Mara wasn't supposed to go—but Janet had such a good feeling about her that she convinced director Chris Columbus to bring her along. Sure enough, Mara got the part—and then we cast her in *Miracle on 34th Street,* and then she starred with Danny DeVito and Rhea Perlman in *Matilda.*

Like many child actors, Mara came from a showbiz family—her dad was a cameraman; her mother was a secretary. Her mother told me that when Mara was five, she announced her wish to be an actress, like her big brother.

All well and good, the parents thought, but how could they be sure little Mara knew what she was in for? So they staged some mock auditions in their own home, and her mother told Mara that she had gotten rejected at every one. Did she still want to be an actress? Yes, Mara replied. She understood how tough the business could be—she just loved to act.

Everybody adored working with Mara, and she seemed to have an amazing career ahead of her. Then, sadly, her mother became ill with breast cancer while Mara was making a movie and died soon after, when Mara was about nine or ten. Something seemed to go out of her after she lost her mother, and she hasn't acted in several years. She was a lovely actress, without any of the mugging or cuteness you sometimes find in child actors—she didn't have a phony bone in her body. We hope she either finds her way back to the screen or discovers something else she loves equally well.

JANET

When I'd finally found the babies for *Baby's Day Out,* I could return to my old worries: Would they start walking before shooting ended? The worry was especially maddening because, once shooting began, there was absolutely nothing I could do about it. (Jane once suggested hobbling the little darlings, but I thought that was going too far.)

I did stay in touch with the baby wrangler, though. (The term "wrangler" goes back to the days when actual horse wranglers were part of the crews of Hollywood's early Westerns; now we have animal wranglers and baby wranglers and even actor wranglers, who manage the traffic at big auditions or on complicated shoots.)

I don't know what I thought staying in touch would accomplish: I guess I wanted to be ready to leap into action if we needed to find substitute babies—though I had no idea how that would work. Would we try to fake in the new kids for the old ones, using tricky side shots or back shots, and hope that no one would notice? (Sometimes directors do this with adult actors when a cast member dies.) Would the whole movie get scrapped?

You can imagine my relief when I got a call on the very last day of shooting. "It's okay," the baby wrangler told me. "We made it." Then he dropped his bombshell. "One of the kids is still crawling, but the other has just started to walk." If shooting had lasted one more week—it didn't bear thinking about. Thank heavens, the casting gods were with us once again.

JANE

Another day the casting gods were with us was while I was casting *Alex & Emma* for Rob Reiner. *Alex & Emma* is essentially a budding love story between a writer, played by Luke Wilson, and the stenographer who comes to work for him, played by Kate Hudson. The plot thickens later in the film when Wilson's girlfriend, the stunningly beautiful Sophie Marceau, reappears to interfere with the new romance.

As it happens, the Sophie Marceau character had two children, a girl around five and a boy around seven. Imagine the casting nightmare: young children, authentic French accents (yet a good enough mastery of English that the audience could understand their dialogue), and attractive enough to seem like the children of Sophie Marceau, who is one of the most beautiful women in the world.

I put out a breakdown, which usually gives us at least a handful of usable candidates. Nothing. I started calling agents. Still nothing. Finally one of the agents I called told me about the daughter of a costume designer she knew. The little girl was adorable, five years old, and Francophone. Problem solved—halfway.

"Hey, Rob," I tried in a desperate phone call. "I still can't find the little boy. What if there's, like, only *one* child?"

"Noooooooo," Rob said firmly. "We need two kids. Find the boy, Jane."

The search went on in its fruitless way, and I was starting to tear my hair. Then one day I was out walking my dog, a little later in the morning than usual. Suddenly, as I turned a corner, I caught sight of a woman and two children—a girl about ten and a boy about seven—coming out of a house, all speaking French. And the boy was a breathtakingly adorable kid—his face, his eyes, his little you-can-only-buy-it-in-France outfit.

"Excuse me," I said, breaking in on the happy family scene, "but do you speak English?"

They did, though they couldn't help wondering what a local woman with her dog was doing asking them about their language abilities.

"This is going to sound very strange," I admitted. "But I'm a casting director working on a film for Rob Reiner—"

"I am sorry," said the mother. "I do not know who this Rob Reiner is."

"Um, well, he directed *The Princess Bride*—"

I'll never know why, out of all Rob's films, that was the one I chose to mention. But the mother's eyes lit up immediately.

"Oh, my God," she said, pointing to the seven-year-old, "that is Alexander's favorite film. He can recite every one of the lines of Prince Westley!"

Magnifique. I went on to explain that I wanted to audition Alexander to play the son of Sophie Marceau—of course, she had heard of Sophie Marceau—and asked her to contact me if he might possibly be interested in reading for us.

I didn't even have a business card with me, just a plastic bag for picking up dog poop. I wrote down my name and number on a piece of paper from the mother's purse, certain that this elegant woman must think I was a raving lunatic, if not an actual child molester.

Days went by, and I had just about given up when the mother finally called. "We've talked about it," she explained, "and Alexander thought it might be fun to try out."

It turned out that they'd just come over from France, because the father had gotten a job at an insurance company. They didn't even live in the house where I had found them— they were only looking to see if they wanted to rent it.

The boy came in to read, and of course he was absolutely fabulous. Rob fell in love with the kid and gave him all the lines that had formerly gone to the little girl.

Then we ran into trouble. Although the father had legal permission to work in America, the son did not. At the ripe old age of seven, he wasn't expecting to earn any money here, so no one had bothered to get him a work permit. It ended up costing far more to rectify his legal situation than to pay his salary, but by that point, the boy was really into the project, and Rob felt that he couldn't take the job away from him. Besides, there wasn't anyone else whom we liked. And the whole convoluted way we'd found the kid seemed to be part of his charm—after a story like that, how could we not use him?

Every so often, we do find people through such circuitous routes, though I'm loath to admit that to any actors out there who might be reading this. Yes, once in a blue millennium someone brings himself to your attention outside the usual channels. An actor showed up at a casting session once without an appointment—somebody must have told him that I was looking for a football player—and sort of bluffed his way onto the schedule. "Are you crashing my casting session?" I asked in disbelief when I realized what had happened. It wasn't all that obvious—he sure *looked* like he belonged with all the big, hulking guys in the waiting room— so we let him read, and of course he was perfect. Who knows why his agent hadn't submitted him, or maybe we just hadn't seen the picture, but he looked like what I needed and he could say the lines, so he got the job. But actors, please don't try to crash our casting sessions! In every other possible instance, I promise you, you'll only get yourselves into a situation where we won't ever agree to see you again.

Anyway, the French kid, Alexander Wauthier, was wonderful, and although I don't believe he had any plans to become an actor, I'm sure he had the time of his life shooting the film. My favorite thing about his audition was that when we read his scene together, he very politely but firmly corrected my French. Yes, Rob agreed. That was the kid we needed.

☆

One of the hardest parts about casting children is keeping yourself from getting emotionally involved with the ones who don't make it. Of course, that can happen with adult actors, too—we're only human. You tend to develop attachments to the people you bring in, especially after a few callbacks, and you find yourselves rooting for them to get the part. Then the director says, "Noooooooo, I don't think so," and since it's ultimately his vision you're supposed to be serving, that is definitely that.

When I was casting *Stand by Me* for Rob Reiner, one of the boys up for the leading kids was a child named Chance Quinn, whom I absolutely fell in love with. He was adorable—sweet, polite, smart, talented—and I was rooting for him like you wouldn't believe.

We had an amazing roster of talent trying out for *Stand by Me*. Finalists for the various boys included Ethan Hawke and Sean Astin—who didn't get cast—and Kiefer Sutherland, Corey Feldman, River Phoenix, Casey Siemaszko, and Wil Wheaton, who did.

Kiefer had come into town right out of Canada and we'd already seen him on a general before calling him in for this picture. He'd done *The Bay Boy,* a Canadian movie, in 1984, that had sort of put him on the map, and then of course, he was Donald's son. So when he came to L.A., all the casting directors had wanted to meet him. He was absolutely perfect for the older juvenile delinquent brother—and the relationship he developed with Rob later led to him being cast without an audition in *A Few Good Men.*

River was up for Chris Chambers, the slightly older kid who's the hero's best friend. He had an exquisite face and a kind of physical beauty that stood out even among the usual run of gorgeous Hollywood kids, but he also had real depth. The sense of compassion and love he was able to convey stands as one of the most moving portraits of male friendship I've ever seen.

The Phoenix family was extremely close, and most of the kids had taken up acting. The family had performed as a singing group, and they were all dedicated artists—and vegans. I remember River earnestly explaining to me that he never wore a leather belt or any kind of shoes but sneakers because he didn't believe that animals should suffer just so he could be well dressed. When we went on location for *Stand by Me,* instead of putting the parents and child actor up in a hotel room, we paid for a Winnebago so the entire family could camp out. We gave them all of River's food allowance, too, so he could stay on the family's macrobiotic diet instead of eating whatever craft services had cooked up. "They live on nuts and berries," River's agent, Iris Burton, had told me facetiously. But they were a terrific family. It was fun seeing them years later when we cast Joaquin (then known as Leaf) for a role in *Parenthood* (as the kid who keeps jerking off in the bathroom).

Corey was also an outstanding kid, although my sense is that he had a troubled home life. When he came to the *Stand by Me* callbacks, he was the only kid who showed up without a parent. He must have been fourteen at that point, and he obviously hadn't driven himself to the studio. When I asked where his mother was, he shrugged and said, "She'll be back later to pick me up."

Maybe that's why he was such a natural for the part of the troubled kid. He'd originally come in to read for the role eventually played by River. Granted, that part was also a troubled child, but when I saw Corey, I thought he might be more right for Teddy Duchamp—the wild boy whose "loony" father periodically abuses him, the daredevil kid who gets the other boys to dash across the rickety bridge. I gave him the sides for that part and when I went back out to the waiting room, he grinned at me.

"So, this is the Robert De Niro role, right?"

I guess if there is such a thing as a twelve-year-old Bobby De Niro, Teddy Duchamp *was* the Robert De Niro role, and once we'd seen Corey read it, we knew we didn't need to look anywhere else. At callbacks, he soon figured out that he'd gotten the part, since he was the only one who ever read it, while we mixed and matched the other three. When callbacks were over, he waited patiently for whoever was picking him up, and I wondered what kind of reaction his family would have when we cast him. I never found out, because on location, when all the other kids were accompanied by parents, he had a twenty-one-year-old guardian. He spent a lot of time with the Phoenixes on that shoot.

Corey's career was very big in the 1980s but then it sort of took a dive. I didn't stay in touch with him so, beyond what I read in the papers, I don't know what happened. I just know that on *Stand by Me,* he was a terrific actor and a joy to work with.

But the kid who'd really won my heart was Chance. After the callbacks were over, I was sure he was the rightest kid for Vern Tessio, the fat kid. We spent hours looking at the tape, and looking at the tape, and looking at the tape again. Finally, Rob called and said, "You know, I think I'm going to go with Jerry." That was Jerry O'Connell—now perhaps best known for his role as the extremely sexy detective Woody Hoyt, Jill Hennessy's recurring love interest on the TV series *Crossing Jordan.* Jerry was the youngest kid in the cast—only eleven, while most of the other boys were twelve and thirteen. River, the oldest of the group, turned fourteen while the picture was shooting. I guess Rob thought that Jerry's extra degree of youth made him that much more touching and vulnerable.

I was heartbroken for Chance, but I just had to let it go. As a consolation prize, we put him in as the son of the Writer at the movie's end—the scene where the narrator is now portrayed as an adult (Richard Dreyfuss), and his own kid comes in and says, "Come on, Dad, you said we'd go fishing."

One of the nice things about having cast kids for all these years is watching "our children" grow up. Recently Jerry came in to audition for *The Holiday.* He was funny and terrific, but alas, he didn't get the part. Given his starring role on the TV series *Crossing Jordan,* we counted him a success nonetheless.

We're also proud of Thora Birch (*Ghost World, American Beauty*) and Leonardo DiCaprio, both of whom we cast in the short-lived TV version of *Parenthood.* You could tell that Thora was the kind of performer who was never going to agree to selling cornflakes. Even as a kid, she had that serious old-soul quality, and she was always a serious actress. And Leo—well, Janet vividly recalls that the first time she saw him, she literally gasped. She'd just opened her office door, and there was this Raphaelesque angel sitting in our waiting room. At that point, Leo was there to read for Ponyboy in the TV version of *The Outsiders.* Although he was still a little young for that part, we did give him the one-shot role of a boy who gets beat up by a tough girl. We thought he was terrific even then, and we weren't surprised when he went on to bigger things.

Winona Ryder was another kid who had an extraordinary sense of herself. When she was twelve, I tried to convince her to do a film called *Labyrinth,* directed by Jim Henson. "Don't you want to meet the man who created Kermit?" I asked plaintively—but Winona was a punky, bohemian kind of kid who had no interest in the Muppets. (We went on to cast a young Jennifer Connelly in that part.) Winona eventually let us cast her in *Beetle Juice,* after she finally came around to thinking that all the dead people were cool.

Natalie Portman also knew what she wanted from a very young age. We tried to use her in *North,* but for whatever reason, it wasn't a movie she wanted to do. Even at age twelve, she was never interested in "just another part"—she wanted only extraordinary parts in movies where she was the featured player. She was serious, dedicated, and ambitious, but she also had a winsome, little-girl quality that was very appealing.

A girl we did end up using in *North* was Scarlett Johansson, who was one of the cutest kids we'd ever seen. Like most child actors, she was quiet and serious on set, and rather shy between takes. It was clear even at a young age that she wasn't just a beautiful kid but a budding serious actress—a couple of years later, she made a low-budget movie called *Manny & Lo* about two sisters who run away from foster homes and kidnap a kind of mother figure whom they think will help them. It was a demanding part, and she did an extraordinary job. She went on to do brilliant work in *The Horse Whisperer* and in *Ghost World,* another quirky independent film where she co-starred with Thora Birch as a frustrated teenager trying to make sense of a painfully constricted suburban world. Her current success is no surprise to any of us who've followed her work.

One of my favorite child actresses is Dakota Fanning—

so serious and so good at what she did, she was almost scary. Even at age five, she had real craft; she never just improvised or went on instinct alone. Usually when I work with kids, I become bright, encouraging, and helpful, but with Dakota, I found myself talking to her the way I would to an adult actress. It was a bit disconcerting, dealing with this child as though she were my contemporary and then, later, hearing her say proudly that she was going to join the Girl Scouts and couldn't wait to start selling cookies. (*She* has very good screen parents, too!)

Joey Mazzello had a similar quality. When we saw him read for *Jurassic Park,* he astonished us with his technique: the interesting places he found to pause or the unusual ways he'd vary his line readings. It was a command of the craft that wouldn't have been out of place in a highly trained professional—but Joey was only eight.

Of course, I was only twelve when I started attending the High School of the Performing Arts, and yet I knew exactly what I wanted to do. Over the years, having seen performers like Dakota and Joey, I've wondered if we don't all tend to underestimate children. Some of them, at least, have abilities far beyond the ones with which we usually credit them.

JANET

Some of my favorite kid auditions took place when we were casting *Harry Potter* for Chris Columbus. *Harry Potter* is my kind of literature—I love classic children's fiction—so I noticed when the book got all that attention, and I noticed as well when the buzz started about the film. When I heard that one of the people up for directing it was Chris Columbus, with whom I'd worked for many years, I thought, "Oooh, who knows?" Then I read that Chris had gotten the gig, but that it was going to be shot—and cast—in England.

It sometimes happens that when a picture is shot in another country, Jane and I become what is known as "bad money": the studio sets up the financing so that the money comes from—and must be spent in—Britain or Europe. Chris might bring me in on most of his movies, but doing the production in England almost certainly meant that I wouldn't be working with him.

In fact, even before Chris came on to the picture, Warner Brothers had hired a well-known British casting director to start the search for the kids. They'd done a nationwide search and had even gone on television to invite submissions. Naturally they were deluged with photographs, but for this very special project they needed not only good actors but also kids who fit everybody's very vivid image of the book's characters. Since the novel would have sequels, presumably the movie would, too—so the producers also needed actors who would stay with the roles over the years.

Then Chris got hired. Although he couldn't use us as the primary casting directors, he very kindly brought us on as consultants, charged with looking for British kids in North America. It was a lonely task. Once British kids get over here, they tend to lose that special English quality, let alone their accents. But Chris and I had been working together since his first film, *Adventures in Babysitting,* and we'd developed our own special rapport.

His relationship with the British casting director, on the other hand, was not going so well. To some extent, this was simply because the British had another way of doing things, and Chris wasn't used to it. To some extent it was because he and the woman in question just didn't know each other very

well—and sometimes chemistry is not only about how actors work together.

The British were also very protective of the Harry Potter
story. They were proud of J. K. Rowling's meteoric rise to international fame, and they loved the tradition of boys' school
stories and fantasy fiction out of which the series had been
written. There was already a certain amount of resentment
that an American director was going to bring "their" movie
to the screen, and they had given Chris the mandate that
only British children could be in the film.

Chris had already embraced that mandate. But that didn't
mean he and his British casting director were getting along.

Finally producer David Heyman decided that the casting
situation needed to be changed. He'd met me a few times
and we'd gotten along well. So suddenly I got one of the best
Calls of my life. "Do you think," David said in his cultivated
British voice on the phone, "that you might be able to perhaps come over here?"

This initial query came on Wednesday. On Sunday, David
called again. "Could you possibly, um, come tomorrow?"

Monday was the premiere of *The Perfect Storm,* so I
couldn't leave then. By Tuesday, the story had hit the British
tabloids: "American usurper come to steal Harry for the
Yanks!"

I knew that it was very important to Chris that the children be English—so important that I didn't even audition
the likely American kids. Not just the kids but the adults had
to be British: Robin Williams was dying to be in the film,
and he and Chris were good friends, but Chris wouldn't even
consider him. As for me, I'd grown up with a British mother
and grandmother, and I loved all things English. (When the
Harry Potter project came up, Jane started calling me "Janet

the Anglophile.") What interest could I possibly have in violating British cultural integrity?

☆

Although I'm very happy living in Southern California, all my life I'd cherished the dream of someday working in England, and taking my mother with me. Mom was an English war bride who'd been evacuated from London in 1939 when she was thirteen, had married an American GI in 1945, and had come to America in 1946. She hadn't been back to her native land in all that time, and I'd always wished I could somehow take her to revisit her childhood home. When I realized that I'd be in England for three and a half months, I thought, "Great, I'll bring my mom for a visit!"

But when my mother went to get her passport, she discovered that although she'd been an American citizen for years, she didn't have her naturalization papers. She sent off for them right away, but the whole bureaucratic process might take two or three years.

Still, coincidence marks the life of a casting director, and this incident was no exception. Before I left, I got a call from Dan Furie, a very nice business affairs guy at Warner Brothers with whom I'd worked on *The Perfect Storm*. He had a friend in England who was an actress—would I be willing to meet with her on a general? Sure, why not?

A few weeks after I got to England, I met the young woman. As we were chatting, I found myself telling her my mother's story. "Oh," she said, "call Dan and see if he can get my father to help." It turned out that the actress was the daughter of former actor and ambassador to Mexico John Gavin. And indeed, when I called Dan's office, his lovely assistant offered to put us in touch with their immigration attorney, who offered to explore a couple of avenues. If they didn't pan out, he warned, Mom would just have to wait for the bureaucratic wheels to turn.

Fortunately, the lawyer was able to help, and he called one day to tell me that my mother's papers had gone through. I happened to be riding in a studio car, talking to my mother on my cell phone, when the attorney's call clicked in on the other line. I looked out the window as I got the news and I couldn't believe it. I was on Kilburn High Road—the main street of the part of London in which my mother had grown up.

I thanked the attorney profusely and clicked on the other line. "Mom," I said, looking up at the street sign, "it's okay. You can come over. And you'll never guess where I am . . ."

☆

But that was a few weeks in the future. When I first got to England, thoughts of my mother took second place to the task of getting oriented and hiring an English casting director. We brought on the wonderful Karen Lindsay-Stewart and immediately set up a series of open calls around the country.

Meanwhile, I was amused by the tabloids' shrill charges of Americans usurping their Harry. Neither Jane nor I have ever been the focus of such relentless publicity, before or since. Since I knew the charges were ridiculous—of course we were committed to using British kids!—I was less offended than amused.

Casting kids is never easy, but casting the three top kids for *Harry Potter and the Sorcerer's Stone* was an even bigger challenge than usual. Not only did these kids have to carry a full-length movie based on a famous book—a book that millions of kids and a not inconsiderable number of adults adored—but unless this first film failed miserably, they would almost certainly have to sustain the parts for another several years and as many sequels as their ages would permit. Because we needed the kids to age with us—hopefully through all six sequels slated for the series—they had to be pretty much the right age for the characters. We couldn't consider casting a young-looking thirteen-year-old to play the eleven-year-old Harry; it was too likely that next year, at age fourteen, the actor wouldn't be able to pass for twelve. (In the end, our Harry was eleven, our Ron was twelve, and our Hermione was only ten.)

Plus we had to hire kids who looked pretty much the way their fans pictured them. If a character in the book was described as green-eyed, we couldn't get away with hiring a brown-eyed child. And Harry, Ron, and Hermione were such vividly drawn characters that *everybody* already knew what they looked like. Try finding real kids who fit that image, who are still the right age—*and* who can act!

By the time I came on board, there were actually several strong candidates for Hermione and Ron. But they didn't have a Harry, and they were starting to worry.

Then, once again, coincidence came to our rescue. Young Daniel Radcliffe's mother was a casting director, and his father was a literary agent at the London office of ICM. So he wasn't exactly unknown to the film world, especially since he had played David Copperfield on British TV. Despite his early success, though, Daniel wasn't really interested in acting and had already issued a definitive "no" to the previous casting director. He was far more interested in the World Wrestling Federation.

As we approached panic time, David Heyman ran into Daniel and his father at a play. They knew each other socially, and on impulse, David said, "Please. Let your son come in and read." •

Somehow Daniel was prevailed upon to meet with David, who thought he had real Harry possibilities. The next day he read for Chris, some of the producers, and me, and we all liked him very much. In fact, by that point, we'd found a few kids that I liked. Things were definitely looking up.

We decided to do a full-on screen test for the three main parts, which these days happens very rarely, since you need to assemble a crew, soundstage, and lighting. For Hermione, we tested two girls, one of whom had lots of experience. She'd played Madeline in the movie of the same name, which made her so famous that Emma Watson, the other little girl, recognized her rival when she went in to audition. "Oh, well," Emma thought. "There's no way I'm going to get the part if I'm up against her." But when we looked at the footage, there was no contest: Emma leapt right off the screen. The next day, when we showed the tests to the people from the studio, executive Lorenzo di Bonaventura said, "Wow, can we put her under contract till she's forty?"

Steven Kloves, the writer, agreed. "Can I write for her when she's eighteen?" She just had such presence. Sure, she played a pushy, bossy little girl, but somehow, when she went into her know-it-all routine, it was delicious. When the other little actress started showing off, you kind of wanted to slap her, but Emma made it all seem charming. I think she had some of that same bossy, precocious quality offscreen, so maybe she'd already figured out how to make it work for her.

We also screen-tested several candidates for Harry's best friend, Ron Weasley. At first, Chris and I were on opposite sides of this one. He liked one Ron; I liked the other, who I thought had this adorable goofiness that was just perfect for the hapless but determined Ron. When we looked at the tests a second time, Chris must have seen what I saw, because he switched his vote. Rupert Grint would play Ron Weasley.

Harry turned out to be a harder call. Four boys were tested for the Harry role—but this time, it was a split decision. Some of us liked Daniel; some of us preferred another kid. I was actually in the latter camp. Daniel's rival was a year younger and I thought he looked more vulnerable, and more like Harry. Chris preferred Daniel, but he didn't want to make such an important decision with half the room opposed. It was now late at night, and we decided to adjourn till the next day.

The next morning, I woke up with a different opinion. As I reviewed my memory of the tests, I came to think that the other kid really was about a year too young. Yes, he could show us the vulnerable part of Harry, but Harry wasn't all about vulnerability. He was also about toughness—the mental toughness of a plucky kid who becomes a hero because circumstances force him into it. Harry has to grow into his heroism pretty quickly, and we needed to see that potential from the first moment he appears on-screen.

When we reconvened to review the tests, Chris's associate producer, Paula DuPré, took me aside. She'd worked with him for years, and she had an even closer relationship with him than I did. "Look," she said, "Chris is really interested in what you think. If you don't like somebody, he's going to be terribly concerned."

We reran the tests. As the film on Daniel flashed across the screen, I could see Harry's intelligence, his grit, his ingenuity. I could see the scared kid, sure, but I could also see the budding hero. As the film played, Chris looked back at me and I gave him a thumbs-up. Hello, Daniel—hello, Harry!

☆

Telling the kids was a treat. We called them into the studio the day after the decision, and of course they had to know something was up—why else would we have called them in? The three of them had all acted so grown up when they were there to read, but when Chris gave them the good news, they turned into kids again, jumping for joy.

When they calmed down, we gave them a tour of the studio, with a particular focus on the art department and the creature shop, so they could see how the monsters and magical beasts were made. As they chatted, Daniel let it slip that he hadn't read the Harry Potter books—after all, he was more of a WWF fan.

"Oh, that is so stupid!" said Emma, rolling her eyes in a very Hermione-like way. I couldn't help smiling. Clearly, we'd made the right choice.

☆

Daniel, Emma, and Rupert bonded immediately, forming friendships that would sustain them through the next several years of filming. Meanwhile, we were busily engaged in casting the adults. As soon as I'd been hired, Chris and David and I had all agreed: Maggie Smith was our top choice for Miss McGonagall. As soon as her name came up, everyone said, "Oh, yeah. Who else would we want?" Likewise, J. K. Rowling herself had always thought of Robbie Coltrane to play Hagrid, the groundskeeper, so in effect, she cast that part—but who could disagree? Robbie was perfect.

Most of the rest of the parts were cast with Stars who didn't have to audition or even to meet: nobody was going to ask the likes of Alan Rickman or Richard Harris to come in and read. Some adult actors did come in for auditions, but that all went fairly smoothly. What was more difficult was arranging the contracts with the cream of the British acting aristocracy. The studio, knowing that there would be sequels, would not hire anybody whose character appeared in succeeding books without an option—the right to hire the actor for three subsequent movies at prenegotiated salaries. (Actually, the children were signed for only one sequel, while the adults were signed for three.) Though the studio knew there would be seven books in the series—and hopefully seven films—executives understood that they couldn't prenegotiate so many sequels. Stars at the level of the people we were considering don't often do options, and to make matters more complicated, these deals had to be made "for a price." Because these contracts were negotiated under British Equity—the British actors' union—they didn't include residuals (additional payments to actors based on a film's sales to TV, video, and other mediums). But to sweeten the deals, Warner Brothers decided to give all the actors the residuals that they would have gotten under SAG.

I'm not saying that studios don't always want to make movies as cheaply as they can. But for *Harry Potter*, it was also true that the movie would lean heavily on special effects, no matter who was in the cast. Just as in *Jurassic Park* the dinosaurs got the money, and in *The Perfect Storm* bucks went to the storm, in *Harry Potter* the dollars—or the pounds— went to the flying broom.

We actually got a lot of help from children in our casting efforts—not our kids but the actors'. I lost count of how many people came in saying, "My children (or my grandchildren) told me that I *must* get this role." Richard Harris, for example, who played the venerable Dumbledore, head of Hogwarts, was originally not interested in the movie. Then a grandchild told him, "Oh, no, Grandpa, you'd better get that part!" He ended up loving the role, and of course he was wonderful in it. Everybody was. In fact, *Harry Potter* was the occasion for Jane and me to win one of our three Artios Awards—the special award given each year by the Casting Society of America.

☆

One of my most satisfying moments on *Harry Potter* came when we cast Malfoy, the evil child who becomes Harry and his friends' archrival. Before I came on the project, Tom Felton had been considered for Harry, and though he wasn't quite right for that part, Chris had kept his tape. As soon as I saw his test, I said, "Oooh, that's a good Malfoy!"

We did a screen test with Malfoy and our three leads. He was a more experienced actor than they were: Emma and Rupert had never acted professionally, and Daniel had only played David Copperfield, while Tom had been in *The Borrowers, Anna and the King,* and some TV productions. By the time Tom came on board, the three leads had developed a kind of easy, joking-around relationship with one another and with their work—after all, they were still only ten, eleven, and twelve years old. Tom, though, was thirteen, and all business. And as soon as he started the scene, you could see the other three kids thinking, "Whoa! He's good!"

Immediately, each of the others bore down a little harder. They weren't about to have their own performances look bad compared to his. This dynamic continued throughout the picture, too: the three leads might be fooling around a little bit, and then Tom would come in and be right where he needed to be to make the scene work. Immediately, the others would sharpen their own focus.

Watching them, I had to smile. *That's what actors do,* I thought. When they start acting with a really strong scene partner, a kind of natural competitiveness kicks in and everybody begins working at a higher level. *Harry Potter,* I knew, would be a terrific film, the kind of magical tale that only Chris Columbus could spin. But to me, there was also true magic in what happened to Daniel Radcliffe, Emma Watson, and Rupert Grint as they grew into the actors they had it in them to be.

The rest of the movies were cast in Britain, so Jane and I didn't work on them. But it's been a great pleasure watching Daniel, Emma, and Rupert grow along with their characters, albeit from a distance. Like the other child actors we've cast over the years, they've been professional, dedicated, and determined to make the most of the chance they've been given. They've all brought something of themselves to the on-screen characters that they played—especially Emma, I think—and each of them seems to me to have the makings of an excellent adult actor. Of course, they may someday decide to stop acting, permanently or temporarily. But if any of them wants to stay in showbiz, they've definitely got what it takes.

8 ☆ THE TOUGH SEARCH

JANE

It was in our second month of casting *A Beautiful Mind* that we suddenly ran into trouble.

Up to this point, casting had gone remarkably well—so well that I made a classic mistake: I allowed myself to think that all the film's major problems had been solved.

This happens quite a bit, actually. Whenever I come back from an early meeting and say cheerfully, "You know, I think we can cast this movie right now," Janet always says, "Run for the hills!"

Still, in this case I had good reason to be optimistic. After all, we had the brilliant Russell Crowe, the luminous Jennifer Connelly, and the magnetic Ed Harris. I was getting ready to go to New York to begin the rest of the casting, and we were close to making a deal on the elusive part of Charles, Nash's charismatic roommate and best friend.

Normally an unfilled role—especially one of that size—is never completely off my mind, even when I'm home watching television or out having dinner with David and Cynthia, my grown son and his charming fiancée. Janet and I live in a perpetual state of low-grade anxiety when we're casting a movie—low-grade, that is, until it spikes into full-blown panic. Will we find the people we need? Will the director like our choices? Will the actors upon whom we finally decide say yes? These days there's often another question: Will the studio approve? With the new entertainment conglomerates, micromanagement is all the rage, and if we're not working with a top director, we can find ourselves having to justify even our most minor choices to a studio exec.

But our fears have less to do with who's approving our choices than with the inexorable passage of time. We've got to find the right people for every one of the movie's fifty to one hundred roles—and we've got to do it by the first day of shooting.

Still, even with Charles to cast, I thought we were home free, because Robert Downey Jr. had said he'd do the part. He seemed perfect for the character—charming, unpredictable, madly intelligent, and just a little bit dangerous. Under other circumstances, the money might have been a problem—again, the lion's share had already gone to Russell and Ed, and the budget wasn't all that big to begin with. But any Ron Howard picture carries a certain amount of prestige, and Robert—plagued by recent arrests and tales of drug addiction—was eager for a comeback.

So for a few blessed weeks, I felt I could breathe again. Then one day I opened the paper. "Robert Downey Arrested for Drug Use," I read, and my stomach dropped. No matter how often such sudden reversals happen during the casting process—and believe me, they happen all the time—you never quite get used to them. With the soon-to-be-jailed

Downey clearly out of the picture, the search for Charles began again.

Okay, I tried to tell myself. I've still got two months. But it hardly seemed like enough. Both Janet and I have a near-fanatical aversion to settling for second-best for even the most minor parts, and Charles, while not quite a lead, was hardly minor. We spend the first two-thirds of the movie believing that he's a real person—Nash's best friend, his cheering squad, the person to whom Nash will turn when the espionage gets out of hand. When we discover that he's only a figment of Nash's troubled mind, the blow needs to be devastating, for us as much as for Nash. If the actor playing Charles hasn't made us fall in love with him, hasn't gotten us to buy into Charles's outrageous behavior and his apparent affection for Nash, hasn't convinced us to pin all our hopes on Charles's ability to save his friend, well, then the whole movie will simply fall flat.

Lots of terrific actors wouldn't be right for a part like Charles. First, we could rule out the whole category of working-class and ethnic actors, whom you simply wouldn't believe had done graduate work in math at Princeton in the late 1940s. A young Robert De Niro, Harvey Keitel, or Al Pacino would have had the energy and charm but not the class. Putting them or any modern-day equivalent in the role would simply raise too many questions.

Then there are the actors who simply don't project the razor-sharp intelligence, urbanity, and sophistication that were such a big part of Charles. Actors such as Brad Pitt and Ewan McGregor are charming and charismatic—but you don't necessarily think of them as projecting the intensity and intellectual brilliance of a character such as Charles, a man whose near-genius abilities make him the ideal "soul mate" for Nash. Charles needs to be magnetic, yes, but he must also offer an intellectual foil for Nash while maintaining a certain mystery—an unusual combination of qualities that actors are rarely called upon to embody.

We did look at a whole slew of intense, sensitive guys: Noah Wyle, Mark Feuerstein, Josh Charles, Liev Schreiber, Christian Slater, and Dermot Mulroney. In the right part, any of them might have been extraordinary, but none of them had that certain something we needed for Charles, which would allow the performance to vibrate between a realistic portrait and the larger-than-life quality that gave Charles such a hold on Nash.

John Cusack could have done it. He seems to burn with a bit of extra fire, driven by his own dark secrets, marching to the beat of a drummer that nobody else can hear. But he wasn't available. Who else? *Who else?*

By December, I started to panic. Shooting was due to start in February, and traditionally Hollywood shuts down for the entire holiday month. Basically that left me only January to cast a part for which I'd pretty much run out of candidates. So when longtime colleague and agent Risa Shapiro called our office to ask about some detail of her client Jennifer Connelly's contract, I allowed myself to indulge in a few minutes of therapeutic hysteria.

Risa was someone we trusted, but she was also an agent, so naturally, her first thought was to pitch a client. "Jane," she said, "what you need is Paul Bettany."

"Never heard of him." I wasn't completely averse to casting an Unknown, but I didn't like feeling that I was scraping the bottom of the barrel.

"Take it from me, you'll hear about him. Paul is going to be very hot, very soon."

Although some agents tend to exaggerate, the best ones don't. Why waste everybody's time by sending in someone who isn't right? And we'd worked with Risa for almost as long as we'd been in the business.

"He's this young British actor who's just finished making *A Knight's Tale* for Brian Helgeland," Risa went on. "Brian is wild about him—he plays Geoffrey Chaucer."

Great, I thought. A movie about a medieval English poet. *That* should be interesting. But I did trust Risa—as much as you can ever trust an agent. After all, it's their job to convince you that you want someone you didn't know you wanted.

"Can I see his reel?"

"Well, so far he's mainly done theater, so all that's on his reel is this little movie called *Gangster No. 1,* which frankly isn't going to help you all that much."

"Fine," I said, thinking how difficult it was going to be to sell Ron Howard on an actor whose previous work he couldn't see. "Send him in, and I'll get him on tape."

"Sorry—Paul can't come in. He's in London, doing a play."

"Well, Risa. If he hasn't got a reel, and he can't audition, how the hell am I supposed to consider him for the part? Am I supposed to *divine* what he looks like?"

"Let me make a few calls. Maybe I can get you into the editing room of *A Knight's Tale.* You can at least take a look at the rough cut."

Most directors won't let outsiders look at their unfinished films. But when they believe in an actor and want to help his career, they're willing to allow a casting director to view a bit of film in the editing room. So my anxiety level—and my faith in Risa—led me to the editing room at SONY studios, where the assistant editor cued up Paul's first scene.

I got ready to watch, putting myself into that oddly contradictory condition in which I always observe an actor. First, I prepare to measure the new guy against my own mental image of the actor I hope to find—my vision of the ideal performer who has just the right combination of qualities to make the script work. Then I put myself into a state of suspended judgment, a kind of readiness in which I'll be capable of recognizing something entirely new and unexpected. *Know what you want, but prepare to be surprised.*

The editor punched a button, and the tape started to roll. Paul's character had just been waylaid by robbers who'd taken his clothes as well as his money, leaving him naked as a jaybird with his skinny butt facing the screen. He passed a group of bystanders and, without skipping a beat, doffed an imaginary hat. "Geoffrey Chaucer's the name, and writing's the game!" he said gallantly. And then, still buck naked, he bowed.

That's my guy, I thought, overcome with relief. Bettany's persona fairly crackled off the screen. He was smart, but more important, he was witty, with that offhand sense of humor about himself that the British do so well. Although his Chaucer was eminently sane, I could see that he'd be capable of the mad intensity that Charles would need for the scene where he pushes Nash's desk out of the third-story window. And underneath it all was an endearing openness and vulnerability, qualities that were absolutely crucial for the heartbreaking episodes in which Nash finally refuses to acknowledge Charles. When the assistant editor handed me a videotape of Bettany's three biggest scenes in the film, I felt as though I could breathe for the first time in weeks.

"Boy, this guy Bettany is getting really popular," the assistant editor mentioned. "I made one of these tapes for Spielberg just last week."

I don't remember if I even said "Thank you." I just went flying out the door, pulling out my cell phone as I ran. "Ron," I said as soon as he picked up, "I'm about to overnight you a tape, and you absolutely have to watch it the moment you get it, because I think Steven is interested in this guy for *Minority Report,* and if we lose him now that we've found him . . ." I didn't even want to think about what starting another round of Charles-searching would be like.

Ron, in New York, was calm. "Look, Jane," he said, "I'll watch the tape, but no matter how good he is, I can't just hire this guy without meeting him."

"Just watch the tape, okay?" Just my luck, I thought, if this is the one time in a million when Ron and I don't agree. Obviously, if Ron didn't like what he saw, I'd start looking again—of course, I would. But *please,* I thought as I walked off the studio lot, let me not have to.

JANET

As happened on *A Beautiful Mind,* Jane and I frequently encounter a Tough Search, one of those times when we see dozens or even hundreds of actors and none of them is quite right. A search like this can be an exhilarating challenge, but when it goes on too long, it can become demoralizing.

You sit in the audition room, seeing actress after actress. Okay, she's got to be beautiful, but there's no shortage of beautiful women in Hollywood. It would help if she could act, but in theory, there's no shortage of actresses, either. You'd like to see someone with charm, personality, depth. You hope to see someone who can make some kind of sense from the lines on the page, a performer who can create a character rather than simply "read with expression," like some kind of grammar-school project.

And when you don't find what you're looking for, when after seeing fifty or a hundred women you haven't once had that little "Aha!" bell go off in your head, when the words on the page start not making sense, even to you, you begin to wonder. Are your standards too high? Perhaps they bear no relationship at all to the real world of actors and filmmaking; perhaps you're longing for some fantasy performer whom you're never going to find. Maybe these apparently wrong actors are really not so wrong—maybe you've just become jaded, or frustrated with how many good actors you've had to reject, or too narrow in your ideas of what you want to be able to see the possibilities in someone who's sitting right in front of you. Maybe the director would absolutely love someone whom you're throwing out the door. Or maybe if you said the right words, made the right suggestion, found some new way to put the actress at her ease, maybe then she'd suddenly release an extraordinary performance—a performance that you're never going to see, because somehow, for some reason, you're doing everything wrong.

This kind of internal monologue can go on for hours—or, if the search is tough enough, for days, weeks, or even months. Even after all these successful years, the cumulative sense of failure that can result from not finding anyone who comes close to our ideal can cause each of us to question first our judgment, then our taste, and finally our ability to do our jobs at all.

Then the right person walks through the door—and suddenly it all makes sense. The script doesn't need to be rewritten—it only needed the right actor to bring it to life.

Our expectations were perfectly reasonable—they simply weren't being met. Our judgment is just fine, thank you very much—we had good reasons for not liking what we'd seen so far. If you can make it through a Tough Search, you'll have learned a valuable lesson, though it's a lesson we've each had to relearn, several times: When you can't find what you're looking for, don't blame yourself. You just haven't found it yet.

JANE

We did finally cast Paul Bettany, of course. Ron loved him, and so did Russell—and so did Jennifer, who eventually became his wife. To me, the experience of losing Robert Downey Jr. only to end up with Paul Bettany confirms one of the most amazing aspects of this business: *somehow, it always works out.* In every experience of a Tough Search that I've had over the past twenty-five years, even the ones that begin by losing the actors you think you can't live without, you always end up with someone who seems even right-er than the one you lost. (Unfortunately, I'm not nearly so philosophical when it comes to romance!)

In Paul Bettany's case, casting an actor who was then virtually unknown to an American audience had the additional virtue of making Charles's status—real or imaginary?—even more painful. Because we had no preconceived notion of who this guy was, we got to meet him and fall in love with him in this movie, just as Nash did. And then, when we find out that he isn't real, it's doubly disillusioning. With a more known actor, like Robert Downey Jr., we'd have other fond memories of the actor to hold on to, to dull the pain of losing one of the movie's most attractive characters. With Paul, all we had were the scenes of him being Nash's friend.

Finding out that they hadn't "really" happened seemed—to us as well as to Nash—like an unbearable loss.

☆

Sometimes what makes a Tough Search difficult is the gap between what you think an actor can do and what he or she actually does. Believe me, as a former actress, I totally sympathize with how difficult it can be to audition. It's been more than thirty years since I had to read for a casting director, but I still remember vividly how it felt to sit there, my heart pounding so violently I was sure it could be seen right through my chest. So when I run across an actor who seems as nervous as I was, especially a young actor, I say, "Look. Nothing that happens in this room is going to change your life. Chances are that you won't get this job—that's just the way it is. But I will remember you for the next time. So, okay, now you have nothing to lose!"

Sometimes it works; sometimes it doesn't. But at least I've done what I can to keep people at a level of comfort that allows them to breathe and to function. It's as much an act of self-interest as a gesture of kindness: I'd rather hear the best audition each performer has to give than hear the same nervous, hysterical reading fifteen times.

JANET

One of the things I like most about my job is realizing that it's been years since a particular actor auditioned for me, and I still remember the audition. It's a tribute to an actor's power that—whether he got the part or not—he can make such an impression on me. And that impression may eventually pay off when I bring him in for something else.

Sadly, some actors shoot themselves in the foot by giving

away their power. They think of the audition as what stands between them and the work—they don't understand that the audition *is* the work. Every audition should be done as if you were already on the set and you owned the character. We shouldn't see you floundering around like a fish out of water, trying to figure out what you're doing. You're supposed to do all that work before you ever get to the office. Sure, sometimes it's hard; you're not given much to work with and you have no time. But the actors who come in and own the part are the people we have confidence in. They're the ones we're happy to present to a director, because they'll make *us* look good.

An actress once gave a particularly dreadful audition and then said, "I could do it better if you needed me to."

"*We* don't need anything," Jane replied. "If *you* need this job, then, yes, I think better would be good! At what point would you like to do it better—after you don't get the job?"

Sometimes an actor is afraid to make a bold, clear choice with a character, especially if he or she doesn't have the entire script or if the character is relatively under-written. In our opinion, there are no small parts—especially not in film— but there are definitely under-written ones, characters whose function is more to convey information or to move the action forward; characters the writer has not endowed with any unusual traits or quirky characteristics. In that case, it's the actor's job to come up with something distinctive.

Actors: Think of it from our point of view. When we've had fifty people come in to read the same part, how many of them do you think will be reading it exactly the same way? Even if Actor #2 is mediocre and Actor #47 is terrific, when they both make similar choices, they all tend to blend together. We'd so much rather you make a clear choice—which we may then ask you to change. But at least you've invested something of yourself, put a spark of life into the character, created something meaningful. Sure, there are people out there who will reject you out of hand if what you bring in doesn't match their preconceived expectations on the very first try. But you don't know what they're expecting anyway, so why try to please them? We, on the other hand, will be so delighted to see you do something interesting that we'll do everything we can to guide you back to the interpretation of the character that we know the director is looking for. And even if you're wrong for this part, we'll definitely keep you in mind for the future.

I'll never forget Samuel L. Jackson's audition for the scientist in *Jurassic Park*. We saw him right around the time he played the crack addict in Spike Lee's *Do the Right Thing*—his breakthrough role, which impressed everyone no end, including Whoopi Goldberg, who became his champion. I'd met Samuel on a general when he came to Los Angeles after that film, and I was just as impressed as everybody else, so I jumped at the chance to bring him in for one of the scientists in *Jurassic*.

This particular role hadn't especially been written for an African American actor, but Jane and I always like to bring in ethnic diversity and as many women as we can, if it's appropriate to do so. In a period piece, of course, you often can't get past a world in which all professionals and people in power are white and male; and you certainly don't want everything to look too pat, like a Benetton ad. Hopefully, you find a way to diversify the cast organically.

The part we brought Samuel in for was not only not written for a black actor, it wasn't all that specifically written for personality, either. But Samuel endowed the character with such specificity that we were stunned. I'll never forget his choice to have the character speak incredibly fast, as though he'd been up all night drinking coffee with the guys at the lab. It was a very long scene, and the character had a very wordy set of speeches. Samuel sped through it, killing three birds with one stone: he made us understand the information, he helped the scene move quickly, and he established the character's personality in a way that went beyond but didn't contradict the script.

Steven Spielberg was very much impressed and offered Samuel the part. For those of us in the business, nothing is more exciting than to have an actor give you something you didn't even know you wanted.

JANE

On the other hand, when the director is also the writer, she may know what she wants *too* well. Or at least that's how it seems when you're bringing in actor after actor after actor.

Nancy Meyers is one of Hollywood's few female directors, and she's in the enviable position of knowing that her movies pretty much always make money. She got her start as a writer, and she still creates her own scripts, sparkling romantic comedies that appeal to a female audience. For someone less skilled and savvy, those words might be a death knell—guy-oriented action flicks tend to be far more marketable than women-centered relationship films—but Nancy has managed to carve out a special niche for herself that everyone who knows her has to respect.

I was fascinated, when I first worked with her on *Something's Gotta Give,* to see how Nancy was able to get actors to do what no other director could. A Star at Keanu Reeves's level, for example, is well past the audition phase of his career.

But Nancy is deeply committed to hearing actors read the words she wrote before she casts them, and somehow she managed to get Keanu to audition for her before casting him as Diane Keaton's younger boyfriend. Keanu set a sort of precedent: now Nancy had established herself as a director for whom actors audition, even when they're too big to read for anybody else.

Nancy wrote *Something's Gotta Give* for Jack Nicholson and Diane Keaton (who got an Oscar nomination out of it). When the two big Stars signed on, a green light was pretty much assured. She tried to repeat that process with *The Holiday*, the charming story of two young women—an English "country mouse" and a Hollywood "city mouse"—who just can't face the Christmas holidays after getting dumped by their boyfriends. The women find a home-exchange site on the Internet and each goes to live in the other's domain, where, of course, each of them finds romance. Like *Something's Gotta Give, The Holiday* was written with particular actors in mind: Cameron Diaz and Kate Winslet as the two heroines; Jack Black and Hugh Grant as the guys they end up with.

Before I came on board, Nancy had sent the script to all four actors—and then her troubles began. Cameron had decided to take a year off. She thought it was a really cute script, her agent told Nancy, but the actress needed a break.

Kate loved the script, too—but she didn't love the schedule. As the Englishwoman who finds romance in L.A., she'd have to come to Hollywood to make the movie, and she didn't want to leave London while her kids were in school.

Jack also had scheduling difficulties. And Hugh just plain didn't want to do it. Delightful material, he told us, but he had played that "Hugh Grant" part far too many times. We tried hard to change his mind—since Nancy had written the role especially for him, it was difficult even to read it without hearing his voice—but we didn't seem to be having much luck.

Okay, I thought when I heard the rundown. It's early days—let's not get crazy. I was especially relieved when I heard that before I'd really come on board, Cameron had come around. I have no idea who said what to make her change her mind—I just knew we had one out of four.

Then we started seeing people for Iris, the English heroine. We were open to casting an American actress if she could do the accent—Maggie Gyllenhaal came in and did a terrific job—but we really wanted an Englishwoman. *Bridget Jones* had established that a Yank *could* do a Brit if necessary, but we thought a British-born woman would be more authentic.

Okay, but where were we going to find someone who was British, pretty, Star quality, and funny. It was that last quality that was the kicker. There's an old showbiz story, that's been attributed to many different sources, about an ailing performer visited by a young relative. "It must be so hard to die," the young man says. "No," the old man corrects him. "Dying is easy. *Comedy* is hard." Truer words were never spoken. Any decent actor can make an audience cry, gasp, or sigh in sympathy. It takes a special talent to make an audience laugh. And women, who are rarely asked to be funny, rarely develop that skill.

Maggie had been wonderful, but she was an American. Minnie Driver, a bona fide Englishwoman, also gave a great reading, but Nancy couldn't quite see it. After all, she'd lived with these words for months, crafting the scenes, hearing them in her mind. By the time we came to cast the movie, she had a very specific image of how she wanted them said.

If an actress didn't match the rhythms and cadences that Nancy longed to hear, it didn't much matter what else she brought to the table.

We saw several more candidates, but no one quite met Nancy's expectations. Then, months later, we got a phone call from Kate Winslet's agent asking if Iris was still available. Kate and her husband, director Sam Mendes, had agreed that one of them would always be home with the children. But apparently a job of Sam's had fallen through, and suddenly Kate was available. Did we still want her?

Did we! *The Holiday* had been slated to start shooting in mid-November, but casting delays had pushed our start date into January. We were more than happy to welcome Kate on board, and to juggle our schedule to make things work.

Now, guess what? Those schedule changes suddenly meant that Jack Black could indeed do the film. (Learning that he'd be playing opposite Kate Winslet may also have helped convince him to make himself available.) The production manager rewrote the schedule yet again, and now we had three out of four.

By this time, we knew there was simply no chance of getting Hugh. None. Whatever luck the casting gods had seen fit to grant had now run out, and we were on our own.

So we started seeing funny, charming, and handsome English guys—lots of them. Lots and lots and *lots* of them. Ideally, we wanted a Star—after all, we'd assembled a formidable cast, and ideally, our three A-listers would be joined by an A-list guy. Ideally, too, we wanted someone who was in his late thirties to mid-forties: the part had been written as a widower with two daughters aged six and seven, so you had to feel that the actor we cast had lived long enough to raise a family.

On the other hand, you never know. At one point, Nancy and the studio were really interested in Colin Farrell. I kept saying, "Don't we think he's awfully young for this?" To myself, I was saying, "How do you get from Hugh Grant to Colin Farrell?" Both are handsome, sexy, and not from America, but the similarities pretty much end there. And I never particularly thought of Colin as the kind of guy who specializes in funny and self-deprecating.

When his name came up, Colin was in Florida preparing for Michael Mann's movie version of *Miami Vice,* so Nancy flew there to audition him. It might have worked out, but a lot of political reasons suddenly made the whole relationship too complicated, and it was back to the drawing board.

At another point, we auditioned Ewan McGregor and Clive Owen. We *would* have read Hugh Jackman—he shared the universal opinion that the script was delightful—but he ended up taking a part that he was offered in a film directed by Christopher Nolan. Weighing the offer versus the opportunity to audition, Hugh chose the offer.

I'd been auditioning James Bond candidates at the same time, so we considered several of them for *The Holiday,* including Alex O'Loughlin (too young and not yet a Star) and Daniel Craig (Nancy didn't think he was funny enough—and not yet a Star; he hadn't yet been chosen for Bond). In addition to the potential Bonds, Robert Downey Jr. read for us. So did Aaron Eckhart. Julian McMahon of *Nip/Tuck* fame came in. So did Brendan Fraser. Nancy had a quiet drink with Eric Bana—the recent star of Steven Spielberg's *Munich*—but that didn't seem to go anywhere. She brought in Rupert Graves, Billy Crudup, Dermot Mulroney, Josh Lucas, Colin Firth, and at least two dozen more. Of course I wasn't complaining—after all, I was the one who read the

love scenes with these sexy, gorgeous men—but I was starting to wonder if this part would ever be cast. I knew Nancy's
sense of comedy was unerring, and I knew how strong her
casting choices had always been. But *The Holiday* was starting to set a new record for most auditions per part.

Finally Nancy settled on Jude Law, who in a sense had
been there all along. She hadn't initially wanted to consider
him because he and Kate Winslet had just finished shooting
All the King's Men, and she thought it might not make sense
to pair them up again, even though in her film they'd be
playing brother and sister. But after seeing what seemed like
all the other guys on both sides of the Atlantic—with some
from Australia thrown in for good measure—she offered the
part to Jude, who, luckily, took it. Of course, Jude's so good,
when most people see the movie, they'll probably think the
role was written for him. And that's as it should be. For casting to really be successful, it has to be invisible.

JANET

Sometimes it's scheduling that makes a Tough Search
tougher, or that turns what should have been an easy decision into a difficult one. There are lots of ways to work around
scheduling conflicts, but there are also lots of ways such conflicts can make everyone's lives more difficult.

For scheduling purposes, actors fall into two categories:
day players, and everybody else. As the name suggests, day
players are hired by the day for relatively small parts. Actors
in larger parts are hired by the week (with a fixed weekly fee
that we've negotiated with their agent) or for the length of
the picture (for a flat fee that we've negotiated with their
agent). The Screen Actors Guild demands that actors at all

levels get the SAG minimums—whether daily, weekly, or per picture—but actors can and often do ask for more.

If a day player is offered a significantly better role in another film, he or she is legally allowed to break the contract with you. And if you hire a day player, you're also allowed to break the contract.

If an actor higher up the ladder is offered a better role, they're legally required to stay with you once the contract has been signed, and you're required to pay them for however many weeks you first contracted for, even if their part gets written out of the script. Frequently, though, an actor hired at this higher level will beg for permission to take a better part somewhere else. I remember when Jane cast Dylan Walsh—now known for *Nip/Tuck*—in *A Few Good Men*. He'd not only been hired but the cast had already had its first read through—that inspiring one with Jack Nicholson. Then Dylan got a call from his agent: he'd just been offered a major part in a Bernardo Bertolucci movie. Rob Reiner was sorry to see Dylan go, but no way was he going to keep a young actor from furthering his career. We said a regretful goodbye to Dylan and replaced him with Noah Wyle (best known for his work on the TV series *ER*). Sadly for Dylan, the Bertolucci film was canceled—and by then it was too late to get back into Rob's movie.

We had a similar situation on *The Perfect Storm*, though with a happier ending. We'd originally cast Susanna Thompson as the intrepid woman in the sailboat—Susanna, whom Jane had used as Alec Baldwin's supportive second wife in *Ghosts of Mississippi*. I needed to close her deal quickly because we had to fit her with custom-made safety gear, but her agent kept not calling me back. Something was up! Finally her agent phoned. This was the hardest call of his life, he told me, but would we let Susanna out of *The Perfect Storm* to take a regular role on Sela Ward's new hour-long TV series, *Once and Again*? The situation might easily have turned ugly, except for the fact that Tony Award–winning Cherry Jones had been a strong runner-up for Susanna's part, and she was still available. Susanna went on to a few seasons on TV, Cherry was her usual lovely self, and we knew we'd use Susanna some other time.

Scheduling problems tend to have ripple effects, too. When Nicole Kidman broke her rib on *Moulin Rouge* or when George Clooney hurt his back on *Syriana,* it didn't affect only them. It also meant that all the actors who hadn't finished shooting on those films were suddenly going to be delayed, whether they had made promises to other movies or not. Other things can go wrong, too, such as problems with the location, uncooperative weather, or malfunctioning equipment—you just never know.

A production is legally entitled to refuse to accommodate an actor's schedule, though sometimes people will try to give an actor a break if it doesn't affect the timetable for the production. Often, though, scheduling tangles just can't be worked out. It's not only dates that cause problems. Other common conflicts concern the actor's appearance (one movie wants him with long hair and the other has cast him as a Marine sergeant), weight (someone is supposed to gain weight for one part but not for the other), or physical maturity (heaven help the casting director who has to hire a twelve-year-old: you never know when a boy will lose his childlike soprano, when a girl will sprout breasts, or when kids of either sex will shoot up a few inches). When you consider how many movies and TV shows are constantly being shot, and how many actors are constantly being hired, it's a wonder any schedule ever works out!

JANE

One of my favorite Tough Searches was for Rob Reiner's *The Princess Bride.* Two of the parts were especially tricky: Buttercup, the princess; and the Giant.

I asked the writer Bill Goldman for his definition of "giant"—just how big and tall a guy was I supposed to find?

"Oh, you know," he replied. "Someone like André the Giant."

I didn't know who André the Giant was, but I didn't want to admit that to Bill. When I got back to the office, I asked our vice president, Michael, who André was, and he looked at me as though I'd been living in a cave.

"André the Giant is a major wrestler," Michael explained patiently. After commiserating on my ignorance of professional wrestling, Michael kindly agreed to contact the World Wrestling Federation to track down André and any other guys who might be right.

Unfortunately, André wasn't available. Although he loved the idea of playing a fairy-tale giant, he had some wrestling dates worth half a million dollars that he simply couldn't afford to pass up.

As Michael sought out other professional wrestlers, I went from agent to agent, looking for someone who had the physical presence—no one under six foot eight need apply—as well as the character's warmth and charm. I met every big, tall man I could find, including people from all walks of life who weren't necessarily actors. Incredible Hulk

Lou Ferrigno also came to meet with Rob, who thought we could use the ordinary-size Lou only if we redefined the giant as "the strongest man in the world."

Of course, most real-life giants have some sort of debilitating disease, which makes them too weak for the rigors of filmmaking. I'll never forget one candidate in London, a man who was nearly eight feet tall. He sort of loped into the room—his gait was like a crane's—and extended his hand down to where I was. I felt like a baby as I reached up to take his hand, which enveloped mine like a catcher's mitt.

"I've read the script, and there seems to be a great deal of physical action," the man said in his impeccable British accent. "But you see, I have a rather awkward center of gravity. Perhaps you might be able to use a stunt double?"

I looked up at his towering height and tried not to smile. A stunt double has to match the actor's size and shape well enough that the audience can't tell that a switch has been made. "I don't think there's anyone in the world who could double for you."

For a time we thought we'd found our man—a very tall actor who'd already been signed for *The Witches of Eastwick*. But because of the scheduling conflict, the *Witches* casting director refused to let the actor even meet with Rob.

"Look, I'm offering this guy a part where he gets to be a hero—and in your film, he barely speaks and is basically just a sight gag," I pointed out. Too bad. As we'd already discovered, a good giant is hard to find, and the *Witches* casting director was taking no chances on losing his. Although technically the actor could still have gotten out of his *Witches* commitment, he felt morally obligated to the production, and so he gave up his chance at the part of a lifetime.

Then one day we were in the middle of auditions in London when a call came in from Michael. A woman at the World Wrestling Federation had just called to inform him that André's dates had fallen through and he was available. André was on his way from his home in Brussels to his next gig, but he'd have a brief layover in Paris. Perhaps Rob could meet with him in the VIP lounge at Charles de Gaulle?

We halted the casting session immediately, and Rob and producer Andy Scheinman booked a flight, grabbed a taxi, and dashed to the airport. On the flight over, knowing that English wasn't André's first language or even his second, Rob recorded every one of the Giant's lines on a portable tape recorder. When they met, after chatting a bit, Rob said, "Look. You've got the part—you're the guy. Here are all your lines. Learn them—say them just like this."

So when the Giant calls out during the heroic rescue, "Hello, Lay-dee!"—that's Rob Reiner. The entire performance is composed of Rob's timing and André's heart.

André was a warm, wonderful, sweet man who carried around a video of *The Princess Bride* until the day he died. He was so proud of getting to play the gentle but heroic Giant—and I was so relieved to be able to cast him.

☆

"Next," I said wearily. Our assistant nodded and jumped up to bring in the next actress, as I looked skeptically at the lovely features gazing out of yet another head shot. Finding the most beautiful girl in the world isn't as easy as it sounds.

The Princess Bride is based on the William Goldman novel of the same name. While both movie and book featured a treasure trove of quirky character parts—the mercenary kidnapper eventually played by Wallace Shawn, Mandy Patinkin's vengeful Spanish aristocrat, André the Giant's giant—its heart belonged to Buttercup, the beautiful peasant girl chosen by the evil Prince Humperdinck to be his princess bride.

"I haven't done all that many movies," the next candidate confided. No kidding, I couldn't help thinking. We had run out of real actresses some time ago. Now we were looking at models. "Vapid, vapid, vapid," Janet had commented one day. "You've got that right," I answered.

"There is no greater hunter than Prince Humperdinck," the auditioner read, stumbling over the awkward name. "He can track a falcon on a cloudy day. He can find you."

I don't believe you, I thought, looking at the lovely woman's casually styled blond hair, her wide-set blue eyes, her stunningly high cheekbones. *I don't believe you'd use the word "falcon" in ordinary conversation. I don't believe you'd wear a princess's robes. And, most important, I don't believe you're wracked with pain for the one true love who abandoned you five years ago.*

"You admit to me you do not love him," I read, feeding the actress her line.

"He knows I do not love him," the actress replied. That "do not" was crucial—a touch of fairy-tale language that lifted the scene out of colloquial speech—but I could see that this auditioner would have been a lot more comfortable just saying "don't."

"Are not capable of love, is what you mean," I read: scornfully now, trying to goad yet another auditioner into a glorious display of matching scorn.

"I have loved more deeply than a killer like yourself could ever dream," the actress read back. *Nope, sorry,* I thought. *I get that it's an over-the-top line, honey, but it's your job to make it work.*

Most models haven't been trained to create anything beyond what they already are. Usually all they have to do is stand there and look pretty. In fact, it's probably better if they *don't* create vivid characters, so that viewers can read whatever they want into those blank, lovely faces, imagining themselves wearing the model's clothes or riding beside her in that sleek new car. For a movie, though, you need to be able to take one look at the actress and feel that you know who she is: Quick-tempered or sluggish? Agreeable or defiant? Basically at peace with the world or troubled by a tragic blow from which she has not yet recovered? Models aren't used to making those kinds of choices—but we needed someone who could.

"All right," I said as gently as I could when the audition finally ended. Although we might share our excitement with a terrific performer, both Janet and I do our best never to let an actor know that we thought an audition didn't go well. First of all, it's only polite. Second, it's not our place to offer career counseling. Third, you never know. Maybe they were just having an off day, or weren't right for the part, or were held back by some other obstacle that would one day vanish, freeing them to be terrific some other time. Best to stay as neutral as possible and focus on the job at hand.

We also try try not to be overly encouraging. Years ago, I worked with a director who shall remain nameless who always made every actor feel as though he or she had gotten the job. He'd start talking about wardrobe, or when we'd be on set, and the elated actor would leave, sure he'd just been hired. Then his agent would call and ask me, "So when is my guy starting?" "He's not," I'd have to tell them. After several dozen calls of this kind, I finally told the director, "Listen, when people leave a casting session, just say 'thank you'! You've made them all think they have a job, and now *I* have to take the job away from them."

"I'm just trying to be kind," the director said, rather huffily.

"Well, cut it out," I told him. "Otherwise I'm going to have all their agents call *you*." Kindness is one thing. Setting people up for disappointment is something else again.

Actors, of course, could teach the CIA a thing or two about how to dissect obscure information. They will spend hours obsessing about exactly what the casting director meant by "Thank you very much," even though they secretly know that those four words can mean anything from "We thought you were great" to "You're great but not right" to "Never darken our doors again." (Or, possibly, just "Thank you very much.") Experienced actors know about canceled callback sessions and mysteriously disappearing parts, although once they've been asked back, even if it doesn't pan out, they at least have the comfort of knowing that someone thought they were good. It won't pay the rent, but it might lift their spirits.

☆

Despite the cute name, Buttercup is meant to be a tragic figure. Although early in the film she finds her true love, Westley, he soon disappears into the clutches of the Dread Pirate Roberts, who, as everyone knows, never takes prisoners. Faced with a life of loneliness, Buttercup agrees to marry Prince Humperdinck, but her heart isn't in it. She spends most of the rest of the movie longing for her lost love, interspersed with occasional suicide threats which she hurls at the Prince: "If you marry me this evening, I promise you I will be dead by morning!"

The Princess Bride was meant to be played tongue in cheek, a cunning take on fairy-tale clichés. Yet for all its sly comedy, the film is also suffused with authentic emotion. Buttercup and Westley truly love each other, and each is genuinely brave, passionate, and faithful. Buttercup's part is studded with classic proclamations of love and defiance: "Westley and I are joined by the bonds of love." "I know who you are—your cruelty reveals everything." If the audience doesn't catch its breath every time Buttercup asserts her devotion, there's no movie. Such over-the-top lines call for an actress who can bring real depth to a part, someone who can convey with a single sorrowful look that her heart has broken a long time ago and life has lost its savor; someone who can indicate with a flash of her eyes that she'll never submit— never!—to a man she does not love. In the end, *The Princess Bride* is about the power of love, and Buttercup is the symbol of that power, a woman whose faith in her one true love is so unshakable that it sustains her through a thousand betrayals.

As if that weren't enough, Buttercup must be beautiful— so beautiful that every time someone calls her "the most beautiful girl in the world," you take it as a simple statement of fact. And her beauty must be classical, pure, and unadorned, that apparently natural fairy-tale beauty that you instinctively equate with goodness.

When you think about it, very few actresses have that kind of beauty. Each time Meryl Streep enters into a part, transfigured by her acting, she becomes incandescent—but you wouldn't call her beautiful, not in the simple, innocent way you associate with a fairy-tale princess. When Angelina Jolie comes on-screen, those full lips slightly parted, you can't take your eyes off her—but she's gorgeous, or sexy, or hot; you couldn't cast her as the epitome of beauty-as-goodness, either. Marilyn Monroe, Katharine Hepburn, Julia Roberts— these women are all striking to look at, magnetic, charismatic, but none of them have the kind of unself-conscious beauty, serene and self-assured, that would qualify them to be the heroine of a fairy tale.

At one point, exhausted by the search, I ventured to ask Rob about using Meg Ryan. This was a few years before he cast her in *When Harry Met Sally,* and although Rob has always liked Meg's warmth and her spunky charm, he was skeptical. Meg was undeniably pretty, but Buttercup had to be more than that. Meg was unquestionably endearing—but Buttercup wasn't. Her beauty set her apart from other girls, making her seem aloof and unreachable and yet still, somehow, vulnerable.

"I suppose if we decide that Buttercup is the most adorable girl in the world, we could use Meg," he said finally. "But let's keep trying for most beautiful." I thought about the many vapid beauties we had already seen and wished I didn't agree with him.

It's not as though we hadn't thrown out a wide net. I'd looked through hundreds of thousands of head shots, and I'd called in anyone who seemed to have the right kind of look. Although Janet was working on another movie at the time, she tried to help, too, wracking her brain for classic beauties that she had known. In fact, when you consider all of the Unknowns whom we auditioned for that part, it's remarkable how many of them went on to have careers:

Courtney Cox

Carey Lowell (who later married Richard Gere and achieved a certain notoriety as the assistant district attorney on *Law and Order* after Jill Hennessy left)

Uma Thurman (at sixteen already gorgeous, but too exotic looking)

Kim Delaney (of *NYPD Blue* fame)

Amy Yasbeck (remember her from *Wings* and Mel Brooks's Robin Hood movie?)

Alexandra Paul (who went on to fame on *Baywatch*)

Traci Lind (the young woman who dated Dodi Fayed before Princess Di did)

Yasmeen Bleeth (another future *Baywatch* star)

Sarah Jessica Parker (she's wonderful, yes—but boy, would she have been miscast in this)

Cecilia Peck (Gregory's beautiful daughter)

Plus Marg Helgenberger, Suzy Amis, Kelly Lynch, Lauren Holly, Nancy Travis, Cathryn de Prume, Charlene Tilton, Phoebe Cates, Kyra Sedgwick, Mia Sara, Patsy Kensit, Virginia Madsen, Courtney Thorne-Smith, Amanda Pays, Sherilynn Fenn, Catherine Mary Stewart, and a whole slew of other European and American actresses and models, all of whom were gorgeous, and none of whom was beautiful in the right way. Or else, for a moment, they *did* have the right kind of beauty—and then they opened their mouths.

Usually only one of us—the primary casting director— runs the auditions, while the other is busy casting her own movie. But one day both of us happened to be sitting in on the audition of an otherwise forgettable French model.

"Ah 'ave loved more deeply zan a killaire lak yourself could e-vair dream," she cooed, and a little bell went off as our eyes met. Of course! *Buttercup doesn't have an American accent.* The setting of fairy tales, after all, is "long ago and far away," not down the block where people use slang and colloquial speech. From then on, we asked everyone who auditioned to read the scene in some kind of accent—French, Italian, Eastern European, whatever—just to create that delicious sense of otherness that made Goldman's pastiche of romantic banter seem witty and intentional, rather than stilted and awkward. The accent suddenly made even the bad actresses seem a bit more magical; we could only imagine what it might become in the hands—or the mouth—of a good actress.

When Rob cast the British actor Cary Elwes as Westley, that added one more accent to the mix. André the Giant brought his Belgian inflections to the cast, while Mandy Patinkin came up with a not-quite-parody version of aristocratic Spanish speech. Many of the other characters— Wallace Shawn, Billy Crystal, Carol Kane—spoke with American or even Yiddish accents, so that eventually the mélange of different vocal styles made up a whole alternate world, a much richer evocation of a fairy-tale land than a cast full of standard American speakers could have offered.

Of course, Buttercup's performance wasn't just about speech. In many of her most important scenes, the character was virtually silent, but the camera continually returns to her face for what are known as "reaction shots." When Westley is attacked by an "ROUS," (a "Rodent of Unusual Size," or human-size rat), Buttercup watches in horror, her face registering her distress, her fear, her wish to help, her frustration that she can't. When Buttercup saves Westley's life by agreeing to marry the Prince and sending her true love away—after finally having found him again—it is the sorrow on her face that tells us how she feels, when, overcome by emotion, she cannot speak.

Reaction shots are where you really separate the amateurs from the pros. Even when Buttercup merely stands, fists clenched at her sides, her reaction shots make her an integral part of the fight. Watching a good actor react, you feel that something is moving beneath the skin. The remarkable Haley Joel Osment was a master of reaction shots even as a child; when you view him in *The Sixth Sense,* you see on his mobile little face that he is constantly somehow *doing* something—comforting, rejecting, avoiding, challenging, steeling himself—even when he neither speaks nor moves. Whoever played Buttercup would need that same ability—and so far we weren't finding any beautiful girls who had it.

Then one day I got a call from Eileen Farrell, a relatively minor agent who had her own small agency. Although we'd never met, we had a cordial phone relationship, as often happens in Hollywood, and Eileen got right to the point.

"I hear you're looking for some young beauty to star in Rob Reiner's new film," she said. "What about my client, Robin Wright. Remember her?"

I did remember Robin, though not too favorably. I'd met her through one of the writers on Rob's first film, *The Sure Thing,* who'd suggested the then seventeen-year-old Robin for The Sure Thing whom John Cusack pursues across America. Robin had just gotten into the business, and her audition was unimpressive, to say the least. Nor was she "va-va-voom" enough to play a sex bomb—she simply lacked that particular kind of confidence. I must have been watching *A Chorus Line* the night before Robin's audition, because, in a reference to the phrase "Dance 10, Looks 3" from the show's famous "Tits and Ass" song, I wrote an unusually dismissive note on the back of Robin's head shot: "Looks 10, Acting 3."

Well, okay, a 10 in the looks department wasn't bad, but did I really need to see another mediocre actress? "What's she been doing all these years?" I asked Eileen, trying not to sound as doubtful as I felt.

"For the past year or so, she's been on a soap," Eileen replied. Well, *that's* the kiss of death, I thought. She'll have picked up every bad habit in the book. Because soap operas—excuse me, daytime dramas—are churned out so quickly, an hour's worth of material each day, soap stars tend to learn all sorts of tricks to indicate their emotions quickly and unmistakably. In the business, it's called "mugging"—exaggerated facial expressions that are about as far are you can get from the subtle but powerful reaction shots that we were looking for. Because daytime actors are constantly placed in short, highly emotional scenes, they also learn to turn up their emotions very quickly, going from zero ("Oh, hello, Brent") to sixty ("You unspeakable bastard!") without warning. Goldman's clever dialogue intentionally teetered on the verge of the ridiculous; the whole point was to get actors who could play the outsize fairy-tale quality while finding the genuine emotion beneath. A soap actor, I was sure, would just make it all sound silly.

Still, when in doubt, we almost always see someone. An audition takes only a few minutes of our time; a premature "no" could cost us a relationship with a truly talented performer. And you can't judge an actor on what he or she does at age seventeen. Robin was almost twenty now; maybe she'd matured.

"Sure, I'll see her, why not?" I told Eileen. "I've seen everybody else."

☆

When Robin came into the office, I saw that she was just as beautiful as I remembered. Maybe even a bit more beautiful. Sometimes it takes actors a while to grow into their looks, to develop the confidence to fully inhabit their faces and their bodies instead of withdrawing into themselves. Actors often play other people because they're not comfortable revealing themselves. The irony is that nothing reveals your inner self faster than acting, even if you're playing a fairy-tale princess who lives in a magical land. Some teen actors, like John Cusack, seem to be burning with a desire to show themselves, to hurl themselves into a role and mine it for all the expressive possibilities it contains. Other actors are less comfortable with the business of self-expression, even though they've chosen a profession that inevitably requires it. As I watched Robin smile and introduce herself and thank me politely for seeing her, I wondered if maybe being on the soap hadn't actually been good for her. Having to turn in a highly emotional performance every day, while offering plenty of chances to manufacture phony emotions, can also be freeing. You're churning out the work so quickly, you don't have time to get self-conscious. And because no one is all that concerned about Acting with a capital A, you can relax into your work without worrying about the kinds of judgments that a more demanding director might make.

"Can you do any kind of an accent?" I asked Robin as she settled into her chair. "We've found that these lines tend to work better when they're not read in plain old American."

Robin considered the question. "Well, my stepfather is British," she said. "I do a pretty fair Brit."

"Great—try that."

We began the audition. I'd read this scene so many times by now that I had it memorized, leaving me free to notice the transformation that began the moment Robin picked up her script. Suddenly her face looked different—haughtier, more distressed. There was an aloofness about her, an invisible aura warning me to keep my distance. And despite the fiery, defiant words, her eyes suggested an overwhelming grief, a haunted, sorrowful look that seemed to contradict her youth and beauty.

"I have loved more deeply than a killer like yourself could ever dream," she read, and I thought, *Oh, my God, she's doing it.* "You mock my pain," she continued, and I felt like cheering. No one had ever made that line work before, with the right balance of glorious defiance and bitter sorrow. No one had ever found the truth beneath the comedy, the intensity that allowed the line to be both funny and deadly serious. No one had ever made me see—Buttercup, the princess bride, the most beautiful girl in the world.

"That was a great reading," I told Robin when she had finished, doing my damnedest to be cool and professional. The minute she was out of the door, I rushed into Janet's office. "I have just found Buttercup!" I shouted, literally dancing around the room. "Buttercup *lives*!"

When I calmed down a bit, I called Rob, who was at the Columbia Pictures scoring stage working on the background music for *Stand by Me.* Normally I'd never interrupt a scoring session, but for Buttercup, I asked the receptionist to pull Rob out. "I have just found Buttercup—we finally have our Buttercup!" I told him.

Rob also knew that I would normally never interrupt a scoring session. "All right, who is she?"

"You remember that kid, Robin Wright, who came in to read for *The Sure Thing*?"

"Yeah?"

"Well, it's her!"

"Get outta here," Rob said, his inimitable New York accent growing stronger. *"Her?"*

The conversation began to resemble a scene in a bad comedy. "Yes!"

"No!"

"Yes!"

"No!"

"Yes!"

"No!" A pause. "Really?"

"Yes!" I exploded. "She's perfect!"

"Well, I gotta see her," Rob said. "Get her over here. Now."

Robin had left our office ten minutes ago, and in those pre–cell phone days, I wasn't sure I could catch her. But I dialed her agent and said breathlessly, "Eileen, get your client over to Columbia, right now. Rob wants to meet her." Somehow Eileen conveyed the message and one hour later, Rob and I were sitting with Robin in a borrowed office as Robin read the audition scene in her British accent.

"Well," Rob said when she had finished. "Bill Goldman has got to see this."

We arranged for Robin to come over to Rob's house in the Hollywood Hills that Saturday. Producer Andrew Scheinman was there. So was Bill Goldman, skeptical but willing to see whom we might have found to play the princess he'd created. Janet was there, too—she didn't want to miss this moment. We were all waiting together in the living room when the doorbell rang. It was a typically lovely L.A. afternoon, and the sunlight was streaming into the room. Rob opened the door and there stood Robin, dressed in a simple white dress, her long billowy blond hair framing her lovely face, the golden sun illuminating her with a miraculous glow. *Backlit by God,* I thought, as Janet swelled with pride, Andy nodded, and Rob grinned. Bill Goldman was silent for a moment. Then he smiled too.

"*Yes,*" he said with satisfaction, delighted to see his vision finally brought to life. "That's what I wrote."

9 ☆ WHEN IT ALL COMES TOGETHER (OR NOT)

JANE

One of the trickiest puzzles in the world is how to make sure that a movie comes together. So many different elements have to work—script, cast, crew, design, editing—and not just work in themselves but as part of an effective whole. I'll never forget seeing *The Princess Bride* rough cut—the roughly edited early version of a film, with a temporary soundtrack. Janet and I almost never get called in at this stage, and frankly, we don't have the skills to see past the roughness. So when we saw this early version of *The Princess Bride,* we were shocked. We both adored the book, the script, and the cast. But we thought the rough cut was . . . well, rough.

Then when we saw the final cut, we were shocked a second time. How did it get to be so brilliant? The movie remains one of our all-time favorites. We're constantly quoting lines from it, and it's never on TV that we don't get pulled into watching it, even though by now we've seen it so many times that we can mouth the dialogue along with the actors. But without an editor's eye, we didn't know how to look at the rough cut—just as most people who don't cast movies never really understand that part of the process. Now we avoid rough cuts whenever possible. We wait for the premiere with all the bells and whistles. And we have a bit more sympathy for the vast majority of the world—both "civilians" and industry insiders—who simply don't realize the role that casting plays in making a film great.

☆

Sometimes a movie doesn't work, and sometimes, yes, that's because of the casting. One of the most difficult parts of our job is having to live with the results when the director makes a choice with which we don't agree.

Of course, casting is a back-and-forth process. We'll suggest someone, the director will suggest someone, the studio may have some ideas. If we don't all see eye to eye, Janet and I are willing to fight for our choices up to a point, but eventually we have to remember that the director or the studio has the ultimate say.

Often, too, a casting decision is more a matter of taste than an objective evaluation. Two equally good actors might both be right for a part but each will give the film a slightly different flavor, and you need a strong director to choose the flavor he thinks works best. Usually, even when we disagree with a director, we can at least see what he's going for.

Sometimes, though, a director makes a choice that we think is just plain wrong. Years ago, I worked on a film for which some absolutely wonderful actors auditioned. A young, then-Unknown Jeff Goldblum did a brilliant reading for us, as did Philip Anglim, the Tony Award–winning actor who starred in *Elephant Man* on Broadway. In fact, everyone's work was so marvelous, I wondered how the director would choose.

"They're okay," the director said finally. "But I want to give this part to a friend of mine." He brought the guy in to read, and, to put it bluntly, his friend was not a good actor. The producer was beside himself, and called me to be the arbiter.

"I can't imagine that the director's planning on hoisting himself on his own petard," I told the producer. "He must know that his friend can deliver, and who am I to question him?" I did tell the director that he had some terrific choices and asked him if he was sure he wanted to go with his friend. He did—and no, the friend did not deliver. I wished I could have done more to see that the part had gone to a better actor, but in the end it wasn't my decision. So there are definitely times when we wish the credits could read, "Casting by . . . except for Part X." (I'm sure that directors also sometimes wish they could take back a choice or two.)

JANET

Sometimes, even when you know a casting decision was correct, you can't help feeling a certain sense of wistfulness when you look back and think about the ones who got away. I remember the great Kevin Spacey—then just a Working Actor—coming in to audition for the John Hughes movie *Curly Sue*. Besides being an extraordinary performer, Kevin was an all-round nice guy. There happened to be a piano in the hotel conference room where we were holding auditions, and when I went out to get the next candidate, there was Kevin, playing the piano and singing in a good-natured effort to entertain his rivals for the part. Both he and George Clooney were up for that role, and neither one of them got it. I'll stand by both decisions, but you can't help wondering . . .

JANE

I don't mind passing up a terrific actor for good reasons, but it makes my blood boil when a director or producer turns someone down for what I consider trivial concerns. When Phil Hartman came in to audition for *Miracle on 34th Street,* I thought he was the funniest guy I'd ever seen—I may still be laughing from the audition he gave. But the director—who, to put it kindly, was somewhat arrogant—had no sense of Phil's talent. And why not? Because he perceived Phil as a TV comedian, someone who'd been successful on *Saturday Night Live,* perhaps, but who'd never done a substantial film role. I understand why you need Names and Stars in the major roles, but for smaller parts surely talent and "rightness" should be more important.

Likewise, I recently had a producer ask me about a very talented British actor, "If he's so good, how come he's thirty-six years old and nobody knows who he is?" It was all I could do to keep from replying, "Because people like you refuse to hire him!" Here was a talented Working Actor who'd done a lot of British theater and some film, and he'd come in to do a two-scene part as the guy who dumps the heroine. It wasn't a part that required a well-known face, but because the actor came "without certification," some people were nervous about bringing him on. "Mark my words," I wanted to say, "he will be Somebody, with or without this movie, and two years later you'll be saying, 'Oh, God, we could have had *him*!'"

☆

Sometimes actors don't want parts if they can't relate to the character. For the crazed fan in *Misery,* Rob Reiner originally wanted to hire Bette Midler. But Bette took one look at the script—in which her prospective character literally hobbles the writer she idolizes by driving a spike through his leg—and said, "This is the most hateful character I've ever heard of—why would I want to play this?"

As it happened, Rob had recently seen the Tony-nominated actress Kathy Bates in the off-Broadway play that had been written for her, *Frankie and Johnny in the Claire de Lune.* "She'd be great," Rob said, and sent her the script. I think we were also considering Kathy Baker and a few others, but there was a very short list for that part after Bette turned it down. Of course, Kathy Bates was wonderful in the part that brought this forty-two-year-old Working Actress a Best Actress Oscar—an honor usually reserved for A-list Stars.

Kathy's success was all the more striking because of how little known she was; indeed, a few years later, she still wasn't considered big enough to play the lead in the film that was eventually made of *Frankie and Johnny.* So the part she had created on Broadway—the ordinary working-class waitress longing for love—went not to the stocky, middle-aged Kathy but to the luminous and lovely Michelle Pfeiffer.

Luckily, *Misery* could be made with a lesser-known actress. In fact, part of why that film could come together as well as it did was because it was being produced at a time when you could sell a picture without a Star-studded cast. Today it might be difficult to get the film made with one Star—James Caan—and the unglamorous Kathy, who wasn't even a Name. But Rob had a history of doing successful films with lesser-known actors, and he's never cared about getting huge, extravagant budgets.

☆

Sometimes a film that seems perfect on the page doesn't quite come together on-screen. When I first read the script for

Rob's *Ghosts of Mississippi,* I happened to be on an airplane, and I found the story of Bobby DeLaughter's courage so moving that I had to run to the restroom where I could sob in privacy. How could the film fail to be equally powerful?

We cast much of the film locally, around the Jackson, Mississippi, area, where the real-life story had taken place. As a result, our casting was able to reflect the authenticity of the story to a fairly unusual extent. As one of the police investigators who helps DeLaughter, we cast "Benny" Bennett, a police officer and the real-life son of an officer who had worked on the original case. Bennett gave us a kickass audition as he basically read for the chance to play himself. Although we saw a number of actors who did a fine job, Rob kept saying, "I don't think we've seen an actor who has that sort of authenticity." So we cast Benny, who had a wonderful, relaxed way of working with Alec Baldwin (as DeLaughter). Benny had never had an acting lesson in his life, but he wasn't intimidated by the whole apparatus of filming, and he brought a kind of depth and heart to the movie that we couldn't have gotten any other way. Alec was terrifically impressed with Benny's ability to be comfortable and real in front of the camera, and he kept trying to talk Benny into coming to L.A. to be an actor.

"Well, this is kinda fun," Benny would say, "but I want to go home and do my day job."

Whoopi Goldberg played Myrlie Evers, the widow who insists on reopening the case, but the rest of the Evers family was also cast with real-life crossovers. Myrlie's grown children were played by two of the Everses' sons and by Yolanda King, daughter of slain civil rights leader Martin Luther King Jr., and the best friend of the Everses' daughter whom she was portraying. In fact, Yolanda had been working as an actress for some time—Janet had just used her in *America's Dream,* an HBO project.

With three performers who really had lost a father to racist violence, the scenes in the courtroom took on a whole new intensity. The close-ups of their faces as they wait for the verdict, and then the relief tinged with sorrow when Byron De La Beckwith is finally found guilty, added power, depth, and authenticity, as did the presence of Brock Peters, who played Myrlie's second husband—Brock had actually marched with Evers and been friends with the real Myrlie. The first read through—with so many of the cast having had a real-life stake in the case—was extraordinarily moving.

I'm not sure that the final film quite came together, though, maybe because the participation of so many of the Everses' friends and family inadvertently pulled the movie's focus away from Bobby DeLaughter. Sometimes a movie is defined as much by what it leaves out as by what it includes, and trying to give the Everses' story its due may have detracted from a script that was originally a portrait of DeLaughter's remarkable willingness to stand up against his family, friends, and community. The Everses' courage, while no less remarkable, was a movie in itself, and perhaps one film simply didn't have room for both.

But then I'm a casting director, so in the end, I tend to look at every movie in terms of casting. I remember when Janet and I went to a screening of *The Last Action Hero,* which has the distinction of being the only Arnold Schwarzenegger movie we've ever done—and the only one that ever failed. Quite frankly, it was a dreadful movie—it had been rushed into production, and rushed to be released—and we walked out shaking our heads in disbelief.

Then we heard two guys talking behind us—the stunt coordinators. They were raving about how well the gags— the stunts—had worked. To them, the whole movie was about the gags. Then I heard a props person talking about the props. I have a friend who's a costume designer. To her, the entire movie is about what everybody's wearing. To an editor, the movie's all about the pacing, the way the film is cut. And the publicist feels personally responsible for the success of any film, because he or she was the one who got the word out.

All of us are important, no doubt about it. And who combines all of our work into a single whole? The director. Ultimately it's his job to make sure that the film comes together.

JANET

Sometimes what comes together is the chance for an actor to get the part that will make his or her career. Once, for example, we had two actors try out for *Backdraft*, a Ron Howard film about firefighters. Although a young Unknown named Brad Pitt gave a wonderful reading, in the end, Ron went with the more experienced and better known Billy Baldwin. After all, Brad's main credits, at that point, were a couple of episodes of *Growing Pains* and *Dallas*.

When we offered Billy the job, he'd just gotten cast in a small part in a movie known as *Thelma and Louise*. The producers kindly released him from his commitment so he could take the lead in *Backdraft*—and put Brad into Billy's role in *Thelma and Louise*.

Would *Thelma and Louise* have been the hit it was without Brad? Yeah, you know Geena Davis is making this terrible mistake, and he may steal your money, honey, but you

gotta go for it, don't you? Brad brought intensity, danger, se-
duction to the role, but he also conveyed that his character
had a good heart. He felt so bad that he had to steal from
Geena—and he was *so* gorgeous! I'm not saying that Billy
Baldwin couldn't have done it, but I don't think the audience would have been saying, "Oh, I understand" in quite
the same way. Without Brad, the movie might have seemed
more contrived.

And if things had gone differently, if Brad had gotten the
role in *Backdraft,* would that much larger part have done
as much to launch his career? Would Billy have become a
Superstar if he'd kept his role in *Thelma and Louise*? Those
are the mysteries of casting.

JANE

We witnessed a similar odd intertwining of the careers of
Meg Ryan and Julia Roberts. First, of course, was the phe-
nomenon of *Mystic Pizza.* I have a great fondness for *Mystic
Pizza,* but I'll admit that what makes the movie lovable is not
great filmmaking per se. The movie has a simply extraordinary cast—every one of them—but even they are not quite
what makes that film come together. Instead, it's how the cast
interacts, the way they contrast with one another and play off
one another. Julia, wonderful as she is, was remarkable in
Mystic Pizza not as the movie's focal point but as part of a
joyous ensemble.

Meanwhile, the equally wonderful Meg Ryan was
struggling to gain a foothold. If we were to give a prize for
"the most terrific almost-cast," I think Meg would have to
win it. Coming out of a career in soaps, she read for the
Daphne Zuniga role when Rob Reiner was making *The Sure
Thing*—and although he found her adorable, he thought

Daphne was the righter choice for a repressed and overly earnest girl who needed to learn to loosen up.

Meg went on to a role in the third *Amityville* movie, and then to a small part in *Top Gun,* where she was so good that she just broke your heart. She was Anthony Edwards's girlfriend in real life as well as in the movie—maybe the relationship started there—and in that little scene where he dies and she cries, she was fabulous. As *Thelma and Louise* had done for Brad Pitt, those few moving moments really opened doors for her.

Janet and I went on to put Meg in some of her least successful roles—in *Presidio* and in *Armed and Dangerous.* Then came *When Harry Met Sally,* which we cast for Rob. When you see that movie today, with the effortless chemistry between Billy Crystal and Meg Ryan, it's hard to imagine that casting either of these two delightful actors cost Rob even a moment's indecision, but quite a bit of thought went into both choices. Billy, for example, is one of Rob's closest friends, and although Rob had always liked the idea of casting Billy as Harry, he was worried that working with him might somehow affect their friendship. You don't lose a friend over a stupid movie, Rob thought—but finally he decided to give Billy the part. (Their friendship continues, stronger than ever.)

Initially, too, Rob was dating Elizabeth McGovern, and one day he announced that she would be playing Sally. Then he and Elizabeth broke up, and that was the end of that choice.

Another strong Sally contender was Elizabeth Perkins. But when Rob realized that his ex-wife Penny Marshall had just used Ms. Perkins in *Big,* he decided that was too close for comfort.

Sally was finally a part that Rob could cast Meg in, however. When we brought her in to meet with Billy, it was magic—talk about chemistry! The movie made the most of Meg's adorable qualities, and she was a big part of the movie's success—while the movie turned Meg into a Star. It was the perfect example of the right girl and the right part coming together at the right time.

Ironically, Meg had had to get out of another part to play Sally, a supporting role in *Steel Magnolias*. The producers released her—and hired none other than Julia Roberts to take her place. Meg became a Star, while Julia was nominated for an Academy Award for Best Supporting Actress. Would Meg have been up for an Oscar in that role? Would Julia have made *When Harry Met Sally* the runaway success that it became? Or had the casting gods been busy once again?

JANET

Of course, Meg has paid a price for her stardom. Although she is a complicated person with her own complicated past, her public persona is the perky, bubbly character she played in *When Harry Met Sally, Sleepless in Seattle, You've Got Mail,* and a host of other romantic comedies. Whenever she's tried to break free of that type of role—the tough army officer in *Courage Under Fire,* the steamy lover of *In the Cut,* the boxing promoter in *Against the Ropes*—the public has been reluctant to accept her. They don't think of her as the woman who, in real life, had a passionate affair with Russell Crowe or who has made strenuous efforts to broaden her artistic horizons. They want her to stay the Most Adorable Girl in the World.

JANE

One indubitable sign that a movie has really come together is when it's up for an Academy Award—or, as with

A Beautiful Mind, a whole slew of Academy Awards. Although we usually watch the Oscars at home, I happened to attend the year *A Beautiful Mind* was nominated. While neither Janet nor I is in this profession for the glory, I must admit it was a thrill to sit in the balcony of the plush auditorium, listening to the names being called.

"And the winner is . . . Jennifer Connelly!"

Jennifer, serene and self-possessed, went up to collect the statuette. She looked beautiful, as always. Of course, every actress is beautiful when she accepts an Academy Award, just as every woman is beautiful on her wedding day. But Jennifer has that extraordinary luminosity even when she runs to the corner store for a quart of milk.

"The nominees for Best Director are . . ." Ron was one of the most level-headed guys in the business, but I knew that even he was thrilled by his nomination. When he went up to accept his Oscar, I couldn't help feeling proud, too. After all, we'd been with him since his first studio film.

"And for Best Picture . . ." Although the Best Director award is usually a good indication of who will win Best Picture, nothing in Hollywood is a sure thing, so I held my breath until *A Beautiful Mind* was called. I watched Ron, visibly moved, let producer Brian Grazer take the mike.

I knew that Ron, Oscar-winning screenwriter Akiva Goldsman, Russell, and Jennifer were the names that most people would be talking about the next day. But I knew, too, who had found Paul Bettany, Josh Lucas, little Vivien, and all the wonderful New York actors who had played Nash's colleagues and friends. I knew who had helped create the world within which Nash lived, and who had helped make the period feel real—the texture and depth that were an integral part of the way the whole film came together. I knew that the work Janet and I had done on this movie—on any movie—would rarely receive any public recognition. But I also knew that she and I both had a share in the award that Brian Grazer was accepting.

JANE AND JANET

Winning awards is always fun. But it's not what keeps us going. We're in it for those days when a script comes into our office from a director we've worked with or some exciting first-timer, and we look at each other across our facing desks and grin. We know we've got something really special—a movie nobody's ever seen before, one with a special twist or with real depth, the kind of movie that makes you think differently about your life, or makes you laugh harder than you ever thought you could, or just a movie with characters that leap right off the page. Our minds are buzzing with possibilities for the guy, the girl, the best friend, the doctor, even the woman carrying her poodle across the street in that little bit on page 56—wouldn't Rusty Schwimmer be great for her? And maybe we could get John C. Reilly for the doctor's brother, you know, he's got that great scene with the cop in Act II. And of course, it would be terrific if we could get Brad Pitt or George Clooney for the guy, but if they're not available, how about Vince Vaughn? Although he doesn't have Brad's or George's extraordinary good looks, he really hit his stride with *Wedding Crashers,* and he's a great comedian. Yeah, let's put him on the list.

Or we're in it for the days when we've been at our wits' end about a particular role—it could be as small as that woman with the poodle or as large as the male lead—and some actor comes through the door and gives a reading that brings the part to life. "Oh," we'll say to each other, "*now* I get it. We'd been seeing the guy as kind of a smoothie, a real con man—but what if he's kind of a diamond in the rough, a drifter who comes out with those poetic lines almost by accident, in a way that makes you really believe him? I wonder if the director would go for that—let's show him the tape." Or "You know, I'd started to think that this scene didn't work, but when you hear someone play it *that* way, it makes sense. The guy's not being sarcastic—he really means all the things he says. Only he's got to sound just a little bit embarrassed about how he says them . . ." You thank the actor whose hard work, talent, and insight have made you see things more clearly, even as your hand is already on the phone, ready to tell the director your good news.

Then, of course, there are those other days. When we find an actor who seems perfect for the part—but his schedule isn't. Or an actress whom everybody loves—but her people and the studio can't come to a financial agreement. Or the actors who decide, after days or weeks of deliberation, that they just don't like the script, the part, their co-star, the director, and now, after all that time, our second, third, and fourth choices have also become unavailable.

Worst of all are the days when it really looks hopeless. When we've been to every agent, manager, and little theater in town; when we've combed through the thousands of photos in our files and the hundreds of tapes in our library; when we've already done a nationwide search, sending breakdowns to agents from Albuquerque to Raleigh to Orlando. Where will we find our "Soulful High-School Boy with a Wicked Grin" or our "Sixtyish Weather-beaten Female Bartender" or our "African American Former Basketball Star Turned Bitter and Resentful"? At this point, we start to doubt whether we'll even know them when we see them, so exhausted and discouraged are we, so ready to doubt our own instincts.

And then, the way they always do, the casting gods take over. Some new face walks through the door, or we remember some old face we hadn't considered. Some actor who was tied up miraculously becomes available. Or we see a photo in a magazine, or we go by chance to an "off-Hollywood" play, or a friend calls from New York, or Seattle, or Chicago saying, "Maybe you want to take a look at So-and-So"—and hope springs eternal once more. We don't expect it ever to be easy. But it's always satisfying. And, as we say, it's the closest thing we'll ever know to magic.

ACKNOWLEDGMENTS

JANE

I'd like to thank the Academy—ooh, wrong speech. But seriously, there are a lot of people to thank. The people who made this possible—Rachel Kranz for hearing our voice and getting it on the page, Jeff Kleinman for making it all work out, and Andrea Schulz for her insight and clarity.

Since the prospect of making the Academy speech is slim, I want to take this opportunity to say it's impossible to sum up thus far without being grateful for the love and support of my parents, even though my mother never understood what I did or who the boss was; my brother Michael for teaching me to write my name and other lessons; and dear friends who were there to listen—but most especially my son, David, who has always been willing to go with the flow, whether it meant going off with a babysitter or becoming one himself.

JANET

I'd like to thank Nanna for letting me tear apart her movie magazines to make my first actor picture files when I was ten years old. I'd like to thank my mother for her expectation of truth and her example of tolerance. And thanks to my friend and theatre date, Joe Bates.

JANE

Professionally, I must start with Ralph Waite, who dared to give me that first job; Jennifer Shull, who fostered the care and concern I learned from her; Fred Roos, who was a guiding light; and the directors and producers whose continued employment have made this all possible: Francis Ford Coppola, Ron Howard and Brian Grazer, Rob Reiner, Chris Columbus, John Hughes, Steven Spielberg, Barbara Broccoli, and Wolfgang Petersen. There are many more to be sure, but those people have been a steady beacon for all of these professional years. And the most steady of all, the support of Michael Hirshenson and of my dear partner, right arm, and the other half of my brain, Janet Hirshenson.

JANET

As Patrick Swayze says in *Ghost*, "Ditto" on my gratitude to all the producers and directors we've worked with, and Jeff, Rachel, and Andrea. Jennifer and Fred—reiteration is no crime here. And thanks to Michelle Lewitt Ward, trusted associate.

This journey would, literally, not have been possible without my husband, Michael—the third musketeer. His insistence that I could do this big, scary job. His calmness and clarity of vision during moments of mania throughout the casting process. His business acumen in making deals for our services. His cooking skills. But most of all for his love and companionship all these years. And, of course, Jane Jenkins, who I can't imagine casting without.

INDEX